NEO-CONFUCIAN
ECOLOGICAL
HUMANISM

A volume in the SUNY series in Chinese Philosophy and Culture

Roger T. Ames, editor

NEO-CONFUCIAN ECOLOGICAL HUMANISM

An Interpretive Engagement with Wang Fuzhi
(1619–1692)

Nicholas S. Brasovan

Published by State University of New York Press, Albany

For information, contact State University of New York Press, Albany, NY
www.sunypress.edu

Production, Diane Ganeles
Marketing, Anne M. Valentine

Library of Congress Cataloging-in-Publication Data

Names: Brasovan, Nicholas S., 1979– author.
Title: Neo-Confucian ecological humanism : an interpretive engagement with
  Wang Fuzhi (1619–1692) / by Nicholas S. Brasovan.
Description: Albany, NY : State University of New York, 2017. | Series: SUNY
  series in Chinese philosophy and culture | Includes bibliographical
  references and index.
Identifiers: LCCN 2016031417 (print) | LCCN 2017009866 (ebook) | ISBN
  9781438464534 (hardcover : alk. paper) | ISBN 9781438464541 (pbk. : alk.
  paper) | ISBN 9781438464558 (ebook)
Subjects: LCSH: Wang, Fuzhi, 1619–1692. | Neo-Confucianism. | Humanism. |
  Philosophy of nature.
Classification: LCC B5234.W334 B73 2017 (print) | LCC B5234.W334 (ebook) |
  DDC 181/.112—dc23
LC record available at https://lccn.loc.gov/2016031417

To Amy, Sage, and Alethea

Contents

Acknowledgments

This study is a consummation of research that I began as a PhD candidate in the Department of Philosophy at the University of Hawaiʻi. I am infinitely indebted to my teachers, Roger T. Ames and Chung-ying Cheng, for their extensive and intensive lessons on Confucianism, Daoism, and neo-Confucianism. I am indebted to Ron Bontekoe for his seminars on radical empiricism and philosophical hermeneutics, Steve Odin for his seminars on radical empiricism and process philosophy, and David McCraw at the University of Hawaiʻi, Department of East Asian Languages and Literatures, for his expert lessons on classical Chinese language and culture. I am thankful to Shana Brown at the University of Hawaiʻi, Department of History, for her critical advice to contextualize this philosophical study with a biographical introduction to Wang Fuzhi. Thank you to all of these scholars for their critique of early iterations of this work. I am also grateful to Mary Tiles for her seminar on the philosophy of ecology at the University of Hawaiʻi, which introduced me to the paradigm of ecological humanism.

I am grateful to my colleagues, Clayton Crockett and Taine Duncan, for their instructive discussions on new materialism. Indeed, their scholarship and arguments have persuaded me to change my original position on this interpretive engagement between materialism and neo-Confucian cosmology. I am particularly indebted to Taine Duncan for sharing her expertise on this topic in our collaborative work, "Contemporary Ecofeminism and Confucian Cosmology," in *Feminist Encounters with Confucius* (Leiden: Brill Academic Publishers,

2016). I have reworked my discussion of new materialism here based on the resources and arguments that Duncan and I worked through in our co-authored work.

Thank you to the excellent editors at SUNY Press, Nancy Ellegate, James Peltz, Christopher Ahn, Jessica Kirschner, and Diane Ganeles, for facilitating the editing and publication of this work. I am fortunate to have had the opportunity to work with Nancy Ellegate in the early phases of acquisition and editing of this book. Her vision and effort as the acquisitions editor at SUNY Press played a key role in bringing this work to press. Nancy's work has been essential to a wealth of resources on Asian philosophies published by SUNY Press. Her legacy lives on here and throughout the field of Asian studies. She will be missed by authors and readers alike.

Thank you to the University of Central Arkansas, University Research Council, for support of this research project. Finally, portions of my discussion of modernity and methodology here are iterated in a prefatory article, "Considerations for a Confucian Ecological Humanism," in *Philosophy East and West,* vol. 16.1 (University of Hawai'i Press, July 2016, pp. 842–860). Thank you to the editors at *Philosophy East and West* and the University of Hawai'i Press for permissions to reprint portions of that article here.

Abbreviations of Works by Wang Fuzhi*

ZYW *Zhouyi waizhuan* 周易外傳 (1655)

DSS *Du Sishudaquan shuo* 讀四書大全說 (revised 1665)

ZYXJ *Zhouyi daxiang jie* 周易大象解 (1676)

ZMZ *Zhangzi Zhengmeng zhu* 張子正蒙注 (1679)

SWW *Siwenlu waipian* 思問錄外篇 (c. 1680)

ZYBS 周易稗疏 *Zhouyi baishu*

ZYFL *Zhouyi neizhuan fali* 周易內傳發例 (1686)

ZYN *Zhouyi neizhuan* 周易內傳 (1686)

SYY *Shangshu yinyi* 尚書引義 (revised 1689)

SL *Songlun* 宋論 (1691)

---

*Unless otherwise noted, all citations of Wang's work refer to the *Complete Works of Chuanshan*: 船山全書 (長沙市: 嶽麓書社出版, 1988–1996). See bibliography for further details. I follow the conventions for abbreviating Wang's titles as outlined by Jacques Gernet's list, *Ouvrages de Wang Fuzhi* (2005, 11).

One *yin* one *yang* is called *dao*; continuing it is efficacious; developing it is a natural disposition. Humane persons see it and call it humane; knowledgeable persons see it and call it knowing. . . . Everyday novelty is called flourishing excellence. Procreative creativity is called change. . . . Continuous transformation is called an event. *Yinyang*, unfathomable, is called sublime.

—*Book of Changes, Appended Phrases,*
"Upper Division," 5.1

Introduction

Thesis

To be a person is to be a person-in-the-world. In this project I aim to analyze and amplify this slogan, and present the concept 'person-in-the-world' as a model for ecological humanism. I use the term "ecological humanism" in the sense that it is used in Kerry Whiteside's (2002) work in philosophy of ecology, *Divided Natures: French Contributions to Political Ecology*. As Whiteside defines it, ecological humanism is a theoretical paradigm based on the belief that persons and the natural world are inextricably interrelated events. "The concepts of nature and humanity are bound together in historical-cultural processes, such that what nature is can be understood only in relation to human practices, hopes, and fears—and vice versa" (Whiteside 73). In this view, nature has no essence in itself; likewise, persons have no essence apart from the environments that they inhabit. The thesis of ecological humanism rejects any mode of thought that dualistically distinguishes persons from their natural and social environments. In this vein I propose "person-in-the-world" as a synthetic concept that draws together the concepts of "persons" and "environing world." I use the term "person-in-the-world" to denote complex systems of interactive, causally efficacious, relationships that bind persons and the environing world. In short, a person-in-the-world is a complex system. The concept is unavoidably ecological. A person-in-the-world is a nested hierarchical structure. At the basic level, the nested hierarchical structure of a person-in-the-world consists of a complex, thinking-and-feeling, organism situated within a complex environmental ecosystem. With regard to the presence of a heart-and-mind (Chinese, *xin* 心) within persons-in-the-world, I advance that a neo-Confucian model of persons-in-the-world is neither a materialism nor idealism in the traditional senses of the term. The present model of philosophy is thoroughly non-dualistic in the sense that it precludes person/nature dichotomies as well as matter/consciousness dualisms.

This project is a work in philosophy of ecology and comparative philosophy. My principal aim is to demonstrate that the neo-Confucian philosophy of Wang Fuzhi 王夫之 (1619–1692) presents a cogent model of ecological humanism. Advancing Wang's neo-Confucian terminology, I propose that a person-in-the-world is a complex pattern of energy, *qizhili* 氣之理. In this conception, "person-in-the-world" integrates the person's internal embodied energy and the person's external environmental energy. Wang Fuzhi makes this point in his philosophy of energy, *qi* 氣. He presents his philosophy throughout his work. In his *Reading the Compendium of Discourses on the Four Books*, he says, "Filling the space between the heavens and earth, inside and outside of the lived body, there is nothing that is not energy" (*Du Sishudaquan shuo* 讀四書大全說, hereafter referred to as DSS).[1] In the same text, he continues, "The merging of nature and persons just is continuity of energy" (1052).[2] Wang maintains that energy always structures itself into patterns. Thus, the energy continuum of nature-and-persons, *tianrenyiqi* 天人一氣, is also formulated as continuity of patterns, *tianrenyili* 天人一理.

Wang understands patterns of energy as nested hierarchical structures. He writes, "Myriad patterns systemically unite in one pattern; one pattern contains myriad patterns; they are interconnected and inter-contained" (DSS 1110).[3] With this proposition, Wang states his commitment to the neo-Confucian metaphysical slogan, "pattern is unified, but its divisions are many," *liyifenshu* 理一分殊. Wang Fuzhi envisions the world as an open set of dynamic complex patterns. Again, from the perspective of neo-Confucian ecological humanism, a person-in-the-world is a dynamic patterning or organization of energy. The person qua pattern is nested within broader environmental patterns of energy. Energy continuously flows and transforms through and between patterns.

Wang Fuzhi's natural philosophy provides a conceptual model of persons-in-the-world akin to the model of ecosystems ecology. The relationship between the two theories is such that we can hermeneutically reconstruct Wang's worldview as a creative and cogent ecological humanism for the twenty-first century. An ecosystem has at least two hierarchical levels of systemic organization: a level of environment and a level of organism (Keller, Golley 22). Energy continuously flows and transforms throughout the system of interconnected systems. The energy internal to a person's body exchanges energy with the external systems of the person's environment. As Wang Fuzhi interprets it, "energy is transferred among things through reciprocal interactions of giving and receiving" (DSS 962).[4] Accordingly, from the perspective of a neo-Confucian ecological humanism, neither persons nor the environments that they inhabit can be fully understood without exploring the relationships that bind and constitute them.

Interpretive Methodology

The methodology of this work is hermeneutical in the sense that it carries a message from a distant time and place to the here and now. As Wang Fuzhi took up the Confucian classics and interpreted them in the context of the cosmological vocabulary developed throughout the Song and Ming dynasties, I advance a commentary on Wang's philosophy from the vantage point of twenty-first-century philosophies of ecology. In this vein, my methodology for commenting on Wang's work is akin to Wang Fuzhi's own methods of commentarial philosophy.

Liu Xiaogan 刘笑敢 (2002) argues that Wang Fuzhi's commentaries on the Confucian canon constitute some of the most comprehensive and rigorous work in the history of Chinese commentarial philosophy (32). Liu writes, "The basic model of the Chinese philosophical-hermeneutic tradition is to use a method of interpreting a classical text to advance a philosophical system, erect a structure, or restructure a preexisting paradigm" (ibid.). The model that Liu has in mind consists of two dialectically opposed hermeneutic principles. On the one hand, the commentary should respect, represent, and elucidate the authorial intention conveyed by the text; on the other, the commentary should amplify the meaning of the classic by advancing a novel perspective on the text's philosophy. The novel perspective should express a worldview that articulates the commentator's particular cultural-historical situation and personal interpretation (ibid.).

In light of the first hermeneutic principle, Wang's commentaries should express reverence for the ancestral authors of *rujia* and their cultural achievements. He assumes that the books of the Confucian canon are the medium through which the sages of old transmit their enlightened insights to later generations. Accordingly, the root-texts, *benshu* 本書 or classics *jing* 經, are authoritative voices on the ethics of living as persons-in-the-world. Wang Fuzhi's *Du Sishu daquan shuo* indicates the author's respect for the tradition and the authorial intentions voiced by its canonical texts. Chen Lai (2004) thus writes in his work on Wang Fuzhi:

> Chuanshan held a deep respect for Confucian tradition, Confucian classics, Confucius, Mencius, the Cheng brothers, and Zhuxi [. . .][5] And Chuanshan's *Reading the Compendium of Discourses on the Four Books* is a critical summary of Zhu Xi's school of thought. As a matter of fact, looking through the *Reading the Compendium of Discourses on the Four Books*, one finds that Chuanshan's commentaries are not far from other celebrated literati of his era. Furthermore, he also acknowledges the classical character of the *Four Books*, the authority of the Cheng-Zhu School, the legitimacy of Confucianism, and he takes the meanings of the concepts of the neo-Confucian *School of Dao* to be axiomatic. (45–46)[6]

Though Wang takes neo-Confucian cosmological premises as axiomatic, his interpretive commentaries are far from dogmatic. They are not static reiteration of tradition. Wang Fuzhi's appropriation of Confucian discourse is *critical* and *creative* (ibid.).[7] Thus, his work satisfies the second of the aforementioned hermeneutic principles.

The second principle, which may be dubbed a "principle of creative advance," assumes that the meanings of the classics are open to critical analysis and creative interpretation. Accordingly, it ensures that the tradition retains a kind of pragmatic plasticity and ongoing relevance for generation after generation of Confucian scholars. Indeed, one may argue that it is due to this hermeneutic principle of creative advance that Confucianism is open to engagement and hermeneutic reconstruction from a twenty-first-century perspective.

As a principle of hermeneutic methodology, my investigation into Wang's work takes into account the intellectual history that informs it. In this sense, the project at hand is an attempt at interpreting Wang Fuzhi's texts within their original context. Given Wang's historicity and the breadth of his copious commentarial work, any attempt at accessing Wang Fuzhi's thought must approach it obliquely by taking detours through the *Book of Changes*; *Analects of Confucius*; *Record of Rites*; *Mencius*; *Xunzi*; Song-Ming School of *Li, Lixue* 理學; and Lao-Zhuang Daoism.

Nevertheless, the present project is not principally a work on the history of Chinese philosophy. As I see it, this work is in line with Michael C. Kalton's (1998) call "to see what becomes of the traditional conceptual schema if it is put in complete interaction with contemporary [ecological] understanding, and second, to see what kind of benefit to contemporary understanding might come from thinking from the Neo-Confucian traditions" (80). This approach requires rethinking Wang's original work in terms that are foreign to the text. It requires "reviewing the old as a means of realizing the new," to use a Confucian dictum (*Analects* 2.11).[8] The method is to frame a dialogue between two culturally, historically, and linguistically distinct philosophical traditions with the goal of developing an enriched and multifaceted account of nature and persons-in-the-world. By definition, no dialogue is unilateral. From a hermeneutic standpoint, a dialogue between historically, socioculturally, and linguistically distinct traditions is only fruitful—is only possible—if the dialogical counterparts can be shown to agree on fundamental questions and a shared universe of discourse. Moreover, as in the case of dialogue, such an interpretive method results in the mutual transformation of both neo-Confucianism and postmodern ecology. Again, such a dialogical methodology is akin to Wang's hermeneutic method. Wang echoes the principle of creative advance in the formulation of the *Analects*, where he writes, "The new and old condition each other, thereby renewing the old" (ZYW 1008).[9]

In sum, my intention is to draw from the resources of both traditional Chinese philosophy and contemporary philosophy of ecology to create a theory of neo-Confucian ecological humanism. Before further foregrounding the contemporary hermeneutic perspective of ecological humanism, the discussion now turns to contextualize Wang Fuzhi's authorship with a brief biographical sketch, followed by an introduction to the *Yijing*.

Biographical Introduction to Wang Fuzhi

Wang Fuzhi's biography is an account of an orthodox Confucian scholar during the Ming-Qing transition period of imperial China. Bearing witness to the fall of the Ming and rise of the Qing, he was directly acquainted with the sufferings of social degradation, political capitulation, war, and alienation. Wang Fuzhi was born and raised within a family of orthodox Confucian literati. As a youth he was versed in the classical Confucian canon by his eldest brother, and educated in the polemics of Song-Ming neo-Confucianism by his father, Wang Chaopin 王朝聘. Under the tutelage of his uncle he acquired a deep interest in poetics.[10] "At the same time he was eager to learn about practical affairs, through study in such areas as geography, [and] military techniques . . ." (Yan 80–81). As he would demonstrate throughout his long life of authorship, he loved learning—*haoxue* 好學. Scholars also note the presence of astronomy, calendar methodology, and numerology in Wang's fields of study, and note that Wang Fuzhi was particularly adept at classical studies, historiography, and literary criticism. As we shall see in the ensuing discussion, he held a particular affinity for the *Book of Changes, Yijing* 易經 (Kang 87).[11]

He undertook his early curriculum in earnest: At the age of twenty-four Wang Fuzhi passed the prefectural level civil service examination (*xiucai* 秀才) in his native Huguang Prefecture (modern-day Hunan Province) with an essay on the classical *Spring and Autumn Annals* (Wong, 1987, ix). Shortly thereafter he had intended on traveling North to Beijing to take the imperial level examinations (*zhusheng* 諸生), but as the Ming fell into political collapse, an outbreak of civil unrest and violence occurred. Due to the escalating turmoil, Wang was forced to cancel his plans and return to his home in Hengzhou (Hengyang).

In 1644, when Wang was twenty-five, his father was taken political prisoner by the rebel army of the warlord Zhang Xianzhong 張獻忠 (1606–1644). Wang Fuzhi seriously injured himself so that Zhang's army would not want to conscript him. He is said to have then hidden his brother, and also to have gone to his father's prison to negotiate his release. By "some expedient measure," he secured his father's freedom (Yan 82).[12] That same year, Beijing was overrun by Manchu invaders from the North, and the reigning Ming emperor, Chongzhen 崇禎 (1611–1644), hanged himself. When Wang heard this news, he mourned his "ruler-father and refused food for many days" (Yan 86).[13]

In the several years that followed, Wang first took up arms with a band of Ming loyalists in resistance to the encroachment on southern China by the "northern barbarian" Manchu army. His military resistance was soon overrun by the conquest of the Manchurian Qing dynasty. During this time, the remnants of the Ming government relocated and organized an auxiliary capital in the South, Nanjing. Wang then served as counsel in the refugee court of the displaced Ming prince, Yongming 永明. Bearing witness to political infighting and corruption in the court, Wang became disillusioned with the estranged Ming. In 1651, at the age of thirty-three, he fled from the conflicts of politics and war, and took the path of an orthodox Confucian eremitic scholar. In reference to Wang's plight, Wai-Yee Li (2006) explains:

First, eremitism is a familiar ideal in the Chinese tradition—
a defined niche in the ordering of reality. It summons visions
of a world in which engagement and disengagement, service
and withdrawal, are complementary attitudes, depending
on whether one's circumstances are straitened (*qiong* 窮)
or conducive to action (*da* 達). It implies equanimity,
conscious choice, and a context that accepts this behavior
as reasonable. (8)

Wang's biography speaks for a life lived according to the prescrip-
tions of Confucian ritual propriety, *li* 禮. He strictly practiced actions
befitting a filial son, a respectful brother, and a loyal scholar-official
in his situation. Based on both his biography and the tenets of his
Confucian philosophy, the roles and relationships that Wang Fuzhi
observed must have been central to his self-understanding. As the
sociopolitical structure that supported his personal identity collapsed
under the weight of duplicity, partisanship, and stagnant ineffective-
ness, Wang Fuzhi was thrown into an existential crisis.[14] One the
one hand, he was committed to acting on a humanistic concern for
the survival of his family, social order, and cultural heritage.[15] On the
other hand, he became increasingly aware of his own lack of power
against the complex historical forces that ultimately caused the fall
of his dynasty.

Faced with the apparent death of the sociopolitical order and
the cultural inheritance with which he had identified himself, he was
forced into questioning his personal integrity, alienation, and *raison
d'être*. He viewed the death of the empire as his own. Conveying
his struggle in verse, he composes the "Poem of Sorrow and Wrath"
in which he refers to the Ming as "falling peach blossoms" (Yan
86). And he composed a self-elegy epitaph, in which he writes of
himself as "nursing solitary wrath" and "carrying enduring sorrow"
(Platt 10).[16]

Looking for a resolution to this crisis, Wang turned to away
from society. "Wang Fuzhi considered reclusion a way of dying." Thus
he writes, "Life and death are the affairs of *tian*. How can humans
intervene? Action and concealment are my way of living and dying"

(Li, 2006, 5).[17] He moved deep into the remote mountainous region of central Hunan, where he spent the remaining four decades of his life seeking refuge, guidance. and fortitude in philosophical study and quiet reflection (Platt 10). In his final seventeen years, he lived in a "mud hut 土室" at the foot of "Stone Boat Mountain 石船山" from which he took his penname, Wang Chuanshan 王船山 (Lee 13). As is evidenced by the depth and breadth of his extant works, the author is a literatus *par excellence*.[18] Wang Fuzhi spent his adult life in material poverty, "borrowing the brushes and paper he used for writing from friends and disciples" (Platt 10). And yet the author's wealth is found in his writings: encyclopedic knowledge, philosophical acumen, sincerity, rigor, and intellectual vigor. On this note, Siu-Kit Wong praises Wang's oeuvre: "The sheer quantity is formidable, and both the range and quality could only have been achieved by an intellectual giant" (x).

Wang Fuzhi inherited a hermeneutic disposition for interpreting experience under the categories of classical Confucian and Song-Ming neo-Confucian philosophy. In light of his biography, poetry, and philosophy, I understand Wang's angst as an estrangement from or "death" of his social self—that is, his self-understanding as the locus and focus of interpersonal networks. I suggest, over the course of his forty-year sojourn in nature and textual study, the author sublimated his angst by developing a more inclusive and comprehensive vision of self—an ecological self—a self that is constituted by its relations to the heavens-and-earth and myriad patterns of existence. Although this foray into the psychology of the author may be contested on philosophical grounds, it cannot be denied that Wang Fuzhi significantly advanced neo-Confucian discourse into a comprehensive natural cosmology and philosophical anthropology.

Significance, Symbolism, and Strata of the *Yijing*

In his reflections on the ranks of his Song-Ming forefathers, Wang shows a particular esteem for Zhang Zai 張載 (1020–1077). "In Wang Fuzhi's view, the philosophy of Zhang Zai—whom he admired most highly among the Neo-Confucian masters—is no more than the application of the Way of Changes," *yizhidao* 易之道 (Yan 88). Zhang Zai's *Correcting Youthful Ignorance, Zhengmeng* 正蒙, is an early-Song attempt at developing an idea of *qi* and ideas from the *Yijing* into a comprehensive and systematic cosmology.[19] Zhang's work stands alongside the *Explanation of the* Taiji *Diagram* 太極圖說 by Zhou Dunyi 周敦頤 (1017–1073) as a pillar of Song-Ming neo-Confucianism. Like Zhang and Zhou before him, Wang advances his own philosophy as a critical and creative reading of the *Yijing* and its commentarial sources.

The significance that the *Yijing* has for Wang Fuzhi's philosophy cannot be overstated. Scholars have pointed out that although Wang was erudite with interests in many domains of inquiry, he was particularly adept at classical studies. Of all of his areas of research, he devoted his most profound efforts to studying the *Yijing* and this text above all others takes an exclusive place in his oeuvre (Gernet 104, Kang 87).[20] Over the course of his forty-year exile Wang authored no fewer than six commentaries, *zhuan* 傳, in seventeen fascicles, *juan* 卷, dedicated to the *Yijing*.[21] Attesting to the breadth of his study, the recent compilation of his *Yijing* commentaries (Yuelu Publishing House, 1988) comprises a tome of over one-thousand pages in Chinese characters. Outside of these commentaries, moreover, he draws from the *Yijing* throughout his voluminous corpus (Gernet 104).[22]

Following the lineage transmitted by Zhu Xi 朱熹 (1130–1200), Wang believed that the received *Yijing* was created by *four sages with the same intention*, 四聖同揆. He writes:

> Fu Xi originated the inscriptions of the trigrams and hexagrams (*gua*), and *the patterns of nature and persons* were exhausted within them. High antiquity was simple and unadorned; they did not yet have the leisure to clearly write out their reasoning for the understanding of later generations. Fortunately, diviners (筮氏) were like commentaries [for] the images that they inscribed, and there was not yet any confusion. King Wen arose several thousand years later, and by means of a heart-and-mind that was "unseen yet under a watchful eye, tireless yet safeguarding"[23] he forthwith

grasped the trigram and hexagram images and embodied them. Then he appended the hexagram statements, which provided clear interpretations of the hexagram images [in terms of] grasping, losing, fortune, and misfortune. The Duke of Zhou then further extended the transformations of King Wen's "judgments" to the "lines of the hexagrams" by means of *investigating* the *incipient trajectories of timing and positioning, and by sharpening his morality* (研時位之幾而精其義). Confucius then further brought to light the patterns of reasoning in Wen's and Zhou's "judgments" and "line statements," and he made the *Commentary on the Words of the Text* along with the *Judgment* and *Image Commentaries*. Then he threaded his moral precedents through the alterations [of the original layers of the Zhouyi],[24] making the *Appended Phrases*, the *Discussion of the Trigrams* and the *Ordering of the Hexagrams*. Those who employ prognostication and those who study [the *Yijing*] grasp its significations retrospectively by connecting its different extensions. According to the above, what Confucius brings to light in his discussion of the *Judgment Commentary* and the *Image Commentary* is a guiding principle of clarification, and these two commentaries [clarify] the "judgments" and "lines" of Wen and Zhou; and the "judgments" and "lines" of Wen and Zhou [clarify] the inscribed images of Fu Xi. Four sages with the same intention: Later sages take up and extend the meaning of the former sages, and yet there is not once an increase or a decrease. (ZYNFL 649)[25]

Zhu Xi traced the doctrinal lineage of his school back through the four sages mentioned in Wang's account, and presented Fu Xi as the forefather of Confucian lineage, *daotong* 道統. Insofar as Wang saw himself as part of this ongoing tradition, it can be concluded that he understood his own commentaries as extensions of the four sages' intentions; in this vein, he saw his work as elucidating and amplifying the shared concern of his ancestral forbearers while carrying their way forward through his own life and time.

Jacques Gernet (2005) represents Wang Fuzhi as being *fidèle à la tradition* (104).[26] Gernet's language is unfortunately misleading on this point, for he implies that he is presenting *the* traditional account, as if there were only one. Both Stephen L. Field (2008) and Richard John Lynn (1994) present alternatives accounts of the origins, and like Gernet they both claim to report *the* traditional account of the text's creation. These several studies fail to note the plurality of traditional accounts regarding the genesis of the text. At least three mutually exclusive mainstream lines on the *Yijing*'s origin can be found woven through Chinese exegetical tradition.[27] The Chinese exegetical tradition in general thus contains internal contradictions between these different accounts.[28] If the diversity of traditional narratives is not duly noted in Western sources, then students working with these resources may be left with inconsistent and fallacious accounts of the Chinese exegetical tradition.

Wang Fuzhi's *Zhouyi neizhuan* 周易內傳 (ZYN), or *Inner Commentary on the Zhouyi*, written in the author's twilight years, further speaks for his sanctification of the classic:

> With regard to the root-source, the fine and subtle, with regard to expressing the profound-merging of nature and persons (天人之蘊), the *Six Classics*, *Analects*, and *Mencius* reveal persons' disposition to know nature (人之性知天), yet none of these reaches the depth, meaning, expression and acuity of this (*Yijing*). Truly, the tradition of studying natural disposition (性學) and the essentials of the sages' meritorious efforts (*gong* 功) are disclosed in the *Yi*. (ZYN 532)[29]

In Wang's mature thought, the *Yijing* is not just one text among many. It provides the pinnacle expression of sagacious experience and the most profound articulation of the interconnection between persons and the world. Based on Wang's commentaries, it may be said that he hermeneutically engaged the text in such a sustained and intensive manner throughout his life because he saw in it the fullest explication of the universe. For him, the multifaceted symbolism and textual layers in its totality presents a comprehensive model of the world and persons' place within it.

Wang's *Inner Commentary* represents the *Yijing* as the primary realization of persons' disposition to know nature, "人之性知天." The idea of "knowing nature," *zhitian* 知天, in this context confounds theoretical and practical spheres of judgment. Beyond an objective model or theoretical system, Wang Fuzhi takes up the *Yijing* and its philosophy as a way of life, *dao* 道. He interprets himself, the world, and the relations that bind them together through the categories of the text. In other words, his self-understanding as a person-in-the-world is mediated through his reflection on the symbolism and text of the *Yijing*. Yan Shoucheng (1994) reiterates the point: "It may be said that Wang Fuzhi's adult guideline for behavior, as well as his worldview, was based on his understanding of the *Changes*" (88).

Modern scholarship and traditional Chinese commentators agree that the *Yijing* accrued several layers of symbolic imagery and text over approximately 800 to 900 years of ancient Chinese history. Modern scholars concur that the oldest strata of the text were likely to have been compiled in the relatively early years of the Western Zhou (1046–771 BCE), perhaps as early as the ninth century BCE, but they reject the traditional notion that the authorship of the text can be identified with particular individuals (Field 39, Lynn 4).

Given the traditional accounts of the text's origins in the Zhou, commentators throughout history refer to the received *Yijing* as the *Zhouyi* 周易, *Zhou Changes*, thereby distinguishing it from the reputed divination manuals of the Xia (2100–1600 BCE) and Shang (1600–1046 BCE) dynasties. The received *Zhouyi* as a whole was redacted in the early Han dynasty (206 BCE–220 CE) under the editorial management of Confucian scholars. At this time, the complete text was put into its received form and elevated to the primary position amongst the *Five Classics*, *wujing* 五經, of the Confucian canon.[30] Once it was given the status of a "Classic," *jing* 經, the *Zhouyi* took on the title *Yijing*.

Since the Han dynasty, Chinese commentators have maintained that Confucius (551–479 BCE) is the author or editor of the commentarial appendices, the so-called *Ten Wings*, that accompany the received text. Contemporary sources pronounce a strong skepticism toward the attribution of the *Ten Wings* to Confucius.[31] But doubting Confucius's authorship of the *Wings* is not a new innovation. During the Song dynasty (960–1249), literati had begun to contest the authenticity of certain *Classics* (Gernet 104). The esteemed Ouyang Xiu 歐陽修 (1007–1072), for one, argued that "Confucius could not have written the Ten Wings" (Adler 2002, 72). Scholars in Wang Fuzhi's time similarly took up methods of textual criticism to demonstrate that certain *Classics*, which were considered to be transmissions from high antiquity, were actually compositions of a later date (Gernet 104).[32] Despite the rising tides of skepticism regarding the origins of the *Classics* during his era, Wang Fuzhi follows *a* traditional line.

The biography of the *Yijing* is a unique account of a manual that was originally intended as a tool for prognosticative forecasting, *zhanbu* 占卜 or *bushi* 卜筮, but evolved over time into a treatise expounding a holistic process philosophy and systematic correlative cosmology. (These two elements—prognostic and philosophic—are not mutually exclusive in Wang Fuzhi's worldview.) The primary layers of the *Yijing* served as a prompt book for prognostication in the early Zhou aristocracy. Zhu Xi approximated this truth in his claim, "The *Yijing* was created merely as a divination manual . . . Fu Xi's and King Wen's *Yijing* was originally created for this use" (Adler 2002, vii).

The foundational stratum of the book is constituted by the ordered sequence of sixty-four hexagrams. Even at this initial stage of evolution, the *Yijing* presents a correlative worldview of *yin* and *yang* forces, albeit in the form of purely nonlinguistic graphs. Thus, scholars such as David Keightley argue, based on archeological evidence, an *Yijing*-like method of prognostication and a worldview of complementary, correlative, polar opposition were present in the "Shang dynasty, during the closing centuries of the second millennium B.C." (Keightley 367, 373–375, 385; also qtd. in Brasovan, Duncan 238–239).

The symbolism of the *Yijing* is alluded to in the later textual addendums of the *Appended Phrases* commentary: "Changes have a supreme limit, *taiji*: this produces two modes; two modes produce four figures; four figures produce eight trigrams" (*Xici shang* 11.3). Since high antiquity the "two modes" of *yin* 陰 and *yang* 陽 have been symbolized as line segments, *yao* 爻. A broken line segment with a gap in the middle, − −, symbolizes *yin*. A solid-continuous segment, −−, symbolizes *yang*. The two modes combine to form "four figures, *sixiang* 四象," which populate the complete "set of possible *couplings* of these two segments, ⚌, ⚏, ⚎, ⚍. These four figures represent the interactions of *yinyang* in their simplest forms" (Brasovan, Duncan 239). The eight trigrams, *bagua* 八卦, emerge out of the "four figures." The trigrams are representations of *yin* and *yang* interactions on a higher level of complexity (Brasovan, Duncan 239). Each trigram has three positions, *wei* 位; each position is exclusively occupied by either a *yin* or *yang* line:

☰	☳	☵	☶	☷	☴	☲	☱
乾 Qian	震 Zhen	坎 Kan	艮 Gen	坤 Kun	巽 Xun	離 Li	兌 Dui
Sky, Yang	Thunder	Water	Mountain	Earth, Yin	Wind	Flame	Lake

Some of the symbols are iconographs of the experienced phenomena: thunder is *yang* rising; the lake is *yin*, soft-water, over *yang*, solid-land. Finally, the *Yijing* systematically models the evolution and diversification of complex organizations of *yin* and *yang* modes of *qi* 氣 by further pairing each of the eight trigrams with one another, which yields an ordered set of sixty-four hexagrams, 重卦. Following the same structure as the trigrams, each hexagram is made up of a unique combination of six *yin* or *yang* lines. Take, for example, the first two hexagrams in the received text, Qian ䷀ and Kun ䷁, and the final two hexagrams, Jiji ䷾ and Weiji ䷿. As seen in the imagery of the symbols themselves, each situation in nature is here understood as a structure of *yin* and *yang* modes of *qi*. In his recent work on the role of patterning energy (*wenqi* 文氣) in classical Chinese aesthetics, Ming Dong Gu articulates a concept of structure that is directly applicable to the trigrams, hexagrams, and their ontology of energy:

A pattern is a distinct structure. *Wenqi* [patterned energy] is not a chaotic and amorphous energy flowing and floating aimlessly; it is a structured and structuring force . . . At the same time it is also a totalizing force . . . [As such, a] structure is an arrangement of entities that embodies three fundamental ideas: wholeness, transformation, and self-regulation . . . A structure is not static but dynamic. It is endowed with an internal fluidity that inheres in each of the component parts . . . Moreover, a structure is capable of transformational processes; a structure is self-regulating. (37)

The second layer of the *Yijing*, which was also committed to the manual during the early Zhou, provides two categories of text: (1) a "hexagram statement," *guaci* 卦辭, or "hexagram judgment," *guatuan* 卦彖, associated with each hexagram; and, (2) a respective statement, *yaoci* 爻辭, or judgment, *yaotuan* 爻象, corresponding to each line of each hexagram. The language of much of this level of text is archaic and enigmatic from a modern hermeneutic perspective. The manual was transmitted through the centuries and the original context of its claims had faded into antiquity. Over the passage of time, meanings of the initial judgments became opaque to interpreters in China as early as the Spring and Autumn Period (722–479 BCE). On this point, Wang Fuzhi's biography of the *Yijing* is instructive: Confucian literati, *ru* 儒, saw a need for appending exegetical explanation to the original layers of the text. It would appear that the hexagram and line judgments alluded to significant events or culturally relevant images for the authors and intended audience of the text. The texts would have called to mind a value judgment of the emerging phenomenon in relation to one's situated experience or position within the context of the event. When used in forecasting, the texts provide a positive or negative response for a charge asked of the text. The statements use evaluative terms, "grasping, losing, fortune, and misfortune," as attributes of naturally occurring phenomena so as to convey the qualitative experience of each event. When misfortune is in the forecast, one ought to avoid the situation symbolized by the hexagram. The statements provide a baseline for deliberating over one's course of action; they provide a guideline for discerning the efficacy of action.

The third and final sedimentary layer of the received *Yijing* is a set of seven commentaries, *zhuan* 傳. The final layer may be read as a philosophical systematization of the correlative cosmology and axiology tacitly contained in the older strata. In the received text,[33] three of the seven commentaries are subdivided into two parts each, thus yielding ten total sections of commentary.[34] Collectively, these ten sections are referred to as the *Ten Wings, Shiyi* 十翼, or simply *Commentaries on the Changes, Yizhuan* 易傳. The "*Xici* or *Appended Statements* commentary—integrating man and nature through the medium of the *Yijing*—is arguably the most sophisticated (it is certainly the most subtle) statement of the correlative thought that has been so fundamental to all of China's philosophical systems" (Shaughnessy 1).[35] Correlative cosmology and integration of persons and nature (*tianrenheyi* 天人合一) thus become cornerstones for an *Yijing*-based, neo-Confucian, ecological humanism.

In taking up study of the *Yijing* and Wang Fuzhi's philosophy, we are confronted with a radical process philosophy and correlative cosmology. In this context, every thing, *wu* 物, is an event, *shi* 事. And every event is created and constituted by *yinyang* interactions. The *Appended Phrases* defines the processual *way* of the world, *dao* 道, specifically as a continuity of *yin* and *yang*: 一陰一陽之謂道 (*Xici shang* 5.1). The terms "*yin*" and "*yang*" have no meaning in and of themselves; that is to say, neither *yin* nor *yang* has any essence in itself. They are always defined as a mutually implicative and correlative pair. In terms of cosmology, *yin* and *yang* refer to opposing yet complementary modalities of *qi* energy. *Qi* always functions as *yin* and *yang* interactions. From the simplest and smallest to the most complex and magnanimous states of affairs, everything is explained in terms of *yin* and *yang* transactions. So, the extension of these concepts covers all phenomenological and conceptual oppositions: heavens above and the earth below; noble and base; movement and rest; hard and soft; fortune and misfortune; celestial image and concrete form; male and female; going and coming; initiating and complying; contracting and expanding; animating and embodying; outer and inner; sun and moon; day and night; inhale and exhale; concealment and disclosure; summer and winter; north and south; ease and difficulty; continuity and discontinuity, etc. The ongoing change (*shengshengzhiyi*) of the world is a cosmic interplay of interactive forces, respectively and relatively referred to as *yin* and *yang*. *Yin* and *yang* are general explanatory categories used to interpret how various opposing phenomena spontaneously interact, transform one another, and transition into one another. In the discourse surrounding the *Yijing*, all events are interconnected to one another—and regulated by each other—in greater and lesser degrees through a pervasive continuity of *yinyang* interrelationships. In Wang Fuzhi's philosophy, the dynamism, coherence and holistic unity of the cosmos emerges as a complex system of *yin* and *yang* forces of *qi*.[36]

Disambiguating Ecological Humanism

My intention is to advance Wang Fuzhi's brand of neo-Confucianism by hermeneutically engaging it from a postmodern view of ecological humanism. As an initial point of disambiguation, the sense of *"humanism" in the context of ecological humanism is different from the sense of "humanism" in the discourse of modernity.* In reference of the traditions of the European Enlightenment or modern era of philosophy, "humanism" signifies "anthropocentrism" and "scientism."

   Kerry Whiteside notes that "in the rhetorical field of English-speaking ecologism, 'humanism' often gets confounded with 'anthropocentrism'" (72). This confounded sense of "humanism" is the sense inherited from the "Modern Era" of intellectual history. We may briefly look to Immanuel Kant's rational ethics as a consummate expression of modern humanism. Kant maintains that human beings alone should be categorically and universally treated as ends-in-themselves, never simply as means toward some otherwise contrived end. He holds that if everyone acted in line with their duties to respect the integrity and autonomy of all persons, then society would become the ideal kingdom of ends. In tandem with this categorical imperative is the belief that human beings are the sole, rational, autonomous, moral agents in the world. Only those values that are postulated by humans and rationally willed for the sake and well-being of all humans are valuable in and of themselves. In short, only humans have intrinsic value. By the same token, every nonhuman (nonrational, nonautonomous) life form and nonliving object is absolutely devoid of intrinsic value. Nonhuman entities are valuable if and only if they serve as means for achieving human ends: they only have instrumental value.

"Modernity's master narratives included a story of human progress through the domination of nature, its objectification, and its subjection to technological control" (Whiteside 141). Modern humanism celebrates instrumental reason and autonomy of the will. In conjunction, these potent faculties enable persons to objectively understand and intentionally manipulate the natural forces of their bodies and environments. These powers enable rational and volitional (albeit partial) domination of nature.

Although the idea of rational domination comes to fruition during the Enlightenment, it is rooted deep within the sedimentary layers of history that underlie modernity. The seeds of the idea are so deep that they are said to have been sown at the beginning of time—in *Genesis*. On this account, God created man in his image and charged him to "fill the earth and subdue it; and have dominion over the fish of the sea and over the birds of the air and over every living thing that moves upon the earth" (1.29). The history of natural science demonstrates that "modernity's master narrative" is tied to the biblical narrative of Creation. Whether justified or not, the God-given sovereign right to subdue all other life forms has been consistently and pervasively interpreted throughout history as a sanction for anthropocentric axiology. In time, the doctrine of *dominion* becomes the doctrine of *domination*.[37]

In 1637, with the publication of his *Discourse on Method of Rightly Conducting One's Reason and of Seeking Truth in the Sciences*, René Descartes ushered forth the traditional conception of "dominion" into the modern era. In this text, Descartes sets forth the agenda for modern science and applied instrumental reason to come to understand the objective forces of the world in order to "render ourselves

the lords and possessors of nature."[38] Likewise, during the early establishment of modern science, Francis Bacon sought to restore the
divine mandate of dominion through science and technology, which
Bacon refers to as "mechanical *arts*."[39] This approach and disposition toward nature is one of coercive control, mastery, inquisition,
and conquest of nature through the methodical application of *instrumental reason*. Bacon proposed that science and technology should
be used to "search into the bowels of nature," and "shape nature
as on an anvil."[40] According to the modern scientistic and technocratic understanding, persons are established as autonomous, rational,
agents who are engaged in a struggle versus the objective forces of
nature. The intention of science, in Bacon's words, is "victory of art
over nature" and overcoming the "inconveniences of man's estate,"
that is, the adverse conditions of persons' natural environments (Leiss
78, 83, 85). Characterizing the ideals of Descartes and Bacon, the
nineteenth-century philosopher, Ludwig Feuerbach, thus remarks on
the history and trajectory of modern epistemology, "Natural science
has therefore no other goal than to more firmly establish and extend
the power and domination of men over nature. But the domination
of men over nature rests solely on art [technology] and knowledge"
(65).[41] Ecological humanism critically rejects the anthropocentric
ethics and scientism of modernity. Indeed, ecological humanism is
an entirely different paradigm from modern humanism. As such, ecological humanism is postmodern.

Though ecological humanism is skeptical of the scientism that
emerged within the context of modernity, it accepts natural science
as an authoritative method for generating justified true beliefs. That
is to say, ecological humanism critically evaluates, generalizes, and
advances the theoretical models that are generated in and adopted
by the science of ecology. In particular, ecological humanism is committed to the naturalism and complex systems theory assumed in
ecosystems ecology. Along these lines, it is committed to the thematic
propositions that David R. Keller and Frank B. Golley outline (2000)
as conditions of viable, contemporary, ecological worldviews:

1. All living and nonliving things are integral parts of the
    biospherical web (ontological interconnectedness).

2. The essence or identity of a living thing is an expression of connections and context (internal relations).

3. To understand the makeup of the biosphere, connections and relations between parts must be considered, not just the parts themselves (holism).

4. All life-forms—including Homo sapiens—result from the same processes (naturalism).

5. Given the affinities between humans and nonhumans, nonhuman nature has value above and beyond instrumental, resource utility for human beings (nonanthropocentrism).

6. Humans have caused serious negative impacts (pollution, anthropogenic extinction) on the earth, leading to the need for environmental ethics. (Keller, Golley 2–3)

In addition, ecological humanism demonstrably exhibits a commitment to a "mitigated scientific realism," in the sense that Keller and Golley discuss in their *Philosophy of Ecology*. With its emphasis on these themes, ecological humanism finds an interesting and interested dialogical partner in neo-Confucianism.

Synopsis

Wang Fuzhi's cosmology is a quintessential expression of the traditional Chinese naturalism that Mary Evelyn Tucker and John Berthrong find so resonant with ecology:

Chinese naturalism in its broadest sense is characterized by an organic holism and a dynamic vitalism . . . Nature is seen as unified, interconnected, and interpenetrating. . . . This interconnectedness is already present in the early Confucian tradition in the *I ching*, or *Book of Changes* . . . This sense of naturalism and holism is distinguished by the view that

there is no Creator God; rather, the universe is considered
to be a self-generating . . . process. (xxxvi)

Though certain components of this broad characterization will need
to be subject to critical review from the perspective of contemporary
ecological science, the natural philosophy of neo-Confucianism opens
the door to an ecological reading of traditional Chinese philosophies.

Berthrong and Tucker suggest a contrast between "Chinese
naturalism" and theistic Creationism. The method of contrasting Wang Fuzhi's cosmology against theistic Creationism has been
employed in the several available English and French monographs
on the philosophy of Wang Fuzhi: namely, Alison Harley Black's
Man and Nature in the Philosophical Thought of Wang Fu-chih (Seattle:
University of Washington Press, 1989); François Jullien's early work,
Procès ou Création: Une introduction à la pensée des lettres chinois, *Essai
de problématique interculturelle* (Paris: Éditions du Seuil, 1989); and
most recently in Jacques Gernet's *La Raison des choses: Essai sur la
philosophie de Wang Fuzhi (1619–1692)* (Paris: Gallimard, 2005). The
first chapter of the work-at-hand surveys these several monographs as
well as contemporary Chinese articles on the naturalistic cosmology
of Wang Fuzhi. Based on this survey and analysis of Wang's original
text, chapter one demonstrates Wang's commitment to a doctrine of
immanent cosmological creativity. Broadly speaking, Wang Fuzhi's
worldview is a natural cosmology. *Anything and everything in the world,
including the world itself, is completely the result of natural causes.* Better,
in Wang's language, every *thing, qi* 器, is a natural transformation of
energy, *qi* 氣.

Again, Michael Kalton duly observes the crossroads of ecology
and neo-Confucianism:

Contemporary thought points toward an understanding of
the cosmos, the world, physical systems, biosystems, ecosystems, and social systems as patterned energy of many
levels and modes: not just pattern and not just energy; not
just multiple and not just one . . . Arguments in this area
and difficulties in explaining causality from pattern/system

downward seem amusingly similar to the interminable arguments of traditional Neo-Confucians about *li* and *qi*. (83)

Fully agreeing with Kalton, I take up a discussion of complex systems
theory in chapter two, and move to demonstrate that Wang Fuzhi's
cosmology of energy (*qi* 氣) and pattern (*li* 理) provides a cogent
theoretical resource, which can only serve to enrich and advance
the postmodern paradigm of ecological humanism.

Before closing chapter two, the discussion further addresses the
question of whether or not "materialism" is an appropriate interpretation of Wang Fuzhi's natural cosmology. What is the meaning of
"materialism" and "only thing doctrine" (*weiwuzhuyi* 唯物主义) with
reference to Wang Fuzhi's philosophy? Wang Fuzhi's philosophy can
be called "materialism" with provisos: (1) provided that "materialism" in this context means that persons, experience, and nature are
constituted by *qi* 氣, or energy; (2) provided that "materialism" does
not exclude the belief that persons and impersonal natural forces
alike are sublime, spiritual, sources, and forces of transformation,
creativity, and life; (3) provided that "materialism" does not imply
that *consciousness*, *life*, and *spirit* are reducible to inert, dead, material substance. In this vein, I maintain, Wang Fuzhi's "pre-modern"
philosophy of *qi* ironically answers contemporary "postmodern" calls
for "new materialism."

Chapter three traces the themes of ontological interconnectedness, internal relations, holism, and dynamism through Wang Fuzhi's
reading of the *Yijing*. There it is argued that the *Yijing* is an attempt
at symbolically and theoretically modeling the complex dynamics
of persons-in-the-world. The case is made for the *Yijing* as a kind of
classical ecography. In this context, we look to Wang Fuzhi's critical
relationship to two divergent schools of thought within the history
of *Yijing* study—namely, the school of Meaning and Pattern (*yili* 義
理) and the school of Image and Number (*xiangshu* 象數).

Chapter four delves into Wang Fuzhi's concepts of 'between
nature and persons,' 'nature within persons,' and 'nature within
nature' (*tianrenzhiji* 天人之際, *zairenzhitian* 在人之天, and *zaitianzhitian* 在天之天). Through analysis of these categories, one finds Wang

Fuzhi in agreement with ecological humanism's fundamental premise of reciprocity between nature and persons. That is, Wang's philosophy presents a means for re-presenting a non-anthropocentric, non-teleological, non-dualistic concept of humanizing nature. To further demonstrate the resonance between Wang and ecological humanism on this point, chapter four makes use of Li Zehou's theory of humanizing nature in the context of traditional Chinese philosophy.

The discussion demonstrates that Wang Fuzhi was an analytic philosopher. He was concerned with providing clarity and precision to traditional Confucian discourse on "continuity between nature and persons," *tianrenheyi* 天人合一. Wang believed that persons have unique capacities of knowledge and moral experience. In this vein, Wang presents a critical adoption and advance of the Zisizi-Mencian tradition of philosophical anthropology.

Chapter five critiques the mundane aspects of Wang Fuzhi's philosophy of religion. In particular, this chapter offers a critical reading of Wang's condescending polemics against the transcendent visions of Buddhism and Daoism. Though mundane in certain respects, Wang's worldview contains a profound spiritual appreciation for the sublimity and procreativity of the world. Moreover, in the tradition of the *Yijing*, Cheng Hao, and Zhou Dunyi, Wang Fuzhi expresses a reverence for life. Finally, chapter six provides concluding reflections and an application of Wang's theoretical edifice to the modern ecological crisis of global warming.

By taking up the position of ecological humanism in hermeneutic engagement with this neo-Confucian perspective, the intention is to demonstrate that the theoretical components inherent in his historically rooted worldview may provide a potent resource for postmodern philosophies of human nature and the natural world. Wang Fuzhi's uniquely analytic, critical, and literal reading of the neo-Confucian tradition represents the discourse as a naturalistic account of persons and the world. The naturalistic representation establishes the discourse as a resource for advancing philosophical ecology. Conversely, the philosophy of ecology (or philosophical ecology) provides a place for recovery and reconstruction of Song-Ming neo-Confucianism in the twenty-first century. The thesis of this work indicates the potential for creative advance of neo-Confucianism and philosophical ecology if and when the hermeneutic horizons of these disparate theories are fused. Developing neo-Confucian philosophical ecology has the potential for advancing knowledge in a post-Darwin/ post-Einstein era of natural science while contemporaneously cultivating qualitative, subjective, and intersubjective experiences that are rightly called religious. A neo-Confucian philosophical ecology offers a fusion of naturalism and humanism. It offers a model of ecological humanism.

1

Natural Cosmology

We begin our discussion by adopting a methodology of contrasting Wang Fuzhi's cosmology against a Judeo-Christian assertion of Creationism. After exploring the antithesis to Wang's cosmology, we move to define key cosmological terms that Wang employs to explain the world in which we live. This discussion takes us into a naturalistic account of the Chinese philosophical terminology of "*tian*." The inquiry then proceeds to analyze Wang's insistent naturalism with regard to neo-Confucian terminology of cosmological creativity. In this context we engage in an extended analysis of neo-Confucian concepts of "great ultimate," "without limits," and "great harmony." Having analyzed this terminology, we will be in position to turn in the next chapter to a synthetic dialogue between the contemporary worldview of ecological humanism and Wang Fuzhi's neo-Confucianism.

Creationism as Antithesis

During his mission to Ming Dynasty China, Matteo Ricci (1552–1610) wrote a treatise in Chinese with the purpose of arguing for the superiority of the biblical Creationism. Employing a popular European analogy of the time, he likened the world to a manmade structure: "Nothing is able to make itself; it must depend on an external being to make it. Pavilions and houses do not spontaneously arise; they are always made by the hand of a carpenter" (Ricci 76).[1] Understanding the world as an artifact, which implies a divine Artisan, stands in stark contrast to the natural cosmology of Wang Fuzhi. Citing Ricci's analogy, Jacques Gernet explains the incommensurability between the Jesuit and neo-Confucian perspectives:

> The argument reproduced by all the missionaries [in seventeenth-century China], according to which it must be that the universe was created by a being exterior to nature, could only have been shocking in a world that did not admit anything beyond nature. The explication of the complexity and the constant evolution of living phenomena by way of a coarse model of action by an artisan on "matter," moreover, would seem to have found difficulty in being accepted. (Gernet 83)[2]

Picking up on this theme, both Alison Black and François Jullien present Wang Fuzhi's naturalism as an antithesis to theistic creationism.[3] The argument, in short, is that Wang Fuzhi's cosmology and the cosmogony of creationism are incompatible. Creationism presupposes the existence of a transcendent external cause of natural world; the cause is an intelligent and purposive agent, which creates the world according to design and teleological plan. Wang Fuzhi's cosmological philosophy asserts none of these propositions.

In the legacy of early Christian missionaries like Ricci, the Chinese term 天 *tian* has traditionally been interpreted in terms of "Heaven." As is demonstrated in the ensuing discussion, however, it would be a categorical error to interpret Wang Fuzhi's concept of *tian* in terms of *heaven*. I follow the arguments of Jullien, Gernet, and Black with respect to Wang Fuzhi's commitment to naturalism. Building upon their arguments, I make the case that Wang Fuzhi's concept of *tian* is better understood as *nature*.

The method of identifying Wang Fuzhi's cosmological thesis by way of contrasting it against its antithesis is instrumental to foregrounding Wang's natural cosmology. Contrasting Wang's philosophy against metaphysical dualism is further propaedeutic to apprehending his reading of the neo-Confucian metaphysics of his Song dynasty forefathers, for Wang saw in them a tendency toward metaphysical dualism and hypostatization of metaphysical first principles. As a case in point, Wang takes a critical position with regard to Zhu Xi's theory of patterning (*li* 理) and energy (*qi* 氣). He argues that Zhu's theory dualistically bifurcates these two categories and reifies the former. Zhou Bing (2005) observes Wang's position along these lines: "On the question of '*li* and *qi*,' Wang Fuzhi expresses a continuity of *qi* ontology and a novel perspective on the inseparability of *li* and *qi*" (5).[4] By the same token, Wang takes analytical caution with regard to his predecessors' interpretation of *taiji* 太極, the cosmological source of the world for neo-Confucianism. *Taiji* is immanent in Wang's philosophy. Through the subtle and cosmic interactions of its inherent forces, the natural world demonstrates an autopoietic capacity to continuously engender novel forms of life and experience. I return to an explication of the central concepts of *tian*, *li*, *qi*, and *taiji* later in this chapter. Before turning to this explication, however, I first follow the lead of Gernet, Jullien, and Black by establishing the antithesis to Wang Fuzhi's natural cosmology.

The cosmogony of creationism depicts the origins of the world as a definite temporal beginning (Black 22, 40–41; Jullien 78). Black introduces the fundamentals of creationism through a philological investigation into the term "create":

The word "create" in English usage is derived directly from the Latin *creare* . . . The critical event for the meaning of the word as it passed into medieval Latin and then into English was its use to translate the Hebrew *bara*, a verb used exclusively in the Hebrew scriptures for the creative activities of God. The consequence was that the root meaning of the word "create" in English usage was inextricably associated with its theological application. (6)

The term *bara* occurs in *Genesis* 1.1: "In the beginning, God *created* (*bara*) the heavens and the earth." Without pretending to give an exhaustive account of the manifold, entrenched interpretations of *Genesis*, Black and Jullien agree on salient implications of the biblical account. In the first case, the act of God "in the beginning" is absolutely unique in the advent of the world. Jullien thus writes, "The minimal justification of God within occidental rationalism is to attribute to him the initial impulsion in the chain of causes and effects that constitute the course of the world" (79).[5]

Neither Jullien nor Black explicitly note the name of St. Thomas Aquinas, but analysis of the rationale behind Aquinas's popular cosmological proofs of God supports their critique. Aquinas's brand of Catholicism is a marked appropriation of Aristotelian metaphysics in order to provide deductive proofs of God's existence. In Article III, "Whether God Exists," of Aquinas's *Summa Theologa*, the author concludes, "There must be found in the nature of things one first immovable Being, a primary cause, necessarily existing, not created; existing the most widely, good, even the best possible; the first ruler through the intellect, and the ultimate end of all things, which is God."[6] God is thus understood as the primary unmoved mover of the world. Insofar as God exists outside of the natural order of causality that governs the world, God is himself supernatural. The categorical distinction between the creator and the creation, or cause and effect, demonstrates that creationism is founded on a conception of external causality. In other words, causality here is a disjunctive relation, radically sundering effect from cause. The Creator stands metaphysically independent of and prior to his dependent creation.

Continuing her analysis, Black identifies three defining characteristics of *creation*:

> Here "creation" seems to denote basically the conscious and deliberate making of something new. In other words, we have (1) an intelligent agent, (2) deliberate action, in the form of making according to an original conception of the maker's, and (3) the thing made, dependent for existence on its source but also distinguishable from it, and new in some radical sense. (Black 6)

Jullien makes this same point in his definition of simple cosmogony and the "philosophical necessity of a primary mover":

At least two traits appear to me to have essentially con-tributed to the conception of this representation: on the one hand, the anthropological valorization of a category of subject-agent as the unique and voluntary instance; and, on the other hand, the ideological valorization of the radical difference between the status of the Creator and his creation. (Jullien 82)[7]

In addition to the commitment to external causality, creationism further presupposes that the cause is an act of a volitional, purposive, rational agent. The Creator conceives of the course of the world in accordance with divine Providence. He creates the world out of nothing, *ex nihilo*, and sets it in motion toward a predetermined end, or *télos*.

Although the biblical account of creation provides a primary archetype for the creationist paradigm, this model is a member of a greater "nexus" of theories that distinguish Western cosmogonies from Chinese cosmologies (Black 7). "The receipt of *Genesis*, as important as it is, finally represents only one possible version of the advent of the world in the midst of a panoply of occidental concep-tions" (Jullien 83).[8] In the family of models that represent creation-ist thinking, yet another primary archetype of the creative agent is found in Plato's *Timaeus* (Jullien 18, 82–90; Black 6–8). Plato's *Timaeus* purports to recount a "true story" of how the world was created out of Chaos by a divine artisan, known as the Demiurge. The Demiurge is an agent who constructs the world according to an intentional deliberate plan. The Demiurge, it is said, contemplates the ideal, eternal realm of Platonic Forms, and constructs the world of change as an image of the eternal. Exercising his capacity for theoretical reason, the Demiurge constructs the world according to an a priori intelligent design (Jullien 84–86). Insofar as the creator has a set form or blueprint in mind for the creation, he creates the world toward a determinate end. The root metaphor underlying the archetype of the creator is that of a divine *craftsman* (Jullien 84 ff.; Black 18). The craftsman is self-sufficient. Again, he is ontologically independent from and prior to his creation. Conversely, the creation is ontologically dependent on and secondary to the creator. The Creator causes the creation to come into being. As an external cause, the creator has also been likened to a watchmaker (Jullien 85). The watchmaker designs the mechanism such that once it is set in motion it will continue to function without further intervention by the maker. The maker sets the gears in place, winds it up, and then steps back while the mechanism continues to synchronically tick in local motion. This version of the creationist paradigm is thus represented as a mechanistic model of linear causation.

As opposed to Creationism and its assertion of a supernatural cause of the world, Wang Fuzhi's worldview presents a naturalistic cosmology. Wang's naturalism maintains that each and every thing, including the world itself, is completely the result of natural causes. On this account, the natural world and its constituent components are all that there is.

Tian 天 qua Nature

The philosophy stemming from Wang Fuzhi's root-categories of *tianrenheyi* 天人合一 and *tianrenzhiji* 天人之際 offers a rich resource for developing a neo-Confucian model of ecological humanism. According to the present interpretation, *tianrenheyi* and *tianrenzhiji* are respectively translated as "continuity of nature and persons" and "interstitial interrelations between nature and persons." This thesis hinges on the recognition that in the context of Wang's work the Chinese term *tian* functionally signifies *nature*. The thesis requires analytical proof that for Wang Fuzhi the concept of *tian* falls under the purview of naturalism.

Li Zhecheng (2003) sheds light on the hermeneutic prejudices that inform Wang Fuzhi's naturalistic understanding of *tian*. "Among the pre-Qin philosophies of China," Li writes, "the scholarly tradi-

tions that chiefly advocate a kind of scientific naturalism are the
Lao-Zhuang school and the school of Xunzi" (56).[9] Li argues that
Wang Fuzhi's understanding of nature reflects the influence of both
of these lines of thought (56).[10] Wang expresses his appreciation
for Xunzi's philosophy in his *Reading the Complete Compendium of
Statements on the Four Books* (*Du Sishudaquan shuo*, 讀四書大全說,
hereafter referred to as "DSS"):

> The venerable Xun was fifty when he began his scholar-
> ship. Zhu Yun began his undertaking of the *Yijing* and the
> *Analects* at forty. As for what they understood, compared
> with the cunning lads of our age, whose understanding after
> all is higher and whose inferior? [. . .] Xun and Zhu most
> certainly pushed to the heights of Shun, Yao, and Confucius.
> They took action without intentional thought, without
> purposive action, and the brilliance of *tian* manifested of
> itself. While young, they were bright and intelligent, but
> did not depend on scholarly study. They avoided techni-
> cal, self-serving, excessive prose and scholars that did not
> practice careful observation. They did not have any confu-
> sion in distinguishing persons from the rest of the animal
> kingdom. How unique! (DSS 852)[11]

For Xunzi, "*tian*" means "*ziran jie* 自然界"—in the modern Mandarin
sense of "natural world" (Zhang and Chen 785).[12] Xunzi's interpretation of *tian* qua *ziran* resonates with classical Daoist natural cosmology.[13] *Ziran* literally translates as "self-so." Wang employs it in this
sense by stating of things: "of themselves they are so" (自然而然).
The Chinese term, *ziran*, is rich in semantic content. To qualify the
cosmos as such means that it is a completely *natural, spontaneous,
autopoietic, auto-regulative, non-purposive, amoral* event. In upholding
this position, Wang Fuzhi, Xunzi and the early Lao-Zhuang authors
are critical and skeptical of the view of *tian* celebrated by Confucius
and Mencius.[14]

Confucius relates to *tian* as a kind of a personified participant
and ubiquitous, immanent force in human affairs.[15] Zheng Xiong's

(2006) work on *tian* in the context of the *Analects* and *tian* in the context of Wang Fuzhi demonstrates that Confucius viewed *tian*, in accordance with the predominant religious culture of his time, as an anthropomorphic and controlling power ("人格力量," "主宰力量") (Zheng 52).[16] Its subjective attributes include affectivity: it appreciates human actions at times, and takes offense to them at others (*Analects* 14.35). *Tian* is held in awe in the *Analects*, for it controls the longevity and death of creatures; moreover, it can enact cultural revolutions, sociopolitical capitulations, and epochal shifts in human history (*Analects* 9.5).[17] Finally, *tian* is purposive, intentional, and deliberate in its actions. In sum, *tian* in the context of the *Analects* is masterful and volitional (Zheng 52).[18]

Though *tian* carries these attributes in the eyes of Confucius, it would be a fallacy of equivocation to identify the *tian* of Confucius as a transcendent God. The metaphysical assumptions of classical Confucianism are inconsistent with the metaphysics of traditional theism. In brief the latter presupposes a metaphysical dualism between a transcendent, independent, ultimate reality, on the one hand, and a concrete, dependent, contingent reality, on the other. The theistic model functions according to a top-down causality. The relationship between God and persons is unilateral: persons depend on God for their existence and identity, but the converse is not the case. The metaphysical structure of the *tian*-person relationship for Confucius is bilateral. In other words, *tian* continuously emerges in positive correlation to the moral and cultural achievements of persons. *Tian* is a *spiritual culture* developed by persons over the course of history, and sustained through ancestral reverence. *Tian* serves as the consummate symbol and collective memory of one's cultural heritage. Whereas the theistic model is based on the premise, God created man in his image, the model of *tian* assumes the opposite. The image of *tian* takes shape in the form of historical figures. This process is explained by Roger T. Ames and Henry Rosemont, Jr.: "Culturally significant human beings—persons such as the Duke of Zhou and Confucius—are 'theomorphized' to become *tian*, and *tian* is itself made anthropocentric and determinate in their persons" (47). *Tian*'s intentions and affective responses are derived from and represent the ideal qualities of sagely persons. *Tian's* personified perspective on any state affairs just is the idealized perspective taken by ancestral spirits, or one's cultural *zeitgeist*. "*Tian* sees as my people see, *tian* hears as my people hear" (Mencius 5A5).

Wang pushes neo-Confucianism toward a fully naturalistic understanding of *tian*. In his worldview, *tian* is fully immanent and completely devoid of anthropomorphic qualities. Thus, JeeLoo Liu rightly states that Wang Fuzhi's *tian* is "the totality of the natural world" (360). In Wang Fuzhi's work, *tian* is nature qua *ziran*. That is, in the context of his cosmology, *tian* is fully natural and spontaneous, *ziranzhitian* 自然之天, as opposed to anthropomorphic, deliberate, and volitional, *yizhitian* 意志之天. A survey of recent scholarship in the field of Wang Fuzhi studies draws attention to this aspect of his thought:

> Cosmic transformations do not have feeling or intentionality. They are without heart-and-mind. That which is called "without-heart-and-mind" is also spontaneous. (Deng Hui 76)[19]

> Wang Fuzhi criticized Confucius's "volitional nature," and transformed it into spontaneous nature. (Zheng Xiong 50)[20]

> Wang Chuanshan believes that nature does not have volition or intention; it only adaptively moves within itself and nothing more. (Li Zhecheng 56)[21]

> Nature is without a heart-and-mind; without purposive activity; it does not have volition; it does not have feelings; it cannot control persons' destiny. (Xiong Lümao and Yang Zhengzheng 27)[22]

Wang Fuzhi makes claims to this effect throughout his work: "*Tian* does not intentionally act . . . Thus, when fortune and misfortune constantly change and the myriad patterns all come to fruition, they spontaneously achieve complete excellence" (Li, 2003, 56).[23] This claim further advances the idea of spontaneous nature by formulating it in terms of non-intentional action, *wuwei* 無為. Wang lifts this interpretive strategy straight from the Daoist playbook. Indeed, a host of corresponding negations or "*wu*-forms" are implied by Wang's appropriation of the Daoist "*ziran*": *wuwei* 無為, *wusi* 無思, *wusi* 無私, *wuji* 無己, *wuzhi* 無知, *wuxin* 無心. Respectively, nature is without intentional action, without deliberate thought, without personal inclinations, without self-awareness, without knowledge. In sum, nature is *without heart-and-mind*.

Lacking a mind and will of its own, *tian* does not judge:

> Raising the hands is an act of respectful salutation; kneeling in formal posture is an act of pride: these are the rituals of people. Nature, however, causes fear and trembling but does not instruct by means of ritual reverence; it establishes and underwrites divisions, but does not direct according to self-conceit. People fear the imperial corporeal punishments of tattooing, amputation, castration, and execution because they invoke condemnation. From the perspective of nature, however, the crippled are so *not* because they were robbers, and the emasculated are so *not* because they are licentious.[24]

Spontaneous nature possesses a sublime power to enact transformations. Wang believes that the anthropomorphic worldview constitutes a diminution of nature's sublimity. Making this point, he rhetorically questions the belief in *tian* as a quasi-personal force: "*Tian* is only *yinyang* and five phases, arising and descending, emerging and retracting in the heavens and earth. Why should it ever condescend to the level of giving orders as such?" (DSS 454). Insofar as Wang Fuzhi's philosophy of nature presupposes the cosmological categories of neo-Confucianism, it should come as no surprise that nature is here regarded as a dynamic holistic structure of energetic forces. That is, *tian* is nothing more than patterns of energy, *qizhili* 氣之理.

Neo-Confucian Terminology of Cosmic Creativity

According to Chen Lai 陈来 (2004), "Wang Chuanshan's *Annotated Commentary on Master Zhang's Zhengmeng* is an interpretation and development of Zhang Zai's *Zhengmeng* [. . .] From the perspective of a theory of origin, the fundamental idea of the *Zhengmeng*'s naturalistic philosophy for the most part comes from the *Zhouyi*, primarily the *Commentaries on the Changes*" (361).[25] Chen Lai here advances the notion that Zhang Zai, Wang Fuzhi, and the *Yijing* are to be read as having a theory of origins. The conjunction of Chen Lai's claim with Jullien's and Black's rejection of reading Wang Fuzhi's work as a theory of origins foregrounds a particular *problématique*, which Wang Fuzhi himself saw in the neo-Confucian tradition.

Wang Fuzhi's dilemma of origins grows out of the question of how to interpret the concept of supreme limit *taiji* 太極 and the generative forces of *yin* 陰 and *yang* 陽 in the context of the *Yijing*'s claim:

Changes have a supreme limit, *taiji*: this produces two modes; two modes produce four figures; four figures produce eight trigrams (*Xici shang* 11.3).[26]

On Black's account, "The general import of his [Wang's] argument was to remove from *t'ai-chi* [*taiji*] the concept of generative source and define it as principle of harmony characterizing *yin* and *yang*" (65). Black's intentions are in the right place; nonetheless, her unqualified claim that Wang did not recognize *taiji* as a generative source is too strong. It is not the case that he seeks to remove the connotations of generative source from the concept of *taiji* altogether, nor is it the case that he sees *taiji* as a creator in the sense of Creationism. Wang Fuzhi is particularly concerned with the tendency of the neo-Confucian tradition to interpret the notion of *taiji* as a cosmogonic (external) cause that precedes the advent of the natural world and its multifarious concrete particulars (Jullien 69).[27] Wang takes a critical posture when analyzing the cosmology of *taiji*, *yinyang*, and the productive activity of engendering, *sheng* 生. He intends for his philosophy to serve as an articulation of the neo-Confucian commitment to an immanent source of creativity, life, novelty, and diversity. In this vein he seeks to purge the neo-Confucian tradition of implying the existence of a supernatural cause of the natural world. He intends to clearly distinguish his philosophy of the *Yijing* from any conceptions of origin that presuppose an atemporal beginning or cosmological priority of one state of affairs over and above all others. Wang maintains that *taiji* is a cosmological source or origin, to be sure, but it is an immanent and participatory source identifiable with the world itself. In a word, *taiji* is the root-body, *benti* 本體, of the world:

> These [*yin* and *yang*] are how *taiji* brings forth the myriad things; becoming the myriad patterns, and giving rise to the myriad events. These are the *root-body* of beginnings and growth. (ZYN 525)[28]

Rather than acting on the world according to a top-down structure, the *taiji* qua root-body is an emergent source of transformation, life, and diversity. As Wang Fuzhi describes it, *taiji* just is the globalized unity of all *yin* and *yang* interactions, on all levels of organizational structures and in all localities.

Although the idea of *taiji* is found in the pre-Qin *Appended Phrases*, *Xici*, section of the *Yijing*, it was not a prominent concept for philosophical speculation prior to Zhou Dunyi's early-Song Dynasty *Explanation of the* Taiji *Diagram* (Jullien 69, Black 65). After Zhou Dunyi, neo-Confucian thinkers "made it the foundation of their representation of the course of the world, the advent of all existence, and the ultimate limit, which amounts to all process" (Jullien 70).[29] Black provides the following translation of Zhou's *Explanation*:

> Without Ultimate—the Supreme Ultimate!
> In the Supreme Ultimate there is movement and the
>   birth of *yang*;
> At the limit of movement: stillness.
> In stillness is the birth of *yin*;
> At the limit of stillness: the return of movement.
> Movement and stillness alternating are one another's root;
> *Yin* and *yang* dividing constitute two modes. (Black 65)[30]

Paraphrasing Wang Fuzhi, Jullien explains Wang's interpretation of "*taiji*" along these lines: "One is not able to go farther, climb higher: because there is no farther and no higher. This ultimate limit is one of void itself, as non-actualization (*wuji*) at the source of all actualization: not the void *qua* non-existence, but on the contrary as absolute plenitude—in its phase of non-actualization it is but all possible actualizations . . ." (Jullien 69–70).[31] Whereas *taiji* refers to the world as a dynamic and holistic unity of all diverse phenomena, the concept of *wuji* is postulated to ensure that the world is understood as an unbound totality. Furthermore, *wuji* is not nothing in the sense of *nihilo*. As absolute plenitude, *wuji* refers to the boundless capacity of the cosmos to endlessly give rise to novel actual occasions from its own internal dimensions. *Wuji* is essentially a negative term, meaning *without limits*; *wuji* signifies that there is no determinate objectified source or limits to the transformations of the world (Gernet 156). In this sense, moreover, the complexity and sublime fecundity of the world is beyond the bounds of reason, and thus opens itself up to profound aesthetic and religious appreciation of nature's sublimity.

To take Wang Fuzhi's stance, Zhou Dunyi's *Explanation* and the *Yijing* passage on which it is based delineate a tightrope of interpretation that must be traversed with the utmost caution. The intention in Wang's argument is to retain *taiji*'s sense of cosmological fecundity and yet avoid fallacies of hypostatization and metaphysical reification. Alluding to this difficulty, Jullien writes of the rich ambiguity of Zhou Dunyi's representation of the *Yijing*: "One is able to interpret it in a more cosmogonic sense, conferring on this limit [*taiji*] a status of a point of departure or of origin, *or* in a purely cosmological sense, by eradication of all exclusive status of anteriority" (70).[32] Wang Fuzhi maintained the falsity of the former, and the verity of the latter.[33] He provides the following warning against misinterpreting Zhou Dunyi's *Explanation*:

Those who misunderstand the *Explanation of the Diagram of the Supreme Limit* say the supreme limit originally does not yet have *yin* and *yang*. [They say] because of movement, then there is the fetal beginning and birth of *yang*, and because of stillness, then there is the fetal beginning

and birth of *yin*. They do not know that movement and
stillness are what are engendered by *yin* and *yang*, and
[*taiji*] originally has them [*yin* and *yang*] contained. [*Yin* and
yang] make the natures (*qingzhi*)[34] of winter and summer,
moistness and dryness, and male and female. The subtle
comingling of *yin* and *yang* (*yinyun*) are prior to movement
and stillness. As for movement and stillness, these are the
movement and stillness of *yin* and *yang*. (Wang, ZMZ, 24)[35]

Chen Lai advances the discussion by explaining that Wang Fuzhi's
emphasis is that *taiji* is the supreme harmony *taihe* 太和 and subtle
comingling of *yin* and *yang* (*yinyun* 絪縕) (Chen 368).[36] *Taiji* in other words originally contains the generative interactions of the two
modalities, and it would be a mistake to conceive of it as a state of
affairs that somehow precedes them (ibid.). In his *Inner Commentary
to the Zhouyi, Zhouyi neizhuan* 周易內傳, Wang comments on the
Yijing's claim that *taiji* produces two modes: "*Yin* and *yang* have no
beginning," he states. "*Taiji* is not something standing on its own over
and above *yin* and *yang*" (ZYN 562).[37] Again, Wang Fuzhi's philosophy is a radical, process, correlative cosmology. He saw the world
qua process as having no determinate beginning and no teleological
end. Accordingly, Jullien further addresses this issue in his work on
Wang's philosophy:

The "virtue" inherent in the grand process that is continuously in operation in the world is that it "embraces all,"
from the largest to the most minute, and that it is also at
the origin of all (that is to say of all the particular actualizations). But there is never "a moment or an existent that
would be able to serve as a point of departure for process,"
of the sort that "all the rest follows it" . . . Just as it does
not have an end, the ongoing movement will not have a
beginning." (Jullien 68–69)[38]

The generative interactions of *yin* and *yang* are always at work in a
perpetual motion. Neither *yin* nor *yang*, Qian nor Kun, is primary

in the cosmological order of things (Jullien 46–49, et passim, Yan 123–124). Each modality reflects, contains, penetrates, responds to, and implies the other. This dynamic interchange between the two modalities does not have any external cause. In other words, the interaction is sui generis, spontaneous and auto-regulative. That is, cosmic creativity is self-so, *ziran*. In agreement with Jullien and Black, Yan Shoucheng makes the case in point in his dissertation on Wang Fuzhi:

> *Taiji* embraces all kinds of the potentials of materials and forces which continuously and spontaneously develop into concrete things and later undergo other, endless transformations. In this sense, Alison Black's interpretation of Wang's philosophy as "expressionism" is applicable—that is it is characterized by innerness, spontaneity, and continuity between the expressive source and the final outcome, and by organic form in which inner and outer are bound inseparably together. (Yan 123)

In sum, there is no *determinate* beginning to the interaction of *yin* and *yang* that one can call *taiji*, nor is there an end. Again, the procreative activity of the cosmos is without limits, *wuji* (Jullien 68–69).

In reference to her translation of Zhou Dunyi's text cited above, Black maintains that her interpretation reflects a traditional neo-Confucian reading of the text, but Wang Fuzhi would not agree with her translation of the verb *sheng* as " 'generate' or '(give) birth' " (65). Black goes on to cite the following passage from Wang Fuzhi's *Minor Commentary on the Zhouyi* 周易稗疏:

> In regards to *birth* (*sheng* 生), it is not the case that what is born is a son, or that which gives birth is called a father. If it were used thus, then there would be a time where there were *taiji* without two modalities, two modalities without four images, four images without of eight trigrams. The birth is the birth of giving rise, as in a person's face giving rise to ears, eyes, mouth, and nose, naturally and completely.

> In their distinction then we name them: this is what is
> now meant by *birth* . . . *Taiji* thus two modes, two modes
> thus four images, four images thus eight trigrams: as in a
> person's face, thus, ears, eyes, mouth, nose. In particular, if
> that which gives rise to what is produced and established
> is divided up and named, then it is two; it is four, and it
> is eight. (Wang, ZYBS, 789)[39]

In this passage Wang pays analytical attention to the verb *sheng* 生.
The term *sheng* refers to the processes through which actual occasions or concrete particulars emerge in the world. As a verb, *sheng* 生
literally translates as "to produce, to bring forth, to beget" (*Mathews*
795). It means "to give birth, to engender." But Wang Fuzhi maintains that the process of cosmological production is not that of a
parent giving birth to a child (Black 66; Jullien 70). If the relation
between *taiji* and the empirical world of protean particulars is thus
characterized as a relation between a parent and a child, Wang wor-
ries that people would get the idea that there was a time in which
the source of particulars could have existed apart from the particulars themselves.[40] *Taiji* refers to the ability of the world to give rise
to itself—in all of its novel and diversified transformations. In the
language of the *Yijing*, *taiji* thus refers to the capacity of the world
to renew itself daily, *rixin* 日新, and create incessantly, *shengsheng* 生
生 (*Xici shang* 6). We return to this particular case in point later in
the context of neo-Confucian spirituality. There we discuss how a
perceived procreative creativity (*shengsheng*) of the world serves as a
source and intention of religious experience.

　　Wang Fuzhi uses *taiji* to refer to the relationship between *yin*
and *yang*, but the intention of this usage is to depict this relationship under its unitary and global aspect. That is to say, it does not
designate the differential functions of *yin* and *yang*. Wang understands
taiji as a mode of generalized latency, where *yin* and *yang*, although
implicitly different, do not actively manifest their difference and are
intimately commingled. In terms of their referent, the synthetic concept of *yinyang* and the concept of *taiji* are the same: They have the
same semantic value, namely, the immanent cosmological source and

perpetual generative process pervading all experience. Analytically speaking, while the *referent* of these two concepts (*yinyang*, on the one hand, and *taiji*, on the other) is the same, the *sense* differs. Whereas *yin* and *yang* signify differentiated modes of process, *taiji* signifies that these modalities interpenetrate and harmonize in a global unity (Jullien 71).[41]

Wang Fuzhi explicitly identifies the notion of *taiji*, the supreme limit, with Zhang Zai's notion of *taihe* 太和, supreme harmony.[42] Following Jullien's interpretation, this equation serves a dual purpose. On the one hand, the notion of *taiji* eliminates the risk, always present, of considering this limit as an origin and point of departure; and on the other, as the communal ground of all actualization, the notion of harmony provides a more distinct characterization of the relationality that constitutes all process (72).[43] Jullien uses the terms "communal ground" (*fonds commun*), "resorption of contraries" (*résorption des contraires*), and "regulative resorption" (*résorption régulatrice*) of "actualizing differentiation" (*différenciation actualisatrice*) to refer to the function of supreme harmony.

The idea behind Jullien's vocabulary is perhaps conveyed more clearly by Wang's claim: "Before there are yet formal particulars, there is originally nothing that is not harmonized; moreover, after there are formal particulars, this harmony is not lost" (ZMZ 15).[44] In the same passage, Wang goes on to discuss supreme harmony in the following terms:

> Supreme harmony is the reach of harmony. *Dao* is the pervasive pattern of the heavens and earth, and the myriad things, thus it is called supreme limit. *Yin* and *Yang* differentiate, but their intimate comingling (*yinyun*) in the midst of the supreme void comes together (*hetong*) and they do not cause injury to one another, they are evenly intermixed (*hunlun*)[45] without interstice, thus is the extent of harmony. (ibid.)[46]

Wang here identifies *taiji* with *dao*, which he defines as the pervasive pattern, *tongli* 通理, binding all of the events of the world together.

Accordingly, *taiji* and *dao* convey the sense that a world is thoroughly interconnected in a global, spatiotemporal, holistic structure. *Taiji* bears more connotations of originary source; *dao* bears the connotation of ongoing origination and sustainment of life, structure, and novelty. *Yin* and *yang* are general categories that refer to phenomenal occurrences on all scales, from the most infinitesimally minute and mundane happenings to the greatest cosmological and sublime occurrences. That they commingle with one another without causing harm indicates that the interconnection of events is functional and productive. Chen Lai explains the key terms employed here in Wang Fuzhi's cosmological thought:

> The supreme harmony and commingling of *yin* and *yang* (*taihe yinyun*) are the initial sources of the production of the myriad things. This is what is contained in the concept of *taiheyinyun*. Because in Chuanshan's [Wang Fuzhi's] cosmological theory, supreme harmony represents the most primitive existence and state of affairs, the separation of *yin* and *yang* and the production of the myriad things both follow from the capacity of the supreme harmony. Nonetheless, it is certainly not the case that supreme harmony only exists prior to the production of the myriad things and merely serves as the cosmological initial source. In reality, supreme harmony still exists after the production of the myriad things. (Chen 365)[47]

Chen identifies *taihe* as a cosmological source in Wang Fuzhi's philosophy. Again, the tightrope must be walked carefully. Given the continuity of harmony before and after the production of the plethora of existents, it cannot be said that *taihe* is a metaphysical being per se. *Taihe* is another way to allude to the unfathomable and numinous coordination of the fecund energies of *yin* and *yang*. Before the emergence of novelty in the world of particular events, *taihe* is the open indeterminate set of conditions that gives rise to the events themselves. In this sense, *taihe* can also be understood as the root-body *benti* 本體 of all that is. The conditions themselves are not singular, but manifold: they are a unity of diversity and diversity in unity. *Taihe* refers to the spontaneously coordinated, patterned interaction of these events, which in turn gives rise to new life and new particulars. *Taihe* is a holistic concept that alludes to the interdependent and creative interactions of all events.

Neo-Confucian cosmology of *taiji*, *wuji*, and *taihe* may very well be consistent with the current scientific theory of the Big Bang origins of the universe. According to the latter theory the cosmos originated approximately 13.7 billion years ago by way of an exploding expansion of an originally infinitely dense and extremely hot concentration of energy. This concentration is referred to as a singularity, which is a singular infinitely small point of infinite density and gravitational force. As scientists trace back the origins of the cosmos to infinity, they hypothesize that in the event of singularity, the laws of physics and the very structure of space-time break down to the point that they are no longer applicable to the structuring and movement of matter. If confronted with the proposition of a Big Bang at the origins of the universe, Wang Fuzhi would no doubt find recourse to interpret the theory in terms of *taiji*, *wuji*, *taixu*, and originary, primordial, energy (*yuanqi* 元氣). The terminology of *wuji* and *taixu* (without limits and great vacuity) are readily applicable to the concept of infinity in which our operational observations and rational comprehensions of the cosmos are abnegated. In short, in locating the origins of the structured cosmos in infinity, Wang would undoubtedly move to maintain that the origins themselves, the singularity from which the cosmos expands is in itself unfathomable. Though the Big Bang may be a determinative event, by Wang's lights, this determinacy originates in indeterminacy.

Wang Fuzhi is a naturalist in the sense that he does not believe that anything exists outside of the natural world constituted by *qi*. Although he recognizes that the movements of *qi* often function so subtly that they are invisible to the human eye, he does not conclude that *qi* has any supernatural status. In place of a transcendent source or principle of the patterned changes and structural coordination of natural events, he advocates an emergent order that is immanent within the world itself. For Wang the operations of *qi* from the cosmic level of *tiandi* to the most infinitesimally small are not fully fathomable by ratiocination; nonetheless, they provide sources for aesthetic and religious appreciations of the dynamically sublime and intricate complexity of the cosmic tapestry. Wang Fuzhi regards the subtle and unfathomable ability of *qi* to transform on all levels of existence as a numinous and sublime quality of *qi*. Wang rejects all modes of thought that postulate, reify, or hypostatize a primary transcendent source of creativity and value in the world. In this respect, he is in agreement with Golley's and Keller's ecological naturalism, which "challenges positions that posit the cause and regulation of the universe as prior to or ontologically distinct from nature itself" (Golley and Keller 12). But the sense of naturalism applicable to Wang Fuzhi goes beyond a simple rejection of metaphysical transcendence; in addition to its negative definition, the axiom of naturalism implies axioms of ontological interconnectedness, internal relations, and holism.

2

Complex Systems and Patterns of Energy

Having provided an exposition of Wang Fuzhi's brand of neo-Confucian naturalism, we now turn to foreground an interpretive perspective of contemporary ecological theory as a position from which to engage Wang Fuzhi in dialogue. Ecological humanism provides a descriptive account of persons-in-the-world. This description is based on the complex systems theories adopted by the science of ecology. This chapter provides an account of the general tenets of the complex system theory at the basis of ecological humanism. Based upon this foundation, we then begin construction of a neo-Confucian ecological humanism. In this vein, the discussion proceeds into an interpretive exposition of Wang Fuzhi's cosmology of *qi* and *li*. Finally, having analyzed Wang Fuzhi's concept of *qi*, the chapter concludes with an argument for critically aligning Wang Fuzhi's philosophy of *qi* with recent developments in postmodern *new* materialism.

A Perspective from Ecosystems Ecology

From Ernst Haeckel's first introduction of the term *Ökologie* into scientific discourse onwards, ecology has refused to abstract, analyze, and understand phenomena apart from their environing conditions. In his 1864 inaugural address at Jena University, Haeckel provided a celebrated description of the science:

By ecology we mean the body of knowledge concerning
the economy of nature—the investigation of the total relations of the animal both to its inorganic and to its organic
environment; including, above all, its friendly and inimi-
cal relations with those animals and plants with which it
comes directly or indirectly into contact . . . By ecology,
we mean the whole science of the relations of the organism to the environment, including, in the broad sense all
the "conditions of existence."[1]

Haeckel identifies ecology as a new Darwinian-based epistemology of
organisms for the modern era. By his definition, the new epistemology
provides an account (*logos*) that attempts to situate an organism or
group of organisms squarely within an environment or habitat (*oikos*).
Haeckel's definition implies that relationships between an organism
and its surroundings are fundamental to the constitution, evolution,
and definition of an organism.[2] From the outset, the discipline of
ecology opened the way for understanding contextually determined
roles and relationships as essentially constitutive of concrete particulars—rather than categorizing roles and relationships as merely
accidental, as they had been regarded in the classical Aristotelian
substance-based ontology. Thus, J. Baird Callicott likewise argues
that from an ecological point of view, "relations are 'prior' to the
things related, and the systemic wholes woven from these relations
are 'prio' " to their component parts. Ecosystemic wholes are 'logically
prior' to their component species because the nature of the part is
determined by its relationship to the whole" (60).
    Throughout the early twentieth century, scientific and philo-
sophical discourse on nature underwent a paradigm shift away from
classical substance ontology and atomistic metaphysics into complex
systems theory and holism. Edgar Morin writes of the early twentieth-
century shift as a kind of Copernican revolution in which classical
categories are overthrown: "Objects give way to systems. Instead of
essences and substances, organization; instead of simple and elementary units, complex unity; instead of aggregates forming bodies, systems of systems of systems" (Morin 1992, 121). The science of ecology

and ecological humanism are very much members of this new-school of nature. During this epochal movement, systems theory was taken up and applied to the still nascent science of ecology. In 1936, famed Oxford botanist, Sir Arthur George Tansley introduced the concept of 'ecosystem' into the science of ecology. Tansley formulates the concept:

> It is the systems so formed which, from the point of view of the ecologist, are the basic units of nature on the face of the earth. . . . These *ecosystems*, as we may call them, are of the most various kinds and sizes. They form one category of the multitudinous physical systems of the universe, which range from the universe as a whole down to the atom. The whole method of science . . . is to isolate systems mentally for the purpose of study. . . . Actually the systems we isolate mentally are not only included as parts of larger ones, but they also overlap, interlock, and interact with one another. (Tansley 64)

Thus, Tansley's original account describes the ecosystem as a complex system embedded within a nested hierarchical structure of complex systems. The consummation of the 'ecosystem' concept enacted a fundamental change in how nature was to be thereafter studied and understood.[3]

A person-in-the-world can be understood as an ecosystem. Each person is a quintessential token of what it is to be a cognizant, communicative, organic system. Each person is a complex, psychosomatic, conscious system embedded within the ever-changing environmental systems of the natural-and-social world.[4] Morin's *Le paradigme perdu* [*Paradigm Lost*] may be cited to disclose the structure of persons-in-the-world as an "ecosystemic relation" between persons and their environing situations:

> The ecosystemic relation is not an external relation between two closed entities: It concerns an integrative relation between two open systems where each is part of the

other . . . The ecological dependence and independence of man find themselves in two overlapping perspectives, which are themselves interdependent: one of the social ecosystem, and the other of the natural ecosystem . . . *L'écologie* or rather *écosystémologie* rehabilitates the notion of nature and the rootedness of man therein. Nature is no more disorder, passivity, or amorphous environmental condition: It is a complex totality. Man is not a closed entity in relation to this complex totality: he is an open system in relations of [relative] organizational autonomy and dependence in the midst of an ecosystem.[5]

Similarly, in their *Philosophy of Ecology*, David R. Keller and Frank B. Golley describe ecological entities in terms of holism, complex systems theory, and ontological interconnectedness: "the boundaries of ecological entities are imprecise, in part because of the entities' openness (porousness or permeability)," they write. "A closed entity would be isolated from its environment; no closed entities exist in nature. An organism continually exchanges matter and energy with the larger system of which it is a part" (Keller, Golley 23). In the language of complex systems theory, persons are *situated* within the world. An individual is *situated* insofar as "it is an interactive part of a system" (Auyang 47). For any concrete particular individual, "being situated is part of its intrinsic character and its behavior is influenced by the situation that is determined by all individuals in the system" (Auyang 118). In this theory, particulars or individuals are not understood as abstract bare elements or absolutely atomic particles (in the classical sense), which bear no *internal relations* to one another. Instead, particulars are situated *constituents* or participants in complex systems of energy flow, exchange and transformation.[6]

The "ecosystemic relationship" is an articulation of "ontological interconnectedness." In terms of ecosystems ecology and Wang Fuzhi's theory alike, persons are connected to their local and global surroundings through continuous exchanges of energy and information. Morin's description provides a poignant hermeneutic perspective for interpreting the complex structure of persons-in-the-world in the worldview of Wang Fuzhi. In particular, Morin's understanding of *la relation écosystémique* serves as a soundboard for reflecting on the dynamic relationships between nature and persons denoted by the core terms of Wang's philosophical ecology: (1) "continuity between nature and persons" *tianrenheyi* 天人合一; (2) "interstitial relations between nature and persons" *tianrenzhiji* 天人之際; (3) "nature within nature" *zaitianzhitian* 在天之天; and, (4) "nature within persons" *zairenzhitian* 在人之天.

Though Tansley was reluctant to align his empirical science of ecosystems ecology with the speculative tenor of philosophical holism, subsequent ecologists like Eugene P. Odum have successfully adopted and applied the terminology of "holism" to ecosystems ecology. Despite Tansley's efforts to distinguish his concept 'ecosystem' from the philosophical theory of holism, ecology remains committed to basic tenets of philosophical holism.

The term "holism" is a neologism coined by South African statesman, general, and philosopher, Jan Christian Smuts (1870–1950):

> Both matter and life consist of unit structures whose ordered grouping produces natural wholes which we call bodies or organisms . . . Holism . . . is the term here coined for this fundamental factor operative toward the creation of wholes in the universe. Taking a plant or animal as a type of a whole, we notice the fundamental holistic characters as a unity of parts which is so close and intense as to be more than the sum of its parts; which not only gives a particular conformation or structure to the parts but so relates and determines them in their synthesis that their functions are altered; the synthesis affects and determines the parts so they function towards the "whole"; and the whole and the parts therefore reciprocally influence and determine each other, and appear more or less to merge their individual character: the whole is in the parts and the parts are in the whole, and this synthesis of whole and parts is reflected in the holistic character of the functions of the parts as well as of the whole. (Smuts 86)[7]

The holistic approach to phenomena posits that the self-nature of any x can only be determined insofar as x is related to other phenomena (Ziporyn 28). A phenomenon only finds its identity and meaning insofar as it is related to other phenomena within a system or world. Moreover, the whole itself is determined and defined not by what it is composed of, or by any unchanging essence, but according to its organization, that is, how its constituent parts relate to one another. There is a reciprocal relation of identity between the whole and its parts: any part is defined in relation to all other parts throughout the whole, and any whole is defined as how its parts are construed, that is, how the parts are related to one another.

Holism is contrasted against atomistic philosophy: the view that the identity of any x is determined in and of itself, apart from its relations to other phenomena. In an atomist metaphysical philosophy the relationships held between things must be accidental and external as opposed to constitutive and internal. In atomism, relationships do not necessarily contribute to the identity of any thing. As Brook Ziporyn suggests, atomism asks "What is X like when the distortions created by the various particular contexts and relationships in which it tends to appear have been removed" (Ziporyn 28). In this vein, atomism is far removed from ecological thinking. Classically speaking, the terms *atomism* and *reductionism* often refer to the same mode of thought. "Ontological reduction is the notion that the cosmos is a composite built out of smaller, simpler units: atoms" (Golley, Keller 73). However, as Morin points out, "Systems theory has reacted to reductionism, in and by 'holism' or the idea of the 'whole.' But, believing to go beyond reductionism, holism has in fact brought about a reduction on the whole" (Morin, 1992, 122). A holistic understanding based on Wang Fuzhi's neo-Confucianism provides a dialectical reinstatement of the individual in relation to the totalistic system in which it is situated. Neo-Confucian modes of holism retain the insight of ontological interrelatedness, and yet they avoid this reverse-reduction or reification of the whole. The person-in-the-world is at once an insistent particular and an energetic phase in a cosmic pattern of interrelated events.

Nature as Patterns of Energy

In the perennial Chinese worldview, *qi* 氣 is an explanatory concept which conveys the experience of the world and its constituent phenomena as dynamic vivacious processes. French sinologist Jacques Gernet provides the following gloss on the term:

> Applied to the broken and continuous lines of the *Book of Changes* or *Zhouyi*, it seems that one can only best translate the word *qi*, a term without equivalent in our traditions, as *energy*. It is the sense that it has in the modern language where the composite *dianqi* designates electricity . . . The Chinese concept of energy has by etymology a sense of "vapor" and has conserved over the course of history the diverse senses of vapor, breath, air, fumes, climate, or even vigor and vital force that can be weakened or reinforced. (159)[8]

Gernet's analysis indicates ubiquitous presence of the term *qi* in Chinese discourse, and correspondingly the ubiquitous presence of *qi* in reality. *Qi* is the continuous energy field that resonates through, constitutes and interconnects all of nature. From the remotest recesses of space (*tiankong* 天空) to the most miniscule pebble, there is nothing that is not fully constituted by *qi*. "The continuous presence of *qi* in all modalities of being makes everything flow together as the unfolding of a single process" (Tu 108). *Qi* is the active vital force driving the continuous transformation of all events. Internal to the lived body it is blood (*xueqi* 血氣), breath (*xiqi* 吸氣), and emotion, as in anger (*shengqi* 生氣). Outside of the body it is atmosphere (*kongqi* 空氣) and meteorological phenomena (*tianqi* 天氣). As the weather always changes, so *qi* is constantly in motion. Though spontaneous, the motions are not chaotic: *Qi* functions according to the self-regulated, patterned movements of *yin* and *yang* (negative and positive feedback loops). In a word, there is no energy that is not patterned, *li* 理.

Wang Fuzhi identifies the interdependence of energy and pattern: "Filling the space between the sky and earth, within people's lived bodies, and external to people's lived bodies, there is nothing that is not *qi*. Thus, also, there is nothing that is not patterned, *li* 理. Pattern moves within *qi*" (DSS 857).[9] The theme of pattern and energy as an inseparable pair is repeated throughout Wang's work. Elsewhere in the same work, for example, he reiterates this fundamental premise: "Patterning, forthwith, is patterning of energy (or energetic patterning, *qizhili* 氣之理). Energy ought to be grasped like this, that is, as patterning. Patterning is not prior, nor is energy afterward . . ." (1052).[10]

Li like *qi* is one of those pugnacious words in Chinese philosophical discourse that refuses to cooperate with any attempt to find a one-to-one correspondence between it and an English term. Again, Gernet's etymological investigation is informative: The term *li*, Gernet explains, originally occurs in the *Book of Odes* without the jade radical that it has in current form. In its original usage it referred to the division of fields for horticultural use. The jade radical was probably added in the normalization of Chinese script that occurred toward the end of the third century (Gernet 199). The character for *li*—the symmetrical subdivision of fields and the interconnected lines interior to jade—suggests a sense of "patterning." Following its original sense, the meaning of *li* developed to signify a natural and harmonious order of particular events. Whereas *qi* functions to explain the dynamic self-presentation of life and process in the world, *li* explains that experience always presents itself with degrees of coherence and structure. *Qi* signifies flux; "*li* is the pattern amidst the flux which provides a means of establishing harmony" (Tucker, Berthrong xxxvii).

The conjoined concepts of *li* and *qi* resonate with contemporary ecology and physics. While Wang Fuzhi's neo-Confucian framework is a kind of holistic cosmology and process philosophy, it affirms the existence and insistence of particularity in the world. Here J. Baird Callicott's essay on "The Metaphysical Implications of Ecology" is instructive. In his exposition of "New Ecology" and "New Physics,"

Callicot provides a language that is strikingly close to that of Wang Fuzhi's neo-Confucianism. Callicott writes:

> An individual organism, like an elementary particle is, as it were, a momentary configuration, a local perturbation, in an energy flux or "field". . . . [E]cological interactions, primarily and especially trophic relationships, constitute a macrocosmic network or pattern through which solar energy, fixed by photosynthesis, is transferred from organism to organism until it is dissipated. Organisms are moments in this network, knots in this web of life. (Callicott 59)

After acknowledging the insistent particularity of organisms and their constitute material atoms, Callicott invokes quantum theory to explain particular organisms and atoms in another frame of reference "are, in their entire structure-from subatomic microcosm to ecosystemic macrocosm-patterns, perturbations, or configurations of energy" (ibid.).

Wang sees a tendency in Song theorists of the Cheng-Zhu school to overemphasize, reify, and hypostatize *li* 理 as a metaphysical principle that is independent from the fluctuating energy that it patterns. Historian Peter Bol notes, "'Neo-Confucianism' is a modern, foreign term. The common Chinese names for this movement are quite different . . . Each of these names emphasizes one aspect of the philosophical discussions at the expense of the other" (78). The term *lixue* 理學 (School of *Li*) as a popular appellation for neo-Confucian thought is a case in point. The lineage of *lixue* is founded on works of Zhu Xi 朱熹 (1130–1200), the "great systematizer," and his intellectual predecessor Cheng Yi 程頤 (1033–1107). "When all is said and done," writes Gernet, "Zhu Xi imagined an ideal *li*, independent of energies and anterior to the formation of beings" (Gernet 201).[11] Gernet continues, "Hostile to abstractions and conscious of an analysis from concrete reality, and following his master Zhang Zai, Wang speculates that the products of the activity of the universal energy demonstrate in an irrefutable manner that this energy possesses in itself the ability to form organized beings" (206).[12] In agreement with Gernet, Alison Harley Black also concludes that Wang Fuzhi regards the *li* of the Cheng-Zhu school as a transcendent principle, a position which he staunchly opposes in favor of the immanence of *li* (Black 61–68). For Wang Fuzhi, in contrast to Zhu Xi, *li* cannot be understood as a principle that governs the movements of *qi* from the top down. *Li* is not a static principle: It *emerges* in and as the pattern of interactive energies. The *li*, being the *li* of *qi* in Wang's philosophy, is here generated in the internal dynamics of *qi* itself. *Li* in other words is the spontaneous and complex organization of *qi*. Insofar as *li* is emergent within the world of flux, it is perhaps better translated as "patterning" rather than "pattern."

A paradigmatic example of holistic thought in neo-Confucian philosophy is found in the slogan accredited to Cheng Yi: *Liyifenshu* "理一分殊." "*Li is continuous, its divisions many.*"[13] The one continuous *li* refers to the experience of the world as an integrative whole. The division and uniqueness of *li* represents the world as a plurality of events—patterns within patterns, and patterns becoming other patterns. Cheng Yi's slogan indicates that one never has a unity apart from the diverse facts that constitute it, and one never has a plurality of facts that do not constitute a unity. As in the case of complex systems theory, the "one" and "many" or "whole" and "parts" are here mutually implicative. Each particular is a unique pattern of *qi*. Insofar as *qi* is continuous throughout the cosmos, each particular can be understood as focal expression of the whole. The idea resonates with Alfred North Whitehead's brand of holism summarized by the slogan: "the many become one and are increased by one" (Whitehead 21). In neo-Confucian discourse, each novel entity is a configuration of the cosmic *qi* that interconnects all things in a continuous energy field. Each particular draws all of the energetic relationships that it has with every other particular into itself, organizes these relationships into a unique pattern, and expresses these relationships in its own way. The one *li* is a cosmic nested hierarchy of patterns. It is a pattern of *qi* transformations or a holistic system of all particular events, but this pattern/structure never has an objective status that can be apprehended apart from a particular perspective. The pattern shifts according to shifting perspectives taken from within the order itself. There is no God's-eye view or universal *arché* to be found in the neo-Confucian account. Rather than a single pattern, the one *li* is an open set of possible ways to experience and imagine the world as a dynamic unity.

Gernet notes that in its current usage the term *li* is used as a translation of the Western terms of "principle" or "reason." But Gernet immediately goes on to claim that it is perhaps better called the absence of reason, "*dénuée de raison (wuli)*" (198). "It is not the reason of logical discourse that excludes all contradiction: it maintains a connection with the idea of putting in order and of natural order. It is neither the Greek *logos* nor the Latin *ratio*,"[14] which would imply a high level of abstraction (Gernet 199). Gernet concludes that in the context of Wang Fuzhi's thought discussing *li* "as an abstract entity, independent of energies and beings is absurd" (199, 202). The order is an order attained by coordination of concrete particulars. Gernet also writes of *li* in terms of systems theory:

> The notion of organization (*li*) and, consequently, that of a system is applied by Wang Fuzhi also to human societies as well as living beings. The institutions of all genres, the mentalities, the collective habits, the dominant ideas form an ensemble which is the culmination of the mutual adaption of these elements, over the course of a long evolution, and constitute a system that modifies itself in a more or less progressive or sudden fashion. . . . (145)[15]

The conjoined force of the concepts *li* and *qi* indicate that the world is a complex dynamic system of complex dynamic systems. From a neo-Confucian perspective the world is comprised by different levels and fields of organized *qi*. This way of understanding *li* and *qi* provides a means for recovering Wang Fuzhi's thought as a complex systemic ecology. Each unique pattern of *qi* contributes to greater global patterns. The global patterns of energy and the unique patterns that constitute it are recursive mutually informing processes. As a basis for ecological humanism, the concepts of *li* and *qi* work together to explain the integration of persons-in-the-world. Persons are complex systems within themselves, but they coexist with and interpenetrate other complex systems on multiple levels. Though they are all interconnected in the patterned developments of cosmic *qi*, they retain their own transient, internal, systemic integrity in the midst of this flux.

Wang Fuzhi's thought provides a paradigmatic example of Chinese natural cosmology. David Hall and Roger T. Ames observe that "in early Chinese natural cosmology, there is no appeal to some substratum or independent metaphysical origin, no 'One' behind the 'many'" (2003, 116). Instead, the source and the emergent events are co-involved in the creative process; in other words, the one and the many are mutually implicative and interactive. Ames and Hall make this argument in their commentary on the *Daodejing*, chapter 42:

> Way-making (*dao*) gives rise to continuity,
> Continuity gives rise to difference,
> Difference gives rise to plurality,
> And plurality gives rise to the manifold of everything
>   that is happening (*wanwu*).
> (Hall, Ames 142)[16]

"Viewed as the creative source of all things that, at the same time, is only experiencable through them, *dao* is both continuity and proliferation" (Hall, Ames 143). Likewise falling within this paradigm of correlative cosmology, Wang Fuzhi's philosophy is neither monistic nor pluralistic. Instead, it is more like a *via media* in between these two extremes—a "pluralistic universe." Depending on one's perspective or emphasis, the world is experienced as a set of continuous conjunctive relations or as a set of particularizing disjunctions. "That is, the multiplicity of things seen from another perspective is the continuity among things: Each unique focus is holographic, entailing its contextualizing field" (Hall, Ames 144). All parts are integrally interrelated with all other parts; they form an organic unity. But the unity is a unity of many particular individuals, and this sense of particularity is retained throughout the cosmology. Again, one finds in this mode of discourse a thoroughgoing commitment to complex holism.

From "Simple" to "Complex" Materialism[17]

Taking up a hermeneutic perspective of Marxist dialectical material-ism, Chinese scholars have maintained that Wang Fuzhi's insistence on immanence and emphasis on *qi* suggests a kind of materialism (Liu 2004). Indeed, this attempt to reconstruct indigenous Chinese philosophies in terms of dialectical materialism was characteristic of Chinese academic and political endeavors during the twentieth century (Tian 2005). Surveying twentieth-century Chinese literature on Wang Fuzhi, one will find the term for materialism used perva-sively. As one twentieth-century editor of Wang's *Zhengmeng zhu* puts it, Wang's philosophy is a *prototypical* or *simple* materialism Wang 1975, 1). Wing-tsit Chan's entry for Wang Fuzhi in *A Source Book in Chinese Philosophy* follows this trend. Chan cites the following passage from Wang's *Outer Commentary on the Book of Changes* in support the materialist reading: "The world consists only of concrete things," writes Wang. "The Way (Tao) is the Way of concrete things, but concrete things may not be called concrete things of the Way" (Chan 694). Wang is in this case asserting his naturalism. According to his expressed viewpoint, there exist no universal principles apart from the natural world of concrete particulars. In terms of contem-porary metaphysics, one may say that Wang Fuzhi is in this regard a nominalist. He believes in the primacy of concrete particulars. Wang carries on his case, "Before bows and arrows existed, there was no Way of archery. Before chariots and horses existed, there was no Way to drive them. . . . Thus there is no Way of the father before there is a son . . . no way of the elder brother before there is a younger brother . . . Therefore without a concrete thing, there cannot be its Way" (Chan 694–695). In a strong sense these lines express an "only thing doctrine," *weiwuzhuyi* 唯物主义, which incidentally is the con-temporary Chinese translation of "materialism."

In a "State-of-the-Field" report on "Contemporary Chinese Studies of Wang Fuzhi in Mainland China," Sky Liu (2004) observes that the materialist reading of Wang Fuzhi has been met by critical backlash. Yan Shoucheng, for instance, serves as a chief proponent of the anti-materialist camp. Dating back to his 1994 dissertation at Indiana University, Yan begins to formulate his opposition to the materialist camp: "In the sense that qi refers to human vital force, the equation of the philosophy of qi with materialism cannot be considered correct" (Yan 125). Fighting the same fight, Tu Weiming vehemently contests the materialistic reading of Wang Fuzhi and his principal predecessor, Zhang Zai:

> Recent attempts to reconstruct the genealogy of materialist thinkers in China have been painful and, in some cases far-fetched. Indeed, to characterize the two great Confucian thinkers, Chang Tsai and Wang Fu-chih, as paradigmatic examples of Chinese materialism is predicated on the false assumption that $ch'i$ is materialistic . . . To them, $ch'i$ was not simply matter but vital force endowed with all-pervasive spirituality. (Tu, 1998, 107)

The anti-materialist argument runs as such: Although qi constitutes concrete forms, it is not matter per se; instead, looking for an English rendition of the term, it may be said that qi has both a spiritual and a material dimension. Along these lines, Gernet cites the incompatibility of the "qi" and "matter" as a justification for rendering of "qi" as "energy" (158). Alison Black likewise maintains that given the lack of isomorphism between "matter" and "qi," it is best to forego the materialist reading and search for an alternative model for interpreting Wang's philosophy (1989, 48). Black critiques Jullien's apologetic reading of Wang as a materialist along these lines:

> "Given Jullien's own cogent arguments about the ineradicable differences between the terms of this Chinese 'materialism' (replete with spiritual and ethical content) and those employed by the West," she argues, "an equally

possible conclusion might be that the categories of ideal-ism and materialism simply do not fit." (Black 1991, 904)

Echoing this conclusion, Jeeloo Liu also maintains: "It is therefore best to abandon use of the term materialism as applicable to his [Wang's] philosophy" (357). In short, the anti-materialist camp main-tains that *qi* has vital, spiritual, and mental qualities that go beyond any simple or traditional category of matter.

The Chinese phrase for materialism, *weiwuzhuyi* 唯物主義, liter-ally translates as "only thing doctrine." As evidenced by the work of Martin Heidegger, the fundamental concept of "thing" cannot be tak-en for granted in philosophy, but must be subject to critical analysis:

> What in truth is the thing, so far as it is a thing? When we inquire in this way, our aim is to come to know the thing-being (thingness) of the thing. The point is to dis-cover the thingly character of the thing. To this end we have to be acquainted with the sphere to which all those entities belong which we have long called by the name of thing. (Heidegger 21)

The "Appended Phrases Commentary" of the *Yijing* states frankly, "*jingqi wei wu* 精氣為物." A preliminary translation of this claim reads, "Pure *qi* makes things." The terms *jing* and *qi* work here as a semiotic pair: *jing* is pure refined *qi*, and *qi* is dispersed *jing*. My initial translation is based on a paronomastic definition of the first character "*jing* 精" in terms of its semiotic associate "*qing* 清," mean-ing *pure*. In addition to "pure," each token instance of the character "*jing* 精" also carries with it connotations of bright luminosity, *ming* 明, and by extension signifies a beautiful quality. In addition, "*jing* 精" is defined in terms of "beautiful, marvelous, wonderful, subtle, sublime, exquisite, excellent, fine, mysterious, and inconceivable": all conveyed by the association of *jing* with *miao* 妙. Moreover, the concept *jing* is strongly related to the ideas of spirit and vigor, *shen* 神. From this proposition, it can be deduced that in Chinese discourse, the fundamental concepts of thing (物) and materiality (*wuzhi* 物质)

are philosophically understood as qualitative terms. The idea that *qi* has a numinous quality suggests that "materialism" in Chinese does not denote an ontological reduction of the world to inert material substance (which in and of itself lacks local motion or efficient causality) as we see in classical and modern Western materialisms.

Citing Gernet's analysis of the miscommunications between Ming dynasty neo-Confucian philosophers and Jesuit missionaries, Roger T. Ames (1997) writes of an incommensurability between the two paradigms of thought: "Believing that the universe possesses within itself its own organizational principles and its own creative energy, the Chinese maintained something that was quite scandalous from the point of view of Western scholastic reason, namely that 'matter' itself is intelligent" (255). Ames goes on to qualify his claim by arguing that "intelligence" in this context does not refer to a "conscious and reflective" capacity, nor does it refer to an intentional, teleological or calculating cognitive power. Instead, the "intelligence" of "matter" in a Chinese worldview refers to the capacity of *qi* to spontaneously give rise to concrete particulars, structures of energy, and their interrelationships.

Insofar as ecological humanism is committed to ecosystems ecology, ecological humanism must conceive of organisms and ecosystems as "the flow of energy and the cycling of matter" (Cooper 25). Nevertheless, ecological humanism advocates retaining a nonreductive, pluralistic, descriptive account of nature. That is to say, from the postmodern perspective of ecological humanism, "nature" cannot simply be reduced to lifeless, mechanistic, material substance (inert matter); instead, nature is at once understandable as material, energy, living, spiritual, and qualitative experience. In this vein, an ecological humanist would appear to be sympathetic with a critique of recasting and reducing Chinese concepts of *qi* in terms of a simple materialism. In other words, the hermeneutic engagement between ecological humanism and *qi*-philosophy provides an occasion to rethink the categories of matter and *qi* alike in terms of dynamic, vivacious, energy. One viable result of the dialogical engagement between the postmodern and pre-modern philosophies at hand is an appropriation of the concept of *qi* as a conceptual resource for contemporary theoretical work in *new materialism*. In this case, Wang Fuzhi's philosophy is not prototypical or simple materialism; rather, it presents a novel and complex materialism.

In response to questions regarding the category of "matter" in and for a viable twenty-first-century worldview, contemporary work in "new materialism" reconstructs and reconceives matter as vital, vibrant, self-structuring, energy. In this vein Jane Bennett (2010) refers to new materialism as a theory of "vital materiality" and "vibrant matter." Vital materiality is complex energy that is at once a particle and a wave. Vital materiality is the dynamic energy that constitutes and connects the entirety of the cosmos. Vital materiality is that energy that has demonstrated its proclivity toward life, self-organizing structures, conscious prehension, and ongoing transformation. With regard to these latter proclivities, new materialists are comfortable investing matter with intelligence, that is, "intelligence" in a similar sense as Ames' use of the term in his aforementioned depiction of *qi*. Rosi Braidotti thus poses the question and reply: "Why is matter so intelligent, though? Because it is driven by informational codes, which both deploy their own bars of information and interact in multiple ways with the social, psychic and ecological environments" (60).

Making the case in point, Mary Evelyn Tucker argues that the substance dualism of modernity, which severs the mind from matter, has resulted in a human experience of "profound alienation from nature and indeed from matter itself" (Tucker 1998, 187). Tucker touches upon the keystone concept of reciprocity in her call for advancing a kind of new materialism: "We have lost a sense of reciprocity with and relatedness to nature, the cosmos, and other species and forms of life, in part because we have privileged the spiritual as a transcendent entity and have drained it from the world of matter."[18] In Tucker's estimation, a new *qi*-based materialism "provides a basis for a this-worldly spirituality that reveres humans and nature as part of a single continuum of *qi*. Empirically, it suggests a rationale for affirming the importance of matter, of sense knowledge, and of the investigation of things in this world."[19] Statements to this effect strongly suggest that a neo-Confucian cosmology is consistent with the mitigated scientific realism needed for a viable twenty-first-century theory of ecological humanism.

Jacques Gernet advances the discussion toward a kind of new materialism by calling attention to the immanent, sui-generis, creativity of energy in the name of *qi*: "Ultimately, there is neither 'matter,' nor 'causes,' nor 'architect,' as was formulated by our medieval scholastics and taught by the first Jesuits to arrive in China around 1600. The universe is through and through, under all of its forms, only energy in incessant and invisible activity."[20] In sum, the philosophy of *qi* depicts the world as a continuous field of autopoietic energy. Persons and all events are herein understood as particular patterns of this universal energy.

Previous attempts at reconstructing traditional Chinese ontology of *qi* have been reductive in the sense that it they have depicted the *qi* philosophy as a kind of prototypical dialectical materialism. In dialectical materialism, matter precedes consciousness. Consciousness, it may be said, supervenes on matter, but is ultimately ontologically reducible to matter. In this reductive sense, *qi* ontology *cannot* be regarded materialistic. *Qi* is not simply *matter as opposed to consciousness or spirit*. *Qi* is at once matter and spirit. *Qi* has an irreducible, non-dualistic, holistic, complex nature. Insofar as it is material, living, prehensive, dynamic, transformative, and self-determining, it is "psychophysical energy."

As such, in the context of new *qi* materialism, matter does not metaphysically precede life and experience. In the absence of substance dualism, what we find in *qi*-philosophy is a kind of neutral monism in which the same energy can be considered simultaneously as matter and consciousness. The concrete particulars that constitute the physical world are *qi*; the experiencing agent and all her mental processes are *qi*. In other words, the subject and object of intentional experience are both configurations of *qi*. In this sense, *qi* may be considered to be a more fundamental category than modern dualistic categories of subject/object and consciousness/matter. *Qi* is very much akin to the concept of energy discussed by J. Baird Callicott's philosophy of ecology: Callicott explains, in the holistic concept of nature adopted by contemporary ecology and physics, "energy seems to be a more fundamental and primitive reality than material objects or discrete entities—elementary particles and organisms respectively. An individual organism, like an elementary particle is, as it were, a momentary configuration, a local perturbation, in an energy flux or 'field.'" (33–34). "Vibrant matter," "vital materiality," "energy," and "*qi*," can be represented as "double-barreled terms," to invoke the language of the father of neutral monism, William James. As James explains, one and the same event is counted twice over in dualistic discourse. On the one hand, these double-barreled terms can be contextualized and parsed so that they refer to the concrete, tangible, world of physics. On the other hand, they can be contextualized and parsed so that they refer to psychological experience. In either case, the terms refer to one and the same world: it is only when the context shifts for their use and interpretation that they come to provide different paradigms for interpreting the same event. The discourse of *qi* and new materialism look to undercut the severances of substance dualism by redirecting our attention to the unified event/experience of persons-in-the-world. As persons and their environments are both constituted by *qi*, the event/experience of persons-in-the-world is an event/experience of *qi* interacting with and transforming itself.

Thus, I conclude, Wang Fuzhi's philosophy can be called "materialism" with provisos: (1) provided that "materialism" in this context means that persons, experience, and nature are constituted by *qi* 氣, or energy; (2) provided that "materialism" does not exclude the belief that persons and impersonal natural forces alike are sublime, spiritual, sources and forces of transformation, creativity, and life; (3) provided that "materialism" does not imply that consciousness, life, and spirit are reducible to inert, dead, material substance. That is, "matter" in the context of a *qi*-based new materialism is not the classical Cartesian "matter" as opposed to "mind." If *qi* is to be reconceived in terms of vital materiality, then it must be understood as a more fundamental category than the dualistic conceptions of matter and mind as discrete, mutually exclusive, substances. Again, the terms "*qi*," "energy," "vital materiality," and "vibrant matter" do not denote Cartesian material substance; instead, they denote a more fundamental, holistic, unified category. Finally, (4) Wang Fuzhi's philosophy is

"materialist" in the sense that it asserts the primacy of concrete particulars, qi 器, as self-determining, natural, patterns of energy. Again,
Wang Fuzhi's "pre-modern" philosophy of qi 氣 ironically answers
contemporary "postmodern" calls for "new materialism."

As stated in the introduction to this discussion, the significance
of the *Yijing* on Wang Fuzhi's philosophy is paramount. Indeed, in
the tradition of Zhang Zai, Wang Fuzhi's philosophy should be understood as a creative, syncretic, synthesis of *qi-li* metaphysics and *Yijing*
process philosophy. The latter presents a holistic vision of the world
as a network of interconnected ever-changing events. Accordingly,
Yijing-based process philosophy shares theoretical underpinnings with
the complex systems theory adopted by ecological humanism. We
turn now to this development.

3

Reading the *Yijing* from
an Ecological Perspective

In this chapter, we take up Wang Fuzhi's philosophy of the *Book of Changes*, or the *Yijing*. We first introduce Wang's interpretive methodology for engaging this text, and demonstrate that this methodology, like his cosmology, is through and through holistic. We then move to inquire into Wang's interpretation of the functionality and symbolism of the text for modelling the complex and dynamic existence of persons-in-the-world. Finally, the discussion shifts to an account of the empirical epistemology endorsed by the *Yijing*, and makes the case that this epistemology is fully consistent with the mitigated scientific realism of ecological humanism.

Holistic Hermeneutics

For nearly two millennia prior to Wang Fuzhi's authorship—dating back at least to the Han dynasty—two major schools of thought vied for recognition as the authoritative theory and methodology for interpreting the multilayered *Yijing*. The two schools are referred to as the Meaning-Pattern, Yili 義理, School and Image-Number, Xiangshu 象數, school.[1] "The *yili* (meaning-pattern) school emphasizes how the Chinese language texts can be read figuratively. The *xiangshu* (image-number) school emphasizes the rationality of hexagram structure and

seeks objective methods for interpreting the text" (Smith 1).[2] Wang
Fuzhi takes a syncretic yet critical approach to these two lines of
thought.[3] Contrary to the Image-Number emphasis on the symbolic
imagery and numerological structure of the hexagrams, and equally
contrary to the Meaning-Pattern emphasis on the textually based
interpretation of the book, Wang critically integrates the rationalistic understanding of the former with the figurative interpretations
of the latter.

Wang understands the *Yijing* in much the same way that he
understands a poem, that is, as an *organic whole* (Wong xiv, 32, 145,
157). The holistic structure of Wang Fuzhi's thought is exemplified by
his hermeneutical understanding of the *Yijing*'s intentionality. Thus,
he expresses his conception of the text as a synthesis of complementary parts:

> "The judgments are the timber; the lines are the resulting-
> function." The timber is made by chopping it up with an
> ax; however, when in the chariot, it is a chariot: the wheel
> and cart—all of it is the chariot. Within particular-tools,
> the timber makes the tool: the middle and sides—all of
> it is the tool . . . Thus it is said, "The same goal, but dif-
> ferent paths, a singular place of arrival but one hundred
> deliberations." (ZYFL 661)[4]

This description calls to mind one of Wang's favored dyadic categories,
ti 體 and *yong* 用. In short, the text is a unified body, *ti*, of disparate
parts; as such, all parts contribute to a singular functionality, *yong*,
or meaning. In his view, the meaning of any part of the text can
only be adequately disclosed when the part is understood in relation
to the totality. As in the world, any part of the text is taken to be
a contextualized, situated, constituent of a system. Wang effectively
argues for multivalent hermeneutic circles between each part of the
text and the whole. In accordance with its structural complexity—the
layers of textual interpretation, and its myriad allusions—the *Yijing* is
a quintessential text for generating meaning. Again, Young-Chan Ro's
description of Yi Yulgok's work on the *Yijing* directly applies to Wang's

view of the text: "The Sixty-four Hexagrams, for example, appear to be a limited number of variations but when taken in symbolic form, they can provide unlimited possibilities of being in the universe" (178). Meaning is generated, in other words, through a seemingly infinite set of hermeneutic circles connecting its disparate parts.

Wang's understanding of the *Yijing* as an organic whole, or an integrative synthesis of parts, may be further elucidated by looking toward the basic hermeneutic circle as it is explicated by Hans-Georg Gadamer:

[T]he movement of understanding is constantly from the whole to the part and back to the whole. Our task is to expand the unity of the understood meaning centrifugally. The harmony of all the details with the whole is the criterion of correct understanding. The failure to achieve this harmony means that understanding has failed. (Gadamer 291)

Wang Fuzhi, like Gadamer, sees understanding a text as an ongoing integration of information provided by the accumulated study of the text by parts. Wang recommends sustained study of the text as a whole through successively working through the parts. His prescription is to study with intense sincerity, *cheng* 誠, so as to exhaustively study the mysteries of the sublime, *qiongshen* 窮神. As knowledge is successively and recursively built up through sustained study, understanding the parts of the text is continuously augmented by new information and context. Understanding is a process of oscillation between part and whole, and the harmony or organic whole of the text is disclosed over time.[5]

Hermeneutic circles are not vicious: they are not closed within the text itself.[6] As a general tenet of classical Chinese cosmology, the ongoing world is not circular in the sense that it keeps coming back to the same without producing novelty (Hall, Ames 28). Likewise, in Wang's reading of the *Yijing*, interpretation spirals out from the text, incorporating information from the other *Classics*, *Four Books*, and commentaries; accordingly, interpretation is intended to funnel new information back into the text. The internal system of the text itself is fundamentally situated within a greater intertextual system.

In Wang's view, moreover, the ancient text and the modern interpreter become contemporaneous through a circle between text and reader—a fusion of horizons:

> Study develops through accumulation; the present and the ancient mutually profit one another, hence [the new] refreshes the old. Thought grasps through an endless effort; [over the course of this process] the subtle and the manifest are mutually successive phases; hence the manifest is found in the subtle. (ZYW 1008)[7]

The *Yijing* is always open to interpretation; indeed, the ancient (encrypted) text and symbolism and content of the book call for it. Each new reader brings a world (or worldview) to bear on the text while bringing the text to bear on a world (or worldview). Through the intercourse of text and world, the text and world continuously attain novel meaning. Wang's prescription for advancing understanding of the book in light of one's own situatedness in time, space, and culture pushes the *Yijing* forward into novel interpretations. Thus the text is able to serve as a basis for dealing with contemporary philosophical crises, namely, the *problématique* of appropriating ancient wisdom for dealing with current issues. In this vein, Wang's hermeneutics justify interpreting the *Yijing* is as a basis for ecological humanism.

As he develops his holistic hermeneutics, Wang Fuzhi launches an attack on previous interpretations of the *Yijing* as being analytically decontextualized and overly speculative.

> Those who explicate the classics grasp the sentence but neglect the section, grasp the section, but neglect the chapter. The tradition from ancient times to present has been sickened by this. Nowadays, the disciples of Yao Hong (Wang Yangming) pick single phrases and thereby extend their presumptions—all of these techniques are like this [. . .]

If one reads books one claim (at a time) and seeks the meaning of this claim (in itself), then the meaning of the claim is necessarily erroneous. How much more so when one seeks to know the complete body and great function of nature-and-persons in the study of the *Yi*? If one takes up one line of a hexagram and seeks the meaning of this line, then the meaning of this line cannot be known [. . .] When one (attempts to) grasp the meaning of one sentence at a time (a sentence in and of itself) and discuss the texts of the former sages, the subtle language of the text remains hidden, and the great meaning is perverted. Insofar as this is the case for the other classics, how much more for the *Yi*! (ZYFL 662, 670)[8]

Wang seamlessly moves from discussing the interpretation of the text into making claims for interpreting the person and the natural world as an organic structure—a complete body, *quan ti* 全體, with a magnanimous functionality, *da yong* 大用. According to Wang, the *Yijing* is not duplicitous or simply a product of human artifice, *wei* 偽. Again, the symbolism and text together constitute an emergent phenomenon, which is taken to be a paradigmatic expression and embodiment of persons' rootedness and ontological grounding, *genben* 根本, in the immanent creative source of the world, *benti* 本體. As a comprehensive model of the integrated person-nature system, the totality of the *Yijing* is more than the sum of its parts. To reiterate, not only are there seemingly infinite meaning-productive relationships between the linguistic and nonlinguistic components of the book, as there are seemingly infinite interrelations between the constituents of the world; in addition, the text like the world requires interpretation at every level for the generation of meaning and value. The interpretation disappears into the text, or is absorbed into the model, thereby becoming part and parcel of the ongoing creation text. In this way, the model opens itself up to incorporate the fundamental situatedness of persons as the heart-and-mind of the heavens-and-earth.

From Wang Fuzhi's perspective, the Image-Number school, represented by Jing Fang 京房 (78–37 BCE) in the Han, and Shao Yong

邵雍 (1011–1077) in the Song, presents a hyper-rational systematization of the numerological-mathematical relations between the different trigrams, hexagrams, and lines.[9] Shao Yong arranges the *gua* and
yao symbols into various charts and sequences according to the binary
structural relationships between the broken *yin* and continuous *yang*
line segments.[10] He then applies these a priori orderings to the natural
world, thereby superimposing mathematically determined structures
onto the changing world.[11] With this methodical approach, Shao
Yong ultimately reduces all phenomena to an underlying numerological structure. Thus, Shao states, "The existence of meanings presupposes the existence of speech; the existence of speech presupposes the
existence of images; the existence of images presupposes the existence
of numbers" (qtd. in Wyatt 20).

The numerological methodology is intended to remove the subjective element from interpretation of the text, by presenting the text
as an objective model of change (Wyatt 20). Although this perspective might find a congenial reception amongst modern positivistic,
reductive, scientistic, mathematical models of ecosystems, it is not
an acceptable methodology by the standards of philosophical ecology—especially ecological humanism. Wang takes a skeptical posture
in relation to the view that the world can be fully understood outside
of an evaluative, subjective, interpretive perspective. In his critical
synthesis of the Image-Number and Meaning-Pattern schools, Wang
can be said to have sought an integration of subjective and objective
modes of understanding the world. To recall a premise set forth in
the methodology of ecological humanism, Wang's philosophy may
be understood here as an instantiation of epistemological pluralism.

At the turn of the twentieth century, William James, John
Dewey, and Alfred North Whitehead leveled a joint attack against
reification and overdetermination of the world by those who would
construct closed, a priori, ratiocinative, philosophical systems.[12]
Looking back on Wang Fuzhi's discontent with Shao Yong and his
ilk from this perspective, it is likely that Wang would have embraced
this critique. Using James's language, it may be said that the Image-
Number school commits a "vicious abstraction"; in Dewey's language,
the school is guilty of "*the* philosophic fallacy"; and in Whiteheadean

terms, it is a case of the "fallacy of misplaced concreteness." In sum, the terms employed by these three philosophers identify a tendency of rationalistic and speculative philosophy to reify abstract models of the world, which are at best only partial accounts, and mistake them for full representation of concrete reality. The Image-Number school abstracts one aspect out of the *Yijing*, the rational-mathematical orders of the hexagrams, and reduces all other meaning of the text (and world) to these structured orders. For Wang Fuzhi, to approach the text in this way is to project an artificial edifice onto the symbols (and the world), whereas the symbols are intended to be grounded in experience, and a posteriori, diagnostic, prognostic interpretation.[13]

The biggest problem that Wang has with the Image-Number approach comes by way of belief that the reductive method produces sterile patterns, which do not model nature's spontaneity and creativity. In the commentarial layers of the book, most notably in the *Appended Phrases*, the text indicates that the *Yijing* is to be taken as a model for (1) ceaseless creativity, (2) novelty, and (3) diversity and nested levels of complexity.[14] Wang Fuzhi will concede that the world does change in accordance with natural patterns, such as from the process of aging, life-leading-to-death-leading-to-life, seasonal- and diurnal-nocturnal cycles, ongoing respiration, expanding-contracting, opening-closing, flourishing-decline, etcetera. François Jullien capture's Wang's position along these lines, "The day and night are like the respiration of the heavens; the summer and winter reproduce the rhythm of the day and night. Only the scale differs. All manifestations are regulated by an uninterrupted going and coming, contraction-expansion, advance-retreat, opening and closing . . ." (Jullien 27).[15] Nonetheless, Wang does not believe that the patterns of change conform to an absolutely determinate structure, that is, a standard or fixed rule, *dianyao* 典要. Indeed, the *Appended Phrases* itself indicates that no such rule is to be found (*Xici xia* 8.1). Following Wang's critique, the Image-Number project of mathematical modeling precludes those of this school from recognizing the *aleatory* nature of change, novelty, and diversity, which is represented in the textual interpretations of the *Yijing*'s symbolic structure. Wang expresses his appreciation for novelty and diversity in nature throughout his work:

The ancients taught us to use heights and depths in study
of the incipient tendencies, *ji* 幾, but we rashly and hastily
employ [their lessons]. In the enumeration of the feelings
of the masses, the feelings are driven into the cages of
names. Reflecting on the world, one can grasp [its pat-
terns]; through study, one can know its patterns (*li* 理)
[. . .] [But the things and the beings themselves (in their
inexhaustible diversity) escape the reflection and study.]
The names and numbers are limited, while in their reality,
beings and things distinguish themselves in infinite species
and subspecies; and if one wants to go to the end of these
distinctions, one is not able to come to an end. The leaves
of a grand tree are counted by the myriads, and amongst
them, one cannot find one that is exactly like another.
How are the names able to limit them? The changes are
infinite. Only one passes in review the events of the day
and the night, nothing is like the anterior states of affairs.
Good weather and rain, here is a reduction to words, which
we are disposed to use. But we never find a time which
does not present the least difference with another. How
can numbers demarcate all of these differences. (SL 276,
qtd. in Gernet 76–77)[16]

Diversity and novelty are thus presented as fundamental characteristics of the world-as-process. Nature's capacity for spontaneously creating novel life forms is inexhaustible and not subject to any absolute
systematization. Rather than closed and determinate, the world is an
open indeterminate system—it is without limits, *wuji* 無極.

    Wang continues this line of thought, emphasizing the transience
and interconnection of all things:

The sixty-four hexagrams are repartitioned in eight palaces
of Jing Fang. It is in the "Before Heavens Diagram" and the
"Nine and Nine Numerical Chart" that we have left Master
Shao [Yong] and Cai Jiufeng. But, investigating between
the heavens and the earth [global-environmental system],

there is nothing that is so perfectly regular. These are only things of the genre "made by man." From the circles that one is able to trace with a compass, of rectangles that one can trace with a square, all of this relevant to human arti-fice; there is never anything of this sort created by nature. The *Yi* says, "(*yin* and *yang*) circulate in the 6 spaces (of the hexagrams); and yet they cannot have an immutable norm." If the *Yi* was able to normalize the [transformations thus], as our sight is able to penetrate bodies, and our ears able to penetrate sounds, we would not still be unable to synthetically comprehend things. Only the Sages were capable of penetrating to the limits of the numinous and reaching knowledge of the transformations. (SWW 440)[17]

The aim of [Shao Yong's] *Huangji jingshi* is written by Zhu Xi's account as "breaking into two," which is to say that everything in the world is mutually opposed. But how could the hard and soft of *yin* and *yang*, and the great and small be mutually opposed? *Yin* and *yang* are *qi*; hard and soft, are substances. If there is this *qi*, then it becomes this substance, if there is this substance then it comprises these energies, how could they be divided? If they could be divided, then substances would be dead bodies, and *qi* would be wondering energy. The small is the young of the great; the great is the old of the small; the young and the old are continuous through a person's life; would the young and old make two persons? The old is achieved from the young through gradual transformations without any divi-sions and sharp boundaries: otherwise, would it be that in one day youth ends and old-age begins? These theories by two and by four, these suppositions and categorical clas-sifications are without relation to the spontaneous order of the nature world. (SWW 441)[18]

Wang Fuzhi does not only insist on the continuity and inherent holis-tic structure of *qi*, but he also maintains a sense of indeterminacy as a fundamental aspect of the world. Wang finds in the world a creative tension between the overall coherence and aleatoric spontaneity of natural transformations. Structure and variance thus come to form a dyadic pair in his worldview as "two indissociable aspects of the same reality" (Jullien 194, 196). These two components are well represented by Wang's insistence on the integration of the categories of *li* and *qi*. As patterning, the former indicates an organic system or body, *ti* 體, of all change. As energy, *qi* drives the world toward creating novel forms of life and fulfillment of particular functions, *yong* 用, or niches within the system.

In reference to the place of indeterminacy in Wang Fuzhi's philosophical system, Alison Black writes, "It was a necessary part of his total conception that one aspect of the universe should elude precise specification . . . This element receives various descriptions at Wang's hands, but it can most comprehensively be described as *shen* 神" (72). Wang derives his conception of *shen* 神 from the *Appended Phrases* claim, "Yinyang are unfathomable: this is called *shen*" (*Xici shang* 5.1).[19] Although the term "*shen*" may be approximately translated into English as "numinous" or "spirit," it does not denote supernatural spiritual presence. In line with his naturalistic philosophy, Wang regards *shen* as a quality of *qi*. Thus, he states, "Outside of *qi*, *shen* has no presence."[20] In his commentary on the *Appended Phrases*, Wang defines *shen* in terms of *miao* 妙, meaning *marvelous* and *mysterious*. He writes, "Shen is *dao* mysteriously going out through the myriad things" (ZYW 531).[21] Wang's claim suggests an experience of profundity in relation to the simultaneous integration and individual integrity of all events. Mysterious is the complexity of the world. He further discusses the very notion of change, *yi* 易, which titles the *Yijing*, as "numinous and mysterious."[22] *Shen* alludes to the unfathomable finesse and subtlety, *jingwei* 精衛, complexity, and magnanimity of cosmic change and structure. Along these lines, the extension of the concept further contains nature's boundlessness, *wuji* 無極, and the invisible, *you* 幽, processes of nature's inner-workings. In a word, *shen* functions as sublime. The quality of *shen* engenders experiences of profound wonder and awe. It elicits reverence for a natural world that is greater than the individual person, and yet provides an intimate place and participatory function for each and every person and thing.

On this point, Wang Fuzhi is again strikingly close to the Korean neo-Confucian thinker, Yi Yulgok. Like Yi, Wang also regarded the hexagram system of the *Yijing* to symbolize "neither a fixed physical object nor a mere mechanical entity; rather, it is a living, dynamic, changing reality" (Ro 177). Moreover, because of the dynamism, pro-creativity, complexity, and open nature of the world-system and its constituent subsystems, the world is a source of "sanctity and mystery" (ibid.). Ro's description of Yi's cosmology likewise serves as an apt summary of Wang's conception of indeterminacy:

> [He] believed the universe could not be completely compre-hended by human intelligence or through human thought processes. He believed that the universe is a "mystery" not to be reduced to the rational or conceptual framework of the human intellectual system. This dimension of mystery causes us to feel that the universe is sacred; hence, we have a sense of awe toward the universe. The universe "manifests" itself to us as much as it "conceals" itself from us. . . . (ibid.)

Although Wang appropriated a sense of penumbral indeterminacy as a positive value into his philosophy of nature, he believed that the *Yijing* yet modeled both the sides of the correlative dyad of determi-nacy and indeterminacy, *you* 有 and *wu* 無; concealed and manifest, *you* 幽 and *xian* 顯; or hidden and illuminated, *yin* 隱 and *ming* 明. This correlative dyad of hidden and manifest is fundamental to Wang's hermeneutics of the symbolism and text. Thus, in the same breath that he critiques the overdeterminate systematization of the Image-Number school, he also critiques the Meaning-Pattern school, which neglects the systematic structure of the world and *Yijing* sym-bolism in favor of subjective, figurative interpretation.

To summarize his critique of the Meaning-Pattern school, Wang argues, there is no *dao* or whole apart from the concrete particu-lars that constitute it. "The world is only concrete particulars and that is all. As for *dao*, it is the *dao* of concrete particulars" (ZYW 420).[23] The critique is akin to the problem of reverse reduction on the whole stated in chapter one. It can thus be formulated by stating that Meaning-Pattern school sought transcendence of the *Yijing's* symbolism, and this marks an abnegation or sublimation of the concrete particularity of each situation in light of the whole.

Wang Fuzhi's critique of the Meaning-Pattern school is directed by-and-large toward one of the traditions early champions, Wang Bi 王弼 (226–249), who lived in the Kingdom of Wei (220–265) just after the fall of the Han dynasty.[24] Steeped in both the Confucian and Daoist traditions of the pre-Qin and Han eras, Wang Bi regarded the *Yijing*, the *Analects*, the *Laozi*, and the *Zhuangzi* alike as signatory allusions to an ineffable reality. As Rudolph Wagner (2000) explains in his magnum opus trilogy on Wang Bi's authorship, reality is not ineffable for Wang Bi because there exists an absolute unchanging Being beyond the empirical realm of beings; rather, the transience and complexity of the world preclude assigning any fixed (nominal or predicative) reference to world.[25] Wang Bi harbors an acute skepticism toward language and ratiocinative systematization as means of providing an adequate metaphysical worldview. He maintains throughout his work that reality can only be pointed to *via negativa* (as in the *Daodejing's* *wu* 無 forms), or by contradictory or metaphorical constructs.

For Wang Bi the *Daodejing* in particular is a marked attempt to "turn discourse against itself," and "make it deviate from its usual [propositional] functioning." One finds a fundamental example in the opening passage of the *Daodejing*, where the functions of the world are referred to as "darkest of dark." The term, "dark," "*xuan* 玄," is a metaphorical means of alluding to the indeterminacy of the world. By "indeterminacy" it is understood that the world can neither be referred to simply as a plurality nor simply as a unity; nothing in the world is a determinate discrete object, and yet all things maintain a persistent particularity—nothing in the world is absolutely reducible to its relations or abnegated in the face of the whole. Rather than reifying the indeterminate aspect of the world as some kind of substance, entity, or object, the phrase "darkest of the dark" shows how the world slips through the hypostasis of denotation. "Through this repetition, the term is kept open beyond itself, exceeding its bounds"

(Jullien 2003, 286). Based on Wang Bi's adoption of this Daoist line, his philosophy is referred to within Chinese philosophic taxonomy as "Study of the Dark-Mysterious," *xuanxue* 玄學.

Perhaps Wang Bi's general disposition toward discourse is best represented in an adage taken from his biography: An interlocutor asked of Wang Bi, "Speaking of indeterminacy, truly it is that which constitutes the myriad things. The sage [Confucius] is not willing to discourse on it; however, Laozi's repeats it without end. Why?" Wang Bi, then replied, "The sage embodies indeterminacy, and indeterminacy cannot be taught; the reason being, speaking is necessarily determinate. Laozi and Zhuangzi have not yet let go of the determinate; ultimately, their exegeses are insufficient."[26] At the end of the day, for Wang Bi, language and symbolism must be put aside, for the world can only be known through unmediated praxis and intuition. Accordingly, he attacked the Han dynasty scholars of the Image-Number school and sought to undercut their methodical systematization.

Wang Bi makes use of a line from Zhuangzi to convey his position on semantic reference: "the rabbit snare exists for the sake of the rabbit; once one gets the rabbit, he forgets the snare. And the fish trap exists for the sake of fish; once one gets the fish, he forgets the trap. If this is so, then the words are snares for the images, and the images are traps for the ideas (meanings)."[27] Wang Bi interprets this claim to indicate that truth is understood by transcending the meaningful world insofar as it is determined by the ratiocinative use of language. The transcendence is not a movement beyond the world; rather, it is an inner movement to "that which" is the world—conveyed in Chinese by the character *suo* 所. Wang Fuzhi adopts a distinction between the world-as-it-naturally-occurs on the one hand, and the world-as-it-is-categorized-by-human-artifice on the other. However, Wang Fuzhi believes that the symbolism and text of the *Yijing* serves as an intermediary, a bridge, between the two.

In a relatively short passage, Wang Fuzhi follows Wang Bi's critique of the Han dynasty numerologists, but Wang Fuzhi reproaches Wang Bi as well:

When the Confucians of the Han dynasty discoursed on images (*xiang* 象), they chose many forced analogies . . . Wang Bi returned to the *dao*, and discarded the Han discourses. He said: "Grasp the images and forget the words. Grasp the meaning and forget the image." However, the (Great) Commentary definitively states, "the Changes are images" (ZYW 1039).[28]

Although Wang Fuzhi agrees that the Image-Number school should be critiqued for their fallacious overdeterminism, to neglect the significance of the hexagrams, their organic symbolism, and their structure altogether is a mistake in itself.

As stated above and is developed further below, Wang Fuzhi took the symbols of the *Yijing* to have grown out of persons' onto-hermeneutic relationship with the natural world. In a somewhat longer passage composed at a later date, Wang Fuzhi continues this line of attack on Wang Bi:

The Qin burned books, but the *Yijing* was taken up as a divination book, and did not suffer this disaster; thus, of the six classics, only the *Yijing* remained a complete book, and afterward its study was prosperous. However, following from this, the *Yijing* fell into disorder. Though the Qin forthwith stripped it away from prognosticators, for a long time it endured and its discussion remained unchanged . . . Those people of the Han who commentated on it did not systematize the teachings of the three sages.[29] And after the Qin, the various prognostic techniques were diverse, confused, and brought disorder to one another. . . . Wang Bi was aware of this meanness, and relinquished these sayings. He singularly took *dao* to be separate [from the earlier methods of prognostication], hidden to some degree in the meaning of the three sages. However, Wang Bi studied the root [of all things] in the Lao-Zhuang [Daoist] significations of vacuity and indeterminacy, and was mystified by *dao*. Accordingly, he writes, "Grasp the meaning and forget the language, grasp the language and forget the images." But he did not realize that the language is integral to the images and the meaning is integral to the language. [This integration of images, language, and meaning] is what is expressed in the world as the profound-merging between persons and nature. How could one forget? (ZYFL 652)[30]

In a strong sense, the hexagrams are symbolic representations of reality. Hence, Kipper Smith suggests that the term "*xiang*" may be translated as "symbol." However, as Young-Chan Ro points out, the very idea of a representational *symbol* is not fully adequate for understanding the nature of the hexagrams and their images. "Here 'symbolic' does not mean a mere formality," writes Ro, "but rather it means a holistic approach, beyond concept, to the reality . . . For example, the trigrams and hexagrams . . . are symbolic *manifestations*, not mechanical representations of the reality of the universe" (176). The hexagrams emerge from Fu Xi's interaction with the world, that is, through his comprehensive observation. The act is creative in that it is an expression of the world as it presents itself to the human interpreter, but the symbolization is not an abstraction; like the person, the symbolism is grounded and sustained by the root-body of the world. Wang Fuzhi conceives of the hexagram-images as nonlinguistic interpretations, creative representations, extensions and expressions of "the phase: insensible passage from one to another of two inseparable opposing terms, of flourishing and decline, of the coexistence of the indeterminacy and constancy . . . which is constitutive of all natural and biological phenomena" (Gernet 73).

Wang Fuzhi's critique of Wang Bi and the Meaning-Pattern school calls on a concept of symbolism that does not radically separate the symbol from its referent. Symbolism, in this case, belongs to the realm of pathos. That is to say, a *gua* is not a symbol in the sense that it refers to something outside of itself; the *gua* is more like an emergent symptom or consummate quality that expresses the full situation as it comes to fruition. The concept of "*xiang*" is more akin to that of a genome than it is to the concept of a "road sign" or a "denotative term." The symbol, in other words, is a microscopic embodiment and expression of the macroscopic situation from which it emerges. In Wang Fuzhi's view, Wang Bi's rejection of the book's linguistic and nonlinguistic symbolism misses the mark on what Yijing's symbols are.

In one critique of constructing the *gua* based on the method used in divination, Wang suggests the idea that the *Yijing* symbolism provides a *cosmography*:

> If one discusses prognostication, then one has three changes whereby one obtains a single inscription taken as the beginning [of a hexagram], step by step, through eighteen transformations, on then develops the hexagram. In the natural development of *gua*, the heaven and earth certainly have their transformation; the myriad things certainly have their patterns; personal affairs certainly have their feelings . . . It is not the case that because of divination one then has a *gua*. (ZYFL 666)[31]

The idea conveyed by this passage is that hexagrams emerge from nature, not from artificial manipulation. The *gua* thereby categorically resonate, *ganlei* 感類, with natural events.

In a recent commentary on Fu Xi's observation and creation of the hexagrams, Kipper Smith provides an analysis of the *Yijing's* symbolism that supports the hermeneutic perspective of reading the tradition as a form of ecological humanism. "It is a text less of culture than of Heaven-and-Earth, of nature," he writes (5). He goes on to redirect his claim, however, by making a case for interpreting the terms of image, *xiang* 象; order, *fa* 法; and pattern, *wen* 文, as demonstrative of the continuity between nature and culture. *Xiang*, or images, are emblematic prelinguistic symbols. The *gua* themselves are interpreted as images of the most prominent situations found in nature-and-society. As images, they are understood as nonlinguistic symbols. Unmediated by linguistic interpretation, images are immediate presentations of the persons-and-nature. According to Smith, "Hexagrams are considered an alternative sign-system, one that offers more potent means for expressing otherwise hidden meaning through their super-linguistic clarity." He continues by citing the *Appended Phrases* line, "The sages set up images (*xiang* 象) to fully express intended meaning (*yi* 意). They established hexagrams to fully express actuality. They attached verbalizations (*ci* 詞) to these to fully express speech" (*Xici shang* 12.2; translated in Smith 8). Based on this claim, Smith concludes, "hexagrams, then, offer various promises—of a clear 'expression of the actual'" (ibid.). Wang Fuzhi, like Wang Bi and others, expresses a concern that propositional discourse and philosophical systematization are ultimately incapable of presenting the incessant and sublime processes that constitute the world. However, Fuzhi sees the *Yijing* symbolism—with the warp and weft, disclosure and concealment of the changing lines—as a model of the fluid structure of the cosmos as a holistic process. This model neither reduces the world to a determinate system, nor neglects the coherence and particularity of the patterns that present themselves in concrete experience. The hexagrams taken singularly and in tandem have a systemic structure; at the same time, the penumbral indeterminacy of transience, chance, and holistic complexity is built into part and parcel of imagery and required interpretation.

For Wang Fuzhi, only when the *Yijing* is taken as a totalizing structure does it provide a comprehensive worldview that overcomes the shortfalls of overdeterminate and hyper-rational, speculative, discursive models. Conversely, when taken as a totality, the book likewise presents an aesthetic order that is grounded in the comprehensive observation of patterns of change. The book can neither be taken as an objective model, nor a prompt for pure subjective interpretative fancy. As it synthesizes nature and persons, so it also synthesizes the subjective (interpretive, indeterminate) and objective (rational, determinate) poles of experience in a hermeneutic circle. Each pole depends on the other, informs the other, and is integrated in the fullness of experience.

Cosmography of the *Yijing*

The cosmology of the *Yijing* maintains that all phenomena exist in the midst of a continuous transition between polar opposition.

Everything in nature is connected in patterns of reciprocal inter-actions and transactions of *yin* and *yang* modes of *qi*. Along these lines Wang Fuzhi holds that natural phenomena constantly undergo mutual reversion and mutual becoming, 相反相成.[32] *Gua* are dynamic presentations in which *yin* and *yang* lines exchange places and move through the different positions of the structure; accordingly, each *gua* can be understood as transforming into other *gua*. This form of process philosophy can be interpreted in terms of A. N. Whitehead's principle of relativity: "it belongs to the nature of a 'being' that it is a potential for every 'becoming'" (Whitehead 22). Along these lines the complete set of *gua* present an organic worldview in which all phenomena are interrelated by their mutual transformability and constant becoming.

The *Yijing* provides a naturalistic account of the world as a coherent, dynamic, self-regulating, holistic system. As such, the phi-losophy of the *Yijing* does not define any given phenomenon in terms of a discrete essence, species or kind: the identity of any phenom-enon does not come by way of analytically extracting or isolating the phenomenon from its environment and attempting to find its atomic core; instead, the phenomenon is identified by the way it functions and alters in relation to other phenomena. In other words, the phe-nomenon is understood according to the role that it plays within the context of its (local and global) environment.[33] Jullien explains that in this context one is not to consider any reality unilaterally (*unilatéralement*) or individually. Without exception each existent has an existential reliance on all other existents. Every phenomenon is *constituted* by its relationships to others. In other words, relationships are internal as opposed to external and primary as opposed to second-ary.[34] That which is apparent in the analysis of any phenomenon is never "*une réalité individualisable.*" No phenomenon, according to the manner of analysis in the *Yijing*, ever attains existence in the world as a singular and autonomous existence; instead, each phenomenon is a phase or *moment* in the midst of a world constituted by interrelated process (Jullien 52, 53).[35] In terms of holism, every part comes to embody, contain, or express the whole in one way or another.

Wang Fuzhi expresses his vision of a complex and holistic world in his earliest commentary on the *Yijing*:

Does the world have radically separable and necessarily mutually opposed things? Searching for such a thing in the heavens and earth, this kind of entity does not exist; searching the myriad things, this does not exist; introspecting into one's thinking-and-feeling (*xin* 心), one is not yet certain or aware of such a thing. The heavens are venerable aloft, and yet they enter the midst of the earth; there is no depth that they do not inspect. The earth is humble below, and yet the earth hoists the horizon, there is no height that it does not penetrate. One cannot take and separate the world [into hard and fast dichotomies] . . . Of the radically separate and necessarily mutually exclusive, the heavens and earth does not have it, the myriad things do not have it, people's thinking-and-feeling does not have it. (ZYW 1073–1074)[36]

Like Zhang Zai before him, Wang Fuzhi takes the *Yijing* to be a "translation of the universe" (Gernet 109). Each *gua* has a complex internal structure of interacting *yin* and *yang* lines, which can be referred to as a vertical dimension. At the same time, each *gua* is constituted by a complex set of relations to every other *gua* in the system, or a horizontal dimension. The interrelationships between *gua* are internal and constitutive, and are symbolic of the correlations that link actual phenomenon. The basic symbolism of the continuous segment of *yang* and the discontinuous segment for *yin* provides a visual representation for conceiving of events as relatively conjoined and disjoined in nature. The idea, in other words, is that all events are porous; all events qua systems are open systems; all events are relatively particular and individual and relatively shared and environmental.

As phenomena are mutually transformable, so the hexagrams have the capacity to transform into one another. In line with their interconnection and principle of relativity, the set of hexagrams is seen as a parsimonious model—a cosmography—of the complex structure, and spontaneous and incessant change that is the world.[37] The set of sixty-four hexagrams do not form an amorphous whole (Gernet 117). They are isomorphic and homologous with the actual world. The fundamental premise of Wang's metaphysics should always be kept close when engaging his philosophy: the world is energy, *qi* 氣, and energy only exists in emergent structures, *li* 理. Within the homologous and isomorphic structures of the world and the hexagrams, each and every phenomenon, *xiang* 象, derives its identity, meanings, and values in relation to the systems in which it is situated. The situatedness or position, *wei* 位, of any phenomenon within the system is constitutive of that phenomenon. As the situation and one's position shift, so does one's identity. Contrary to Aristotelian ontology, the identity, meaning, and value of any phenomenon are not thought to be located in an unchanging essence, which retains its "thisness" regardless of its contextualizing relata. The philosophy of the *Yijing* prioritizes situation over agency.

With regard to the horizontal dimension, it can be said that all *gua* interlock through transformation of the constituent lines— they interlink in a changing *bricolage* (Smith 7; Gernet 110). Wang identifies two primary relations between *gua* to discuss their interconnections, mutual containment, transformation, and mutual expressiveness. The relationships are referred to as: (1) negative, *cuo* 錯; (2) inverse, 綜 *zong*.

The "*cuo*" is an instrument to polish metal, which removes the external (cover) and discloses the internal. The "*zong*" is a woven thread, using the machine it goes, one up and one down (without interruption). The *gua* each have six *yin* and six *yang*. When *yin* is seen, then *yang* is hidden within. *Cuo* removes that which is seen as *yin*, then *yang* is seen. *Cuo* removes that which is seen as *yang*, then *yin* is seen, it is like the relationship between *qian* ䷀ and *kun* ䷁ . . . The *yao* that are seen, up and down they interact and change, it is like holding the thread in weaving, repeatedly, alternately, raising and dropping, as in the relation between *zhun* ䷂ and *meng* ䷃. (ZYBS 788–789)[38]

Many different kinds of change attain in the world. Radical and momentous changes are suggested by the relationship of inversion, *zong*. Subtle and hidden changes are interpreted in terms of the negative, *cuo*. The *zong* relation is attained by flipping a hexagram on its head; the *cuo* relation is demonstrated by substituting each of a hexagram's *yin* line with a *yang*, and vice versa. Within the ordered set of hexagrams in the received version of the *Yijing*, twenty-eight pairs of hexagrams are sequenced according to the *zong* relation: one hexagram is immediately followed by its inverse. The remaining four pairs—"Qian and Kun, Kan and Li, Yi and Daguo, Zhongfu and Xiaoguo"—are related by virtue of being negatives, *cuo*, of one another (Gernet 112).

The sequential *zong* order suggests that the natural world follows patterns of continuous transition between opposites, such as extropy and entropy. Drawing upon the imagery of weaving, Wang makes use of the classical sense of the term, *zong*. The *Shuowen jiezi* defines *zong* 綜 as "a machine for weaving," and identifies the silk radical, 糸, as the significant semantic component of the character. As stated in the previous chapter, the same classical lexicon defines the character *tong* 統, meaning "to unify" and by extension "to unify in a system," in terms of *zong* 綜. Due to the close-knit semiotic relationship between *tong* and *zong*, and based on explicit definition of *zong* in itself, *zong* also signifies a systematic interconnection between the different hexagrams. Each *gua* implies its inverse and is indeed understood as transforming from and into its inverse. But inversion is only one modality of change.

Wang discusses the complexity of the hexagram relations and their ability to transform in accord with the complex nature of change in reality. He alludes to a "network of linkages" as referred to by Cheng's description above. Commenting on the *Appended Phrases* line, "Changing and moving without residing, freely wandering through the six spaces, from up to down without constancy, hard and soft exchanging places, without a determinate rule, only change is suitable"[39] Wang writes:

The *Yi* embodies this as *dao*, thus Qian and Kun established, and Zhun ䷂, Meng ䷃ succeed, the intercourse of *yin* and *yang* cannot abide by sequence; by ten transformations one obtains Tai ䷊, Pi ䷋, [then] eight transformations and one obtains Lin ䷒, Guan ䷓, again transforming and one obtains Bo ䷖, Fu ䷗. Their decline and flourishing is without regular progressive order. (ZYN 605)[40]

The *gua* are not static entities. As symbolic representations of dynamic situations, *gua* are understood as transformational. Each *gua* and each line contained within it is in flux. In other words the individual *gua* and their constituent parts are parsed phases in an ongoing systemic process. Not only does this passage suggest the mutual entailment of opposites, as in the inverted hexagrams here cited, but it further indicates that more than one modality of change is present in the transformation of the hexagrams. In accord with the complex nature of change in the world, the hexagrams cannot be understood as transforming solely according to inversion. If this were the case, then the hexagrams would be subject to a kind of vicious circle in and of themselves: any two inverted hexagrams would be locked in an eternal loop of mutual reference, and unable to become any other *gua* outside of the inversion relation. Therefore, they would be unable to signify the novelty and indeterminacy that presents itself in ongoing experience. The presence of the *cuo*, negative, relationship offsets and opens up the *zong* relationship, thereby, freeing the model from a fixed and determinate rule. The negative incorporates and models the invisible forces and chance one finds in the empirical world.

Recalling the microcosm-macrocosm relationship, which Mary Evelyn Tucker and John Berthrong identify as definitive of Chinese naturalism, each *gua* can be considered an embodiment or expression of all other *gua*.[41] And in words familiar to Wang Fuzhi, each *gua* "contains," *han* 函, the other sixty-three within it. Wang describes this mutual containment in terms of the correlative dyad of the visible and the invisible, or the disclosed and concealed: "One writes *yin* or *yang* six times; the positions, however, have twelve: half concealed, half seen" (ZYW 225).[42] The six lines that are seen are manifest traits of the situation; however, the six unseen lines, the complete negative of the displayed hexagram are regarded as an underlying latent modality.[43] The idea that each hexagram has within it hidden hexagrams, which it expresses, lends support to Alison Black's (1989) reading of Wang Fuzhi's philosophy as a form of expressionism.[44] The six hidden lines are tacit and implied; they are the hidden face behind the expressive face of each hexagram. Insofar as each hexagram is permutated by its negative, Qian, *yang*, also contains Kun, *yin*, but "only in the mode of latency" (Jullien 102).[45] "Similarly," Jullien writes, "all the real possesses at the same time an exterior and an interior, one open and one closed. The hexagram is a double structure, containing the parity of manifest and latency." He continues his explication, "All experience is able to be elucidated globally from this model, for example between yesterday's projects, today's execution, and the transformation of it on another day" (ibid.).[46] Wang Fuzhi expresses his conception of the transformation between invisibility and visibility, indeterminacy and determinacy, concealment and disclosure in a metaphor familiar to Chinese philosophy: the swinging gate, which opens up for disclosure of particularity and closing for concealment within mystery (ZYW 425). What is determinate now is indeterminate later, and vice versa.[47] In his later work, *Detour and Access*, Jullien again nods to this line (using slightly different language): "specific actualization is never trapped in its specificity but remains open to the lack of differentiation, finally returning to it" (286). As soon as beings stand forth, they begin to weaken; hence, they embark on the retrogressive way (*dao*) toward their vanishing.

With reference to the vertical structure of the *gua*, Gernet makes the following claim on behalf of the systems reading of Wang Fuzhi and the *Yijing*:

The position of the lines in the hexagrams is in itself significant. Now, when all the elements together only have a sense by reason of the place that it occupies and that all is not a simple addition of parts, it is here where one is in the presence of a system. One of the ideas frequently expressed by Wang is in effect that of a system. (Gernet 143)[48]

Similarly, Kipper Smith explains, "the hexagram structure becomes a potent set of relationships, not just a collection of six serial places" (11). As in any ecosystem, the inner workings of the *gua* are complex indeed. Each hexagram symbolizes energy-flow, and interactions, exchange, and dynamic tensions between opposing forces on multiple levels. The *Appended Phrases* commentary states, "The movement of the six lines is the *dao* of the three extremes." Wang's commentary on this line reads: "The beginning 2 are the position of earth; 3 and 4, the position of persons; 5 and 6, the position of the heavens. Each position is necessarily significant; the *yinyang* of *qi*, the hard-soft of concrete form; the humanity and appropriate conduct of diposistion: all these intercourse to becoming a complete body and magnificent functionality" (ZYN 515). The numbering of hexagram lines procedes from the base upward. Take hexagram number 63, Jiji, for example:

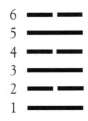

By Wang's explication the bottom two tiers symbolize the hard and soft qualities of the earth; the central two tiers are the virtues of humanity and appropriate conduct of persons; the top two tiers symbolizes the *yang* and *yin* forces within the heavens. Persons and nature are integrated within the six lines of the hexagram. In this integration, each *gua* presents a *totality*, a *globalized* whole, or functional organic system (Jullien 195). Each of the three powers, *sancai*, has a place (niche) to fulfill in the cosmic order. Wang states this: "*Dao* is a continuous becoming, and the three powers are complete, the *gua* is a continuous becoming and the six positions are complete . . . The *dao* of the three powers is a great whole system in a single seed, and the single seed is reflected in the great whole" (ZYW 1064, 1066).[49]

The *Yijing's* symbolic system models change in a number of ways. In addition to the inverse and negative relational-transformations, *gua* also change as lines age from bottom to top. The bottom-most line of any *gua* is considered its youngest line, the top-most line is the oldest. Each line is considered young relative to the line immediately above it, and old relative to the line just below it. Lines are then understood as having a propensity to change according to these relationships. "A young *yin* (*shaoyin*) has in effect the tendency to transform itself into an old *yin* (*taiyin*), and the old *yin* to transform itself in its turn to a young *yang*, which becomes an old *yang* . . . this is what gives a continuous succession of transformation" (Gernet 113).[50]

The lines and their corresponding powers are further integrated within the *gua* through relationships of "responsiveness" or "correspondence," *ying* 應. The responsiveness relationship is based on analysis of each hexagram into its component superior and inferior trigrams. To note, the upper trigram is also referred to as the "outer" trigram, and the lower is referred to as the "inner" thus adding a third dimension to the hexagram. Based on this subdivision, there is a one-to-one correspondence between the first, second, and third lines of *each* respective hexagram. In other words, "responsiveness obtains (in a hexagram) between lines 1 and 4, 2 and 5, or 3 and 6 when one is broken and the other solid" (Smith 11).[51] The above example of Jiji is a paradigm case of obtaining the proper position, *dewei* 得位, according to the relation of responsiveness. Attaining responsiveness is symbolic of harmonization and equilibrium of forces within the situation presented by the *gua*. Not obtaining it presents a case of " 'missing the right positions' (*shi wei* 失位), 'not having the right position' (*bu dang wei* 不當位) . . . and 'lacking correspondence' (*di ying* 敵應)" (Cheng 2011, 408), which indicates an imbalance and instability within the environment—an undesirable and precarious situation for those involved.

More significant than all other qualities of positioning within a *gua*-structure and an actual situation is the positional quality of centrality, *zhong* 中. Cheng writes of the centrality in this context:

> We can see "centrality" (*zhong*) as the right combination of positions and forces, which answer to all requirements of coherence, order, harmony, and concordance in positional, qualitative as well as evaluative aspects . . . *Zhong*

is the right configuration of position and forces that move and develop in the right relationships to other configurations. This means that *zhong* is a structure of harmony, order, and coherence as well as a concordance and process of producing and maintaining more order, harmony, coherence and concordance. (Cheng 2011, 407)

The central position, *zhongwei* 中位, is understood as the place of the organizing, driving, controlling, and integrating force within any system. The Chinese "*tiandi* 天地" most literally translates as "heavens and earth." The phrase always bears connotations of natural environment, habitat, natural world, and *oikos*. The basic spatial relationship implies a sense of a natural hearth that persons occupy in the world: heavens above, earth below, and persons in the middle.

In his exposition of holistic philosophy, Brook Ziporyn (2000) explains that any holistic system has certain parts, or positions, that can be construed as more significant than others. The significance of these positions is that they, above all others, serve as the metaphorical *centers* from which all other points derive their identity, value, and meaning. In other words, all points in the whole derive their meaning, value, and identity only when they are related in some way or another to the center. Any thing has as many identities or meanings as it has relations to the center. To push the notions of center and whole even further, we can say that since any whole is defined as the way in which the constituent parts relate to one another, and the only relation that has real significance is the relationship held between the part and the center, then the whole is completely determined and expressed by the center as it relates to all things. The center itself determines the identities not only of the constituent parts, but it determines the identity of the whole itself (Ziporyn 33). In this sense, Brook Ziporyn argues that the center "is representative of the whole and may be said to include the whole, in some form or another" (ibid. 36). In that the center includes the whole, or represents the whole, one might say that the center is a unity, embodiment, and expression of all of the systems constituents within itself.

In Wang Fuzhi's representation of the hexagram—with the heavens above (lines 5 and 6), the earth below (lines 1 and 2), and persons in between (lines 3 and 4)—persons can be considered central to the structure of the global system. Indeed, the centrality of persons-in-the-world is a belief that Wang presents throughout his *Yijing*-based philosophy. The proposition of persons as the center of the world, however, must be immediately qualified. "*L'hexagramme ne possédant pas de centre unique (entre les traits 3 et 4),*" explains François Jullien in his monograph on Wang Fuzhi's philosophy, "*en même temps qu'il possède deux centres parallèles (les traits 2 et 5)*" (197). Each hexegram is understood as comprised of two primary trigrams: each trigram has in itself a central position, namely, lines 2 and 5, of the hexagram. When understood in terms of the global structure of earth-persons-heavens, then, all three forces equally serve as centers in the world-system. Both nature and persons are central; neither serves as an absolute center; both are relative to one another in their mutually defining positioning within the whole.

Wang Fuzhi believes "[e]verything in the world is unified, [and yet] *there is nothing that does not serve as the center*" (ZYW 1065).[52] Speaking to this claim, Jullien explains that the structure of the hexagram, which is the functional equivalent to the structure of an actual event, is "polyvalent" (197). In contrastive complement to Jullien's explication in terms of "polyvalence," Ziporyn's term "omni-centric holism" provides a more apt description of Wang's *Yijing*-based worldview. Ziporyn writes:

In short, omnicentrism holds that the identity and sig-nificance of any enetite is so thoroughly and completely a function of its relations to other entities—so completely "holistic"—that every identity is a sliding identity whose significance is always susceptible to grounding in something else, always ambiguous, changeable, and instrumental. However, since this is also true of all the other entities in which it is so grounded, every entity equally can and must itself serve as a ground, as a center, as a master signifier from which every thing elsle attains its significance and identity. (38)

One of the peculiar implications of this omnicentric model is that the world, i.e., the whole, can be defined completely by reference to any point within it. Depending upon which point is referenced as the center, the same whole simultaneously takes on qualitatively different (even conflicting) identities. By the same token, the constituent parts of the whole can take on different meanings, identities, and values depending upon which point of the whole is taken to be the center. Since all things must orient themselves around the center to gain any sense of identity, meaning, and value, and there are seemingly infinite centers that can relate to all things in seemingly infinite ways, there is here an indefinite number of identities, meanings, and values that can be equally ascribed to any one point within the system. Also, without changing the content of the whole, there is here an indefinite number of identities, meanings, and values that can be ascribed to the whole itself. There is no "one way" that any thing is. With this insight, the complexity of the system can be understood. The particularity as well as the fundamental relationality of each phenomenon can be accounted for depending on which organizing sub-paradigm is taken as the emphasis, orientation, or center of the explication.

The symbolism of the *Yijing* and its derivative philosophy thereby presents a model for ecological humanism: a nonreductive worldview, which is neither anthropocentric nor ecocentric. Insofar as the system of the world is omnicentric, it is acentric—in the sense that it lacks any absolute center. The complexity of the world-system is thereby modelled by the *Yijing* in that it can account at the same time for the particularity and the interrelationality, as well as the relative stability and relative transcience of any one thing.

Practical Knowledge through Comprehensive Observation

The *Yijing* serves as a basis for Wang's naturalistic cosmology. The symbolic system of *gua* is intended to provide a means of modeling the holistic albeit indeterminate structure of the world and interpreting one's place within it. The *gua* are intended to be an interpretive symbolic system that represents the changing circumstances that contextualize and constitute persons' experience. Knowledge in the context of Confucian philosophy is not merely descriptive: it is also predictive and prescriptive. Wang's interest in the text is not solely epistemological. In Wang's view, the *Yijing* is to be consulted as a normative guide in the event of a moral dilemma: What is the appropriate course of action given a complex and dynamic set of circumstances? In the tapestry of the world spun within the *Yijing*, fact and value (objectivity and subjectivity) are thoroughly interwoven. The natural order is thereby simultaneously conceived of as a moral order.

Implicit in this worldview is the belief that each situation presents itself with a path of least resistance. That is to say, the appropriate, fitting, or right action, *yi* 義, is always determined by one's context. Nature establishes normative demands for the individual in the form of hypothetical imperatives. If one wants to avoid suffering and strife, and cultivate happiness and well-being, one must realize the most efficacious means of attaining and sustaining one's ends-in-view. Absent from this worldview is the belief in an absolute Good, a categorical imperative, or a universal maxim. The idea is expressed by Gernet in his reading of Wang Fuzhi: "There is neither a good nor a bad in and of itself. The good is an affair of situation (*wei*) and of moment (*shi*) . . . One is always only in the presence of relative realities" (91).[53] The hexagrams and the natural occurrences that they embody are neither good nor bad in themselves; rather, they attain their value in relation to persons' ends.

In the context of Wang Fuzhi's neo-Confucianism, the epistemology of mitigated scientific realism, which was introduced in our opening disambiguation of ecological humanism, may be reconstructed as a *mode of being-in-the-world* based on a method of comprehensive observation *guan* 觀 and investigation of things *gewu* 格物. The method differs from natural science and unmitigated realism in that it does not take the intentionality of its phenomenology to be value-neutral. The account of knowledge derived from the method of comprehensive observation is a moral epistemology, for it entails an axiology and normative ethics.

The *Appended Phrases Commentary* (*Xici xia* 2.1) provides the *locus classicus* recounting Fu Xi's original act of creating the trigrams. Here Fu Xi is said to have turned his gaze upwards and *comprehensively observed* the images in the sky. He turned his gaze downwards and *comprehensively observed* the lawful-order of the earth. He *comprehensively observed* the patterns displayed by birds and beasts and the suitability of the earth. He took up that which was near to his lived body, *shen* 身, and that which was far away. From this observation he began to construct the eight trigrams, which are said to be of a penetrating, numinous, and illuminating character. He thereby categorized the affairs of the myriad things.

The philosophical importance of the "*Appended Phrases*" narrative of Fu Xi's originary act lies in the comprehensive observation, *guan*, of the celestial images (*xiang* 象), terrestrial order (*fa* 法), and fauna patterns (*wen* 文), and the codification of these experiences as the eight trigrams. *Guan* is a phenomenology of nature qua "flux and continuity" *biantong* 變通. The account of Fu Xi's survey of the vertical dimension of the world (from the sky to earth) and the horizontal dimension (from his own body to distant regions of space) indicates that the observation described in the text is comprehensive. Indeed, the language of the text alludes to a complete local and global understanding of the world and the phenomena that emerge therein.

Cheng maintains that *guan* provides the methodological foundation for a holistic and systemic account of all things as they are found in nature. On this account, the method requires a sustained observation of natural (cosmological) changes over a long course of time:

> These observations would lead to an understanding of the world with a unity of vision, a totality of scope, to be seen also in a network of linkages and relations as well as a multitude of relevant concrete references and identifications . . . [The] resulting vision of the world is a cosmography of well-placed and well-related powers and processes, namely a dynamical picture of the natural world in which things are to be situated. (Cheng 2011)

The symbolization that is derived from the observation serves as a schema for interpreting minute and particular experiences as well as experience at large. The schema acts as a functional map or model of the cosmos—a *cosmography* in which every natural phenomenon has a situatedness or proper position, *zhengwei* 正位, in correlation with all other events. In terms of *timeliness* and *positioning, shiwei* 時位, this model depicts all phenomena as fulfilling functional niches in a complex system or an ecological order of things. In other words, the "moment and the position provide the two coordinates" in terms of which all processes are understood as functional components of local and global systems.[54]

The *Yijing*-based philosophy of Wang Fuzhi is not a form of natural science, nor does it necessarily result in an anthropocentric instrumentalist evaluation of nature. As Cheng explains in his analysis of *guan* as a method:

> In the formation of the *Yijing* we witness a dynamic unity between theory and action, understanding and practice in the sense that the system of the *yi* symbols is not developed simply for intellectual knowledge, but for understanding the world-reality and life-world for the sake of practice and action. (Cheng 2003, 294)

The continuity of knowledge and action, *zhixingheyi* 知行合一, here instantiates the simultaneous cosmological, normative, and axiological dimensions of Wang Fuzhi's thought. Through sustained and comprehensive observation of the transformations in one's life and environment, *bianhua* 變化, one should come to discern the incipient tendencies and subtle propensities, *ji* 幾, of change within one's situation.[55] One should then engage the changing environment through patterns of initiation and deference; to use Wang's favored dyad, one should relate to the changing environment through initiation, *jian* 健, and compliance, *shun* 順. Recognizing what is within one's locus of control, as in one's *xing* 性, and what is outside of it, as in one's *ming* 命, one responds by positioning certain forces such as oneself within the environment so that the forces harmoniously interact with one another. This requires acting in a timely manner. As stated in the *Appended Commentaries,* "The exemplary person sees, *jian* 見, incipient tendencies, *ji* 幾, and initiates action; he does not wait for the day to end" (*Xici xia* 5.10).[56] Timeliness is hitting the mark every time, *shizhong* 時中 and *zhongshi* 中時; timeliness, alternatively stated, entails neither transgressing the mark nor falling short of it. The ideal of *shizhong* is exemplified by the *middle* ground between two of Confucius disciples: "The master says, 'Zizhang oversteps the mark (*guo*), and Zixia falls short of it (*buji*)'" (*Analects* 11.15).[57] For Wang Fuzhi, *knowledge is a moral capacity.* Again, reified distinctions between fact and value have no place in the horizons of his world-view.[58] Knowledge, on this account, is only complete insofar as it is carried out in space and time (as indicated by the concepts *shi* 時 and *wei* 位). It is embodied, lived, and enacted.

To use an environmental example, if one waits until the water-ways are thoroughly polluted before one attempts to conserve one's reservoir, it is already too late. In light of the ongoing ecological-humanist catastrophe in North East Japan following the tsunami of March 11, 2011, the model can be interpreted in hindsight as a caution for nuclear power sources in areas that demonstrate an incipient tendency to quake and flood, which may be symbolized by the hexagrams *zhen* ☳☳ and *zhun* ☵☳ (the former being named "quake" with two thunder hexagrams stacked on top of one another, and the latter with thunder below water, named birth-throes, indicating a precarious and painful situation).

On this view, to know nature, *zhi tian* 知天, is to know natu-ral patterns, *tianli* 天理. The idea of natural pattern, *li* 理, refers to the coherence, organization, and interconnection of disparate parts, which is in effect a system. Each particular is what it is in relation to all other parts of the system. Thus, following Zhu Xi, Wang regards pattern as *suoyiran zhi gu* 所以然之故, that is, "the reason why things are as they are." In addition to this descriptive sense of *pattern,* Wang also critically advances Zhu Xi's prescriptive sense of patterning, *lishi zhi dangran* "理勢之當然"; which is to say, nature qua pattern is a nor-mative force. Wang Fuzhi writes, "All under the heavens is timeliness and force of circumstance, and that is all. Take advantage of timeliness and accord with the force of circumstance. . . ."⁵⁹ As Wang's philosophy is here proposed as a model for ecological humanism, it thus stands in contrast to an ecology based in scientism. As opposed to a purely factual description of the world, ecological humanism here integrates fact and value within its paradigm.⁶⁰

The normative force of the world, *dangranzhi shili* 當然之勢理, pushes persons and the myriad things toward harmonious accord, *heshun* 和順, with one another. Neither anthropocentric nor ecocentric, Wang Fuzhi's moral epistemology prioritizes situation over agency. Wang Fuzhi recognizes that humans have a power over nature; in a sense, persons direct and order nature, *ren zhu tian* 人主天. But conversely nature has power over persons, *tian zhu ren* 天主人. The relationship is mutually purposive, symbiotic, and conducive toward a general harmonization. From an *Yijing*-based perspective, harmony between natural forces is fecundate; harmony is that which creates and sustains biodiversity. This harmony is conducive to change, novelty, and procreativity (such as *shengsheng* 生生, *yi* 易, and *rixin* 日新 in *Xici shang*, 5.1). The harmony is experienced subjectively, not only as a sensory-aesthetic experience, but also a deep felt existential feeling of ease (*jianyi* 簡易), freedom from anxiety (*wuyou* 無憂), and psychophysical equilibrium and integration (*zhong* 中). "When persons achieve positions in equilibrium (with the cosmic forces of heavens and earth)," writes Wang, "then they can follow the model of the heavens and the earth and be without dread" (ZYN 1037).⁶¹ A consummate experience of peace in one's self, *anshen* 安身, and unobstructed passage in one's daily affairs emerges from the cultivation of practical knowledge.⁶² Acting contrary to the normative push toward harmonization is acting contrary to the procreation of life and coherence within an ecological order. Thus, if one fails to harmoniously comply with the needs and demands of one's local and global environments, one subjects oneself and one's environing systems to accelerated entropy.

Lost in translation, the original Chinese indicates that "change," *yi* 易, which titles the *Yijing* 易經, also bears the significant meaning of "ease and simplicity," *yi* 易. The connection between these two senses of the graph is not at all fortuitous: *change* and *ease* necessarily imply one another in the *Yijing*'s language and philosophy. When one sense serves as the literal meaning or signification in a token use of the term, then the other sense acts as a tacit connotation. Wang's meditation over the symbolic imagery and text of the Guan hexagram indicates that comprehensive observation, *guan* 觀, leads to knowledge.

This kind of experience is at once moral, aesthetic, and spiritual: *moral* in that it is prescriptive and efficacious (intentionally good for increasing the value of life and quality of experience); *aesthetic* in that it brings all modalities of experience (cognitive, emotive, perceptual, sensational) into harmonious accord with one another and the environment; *spiritual* in the sense that is marked by deep and transformative experience of quietude, peace, equilibrium, and calm—a feeling of *being at home* in the world (as in the Greek *oikos*).

Though comprehensive, the observation is always attained from an embodied perspective, a position within the system, as is represented by the reference to Fu Xi's observation of that which is near and far to his *body*. This perspectival position within an environment is constitutive of being a person-in-the-world. Robert Cummings Neville captures this idea in his short article, "Orientation, Self, and Ecological Posture."[63] "To be a person is to have, as constituent elements of the self, orientations, well or badly formed, to ecological matters as well as to all the other orders of the 'ten thousand things.' A self should not be conceived at all except as framed by how it is oriented to the many dimensions or orders of nature" (Neville 265). The person-in-the-world is a situated constituent of the world. Ideas of self and knowledge from this perspective do not presuppose a subject/object distinction. Both the subjective and objective modes of experience are integrated in the fullness of experience. In one sense, interpretation emerges as a consummation of evolving forces and patterns of *qi*: the development of the world has given rise to a particular structure and moment in which a person is present in the world. Interpretation emerges out of the achieved interaction of persons with their situating environment.

As such, the interpretation and evaluation of the world-system occur as part of the system itself. The world-system comes to be self-reflective through the eyes of the persons that inhabit it. In terms more familiar to the tradition, the *Classic Book of Ritual Propriety, Liji* 禮記 describes the situated presence of persons in the world as such: "Persons are therefore the heart-mind of the heavens and earth."[64] Wang assents to and asserts this classical formula in his own work. With the presence of persons-in-the-world, the world is irreducible to its mereological sum.

4

Between Nature and Persons

Ecological humanism asserts a belief that persons and nature are onto-logically intertwined through recursive, interactive, causally effica-cious, historical relations. In short, the concept of *reciprocity* serves as an overarching theoretical framework for the paradigm. Within this framework, the epistemology, metaphysics and axiology are holisti-cally interrelated as isomorphic structures. Thus, the keystone con-cept of *reciprocity* establishes the paradigm's systematic unity. With this in mind, we begin this chapter with an exposition of ecological humanism's novel idea of humanizing nature, an idea of humanizing that entails the reciprocal process of naturalizing.

After foregrounding this perspective on humanizing nature, we then turn to Li Zehou's philosophy of history and the history of Chinese philosophy: Li's theory provides a cogent theoretical resource for advancing the thesis of neo-Confucian ecological humanism. Li's terminology of "humanizing nature" in the context of traditional Chinese philosophy resonates with the terminology of ecological humanism; moreover, Li's theory serves as a means for translating Wang Fuzhi's neo-Confucian discourse into familiar and agreeable terms for ecological humanism. Thus, Li's position provides a triangu-lating viewpoint from which we may further link ecological human-ism to Wang Fuzhi, and thereby hermeneutically enhance and enrich a neo-Confucian model of ecological humanism.

Wang conceives of the relationships between nature and persons as manifold and complex. He does not dogmatically adopt the traditional Confucian slogan of "continuity of nature and persons"; instead, he critically adopts it in conjunction with a complementary concept of "interstice" or "between nature and persons." With this concept Wang advances a two-pronged analytic attack against Daoism, on one side, and earlier Confucianism, on the other.

After presenting Wang's analytical critique of "heterodoxy" and "orthodoxy," respectively, we turn to his natural philosophical anthropology. To this end, we endeavor to uncover Wang's adoption and development of Mencius's account of the heart-and-mind. Finally, before concluding the present chapter, the discussion turns to the deep Confucian tradition of ritual propriety as a particular process of humanizing nature in the context of neo-Confucian ecological humanism.

Humanizing Nature in Ecological Humanism

In its metaphysics, ecological humanism recognizes that the natural ingression and presence of persons-in-the-world effectively results in the transformation of the natural environment into *humanized nature*. In the present context, "humanizing nature" does *not* refer to a unilateral-causal relation in which persons dominate the nonhuman aspects of the natural world. Thus, Whiteside makes the normative claim, "Reciprocity with nature must replace mastery over it as the regulative norm of human activity" (175). The interactive processes involved in humanization result in the emergence (or disclosure) of novel structures, properties and propensities in the world. In the present context, "humanizing nature" also entails the collective evolution of persons in response to the causally efficacious forces that constitute their environments. Humanizing nature is a recursive process or positive feedback loop: persons transform and inform their environments, and the consequent transformations reciprocally inform and transform human existence.

Humanization of nature in ecological humanism is an ongoing historical event. It is "co-evolution of society and nature." In this event, "what must be grasped is not the essential, timeless 'nature' of either but rather the process of their evolution" (Whiteside 51). With this claim, ecological humanism is established as an antithetical alternative to Aristotelian substance ontology. In this rejection of classical metaphysics, the present thesis maintains that neither nature nor persons has any essence per se. Again, persons and their environments are inextricably interrelated through manifold causally efficacious interactions. As a result, persons and nature recursively *institute* and *constitute* one another (Whiteside 26, 68, et passim). As in the Confucian worldview, relationships in the context of ecological humanism are internal and constitutive.

In its axiology, ecological humanism neither accepts the anthropocentric idealization of nature qua instrumental value, nor does it assent to the ecocentric thesis on nature qua intrinsic value. The categorical reciprocity of "persons" and "nature" precludes a centralization of intrinsic value both in persons' self-interest and in the interest of nature in itself. If neither persons nor nature can be understood or said to exist in itself, how could either be valued as such? Whiteside thus reinstates the metaphysics of reciprocity as a basis for developing an axiology of reciprocity: "Neither human interests nor nature exist independent of one another. There is not a nature 'out there' either to be perceived as a function of human interests or to be valued in and of itself" (Whiteside 68). Persons are fully natural, value-additive, creative events.[1] This is not to say, however, that values are necessarily directed toward satisfying persons' self-interests or desires. The question of value here is not a question of who makes the judgment. Ecological humanism will not deny that persons are the world's judges of value. However, it rejects the rationality of judging by determinate teleological principles and a priori decision making procedures. The question of value is a question of intentionality. Having denied both persons and nature the categorical priority of intrinsic value, the ecological humanist has one final option for finding a basis for developing a positive account of value, namely, the reciprocal *relationships* that constitute the person-in-the-world.

In its epistemology and philosophical anthropology, the theory maintains that persons apprehend themselves reflexively in relation to their environment. Persons are fundamentally ecological events.

Philosophical anthropology would miss the mark were it to attempt to abstract and analyze persons apart from the concrete relationships that inform, sustain, and transform them throughout their lives. Conversely, any human understanding of nature is just that: *human* understanding. Knowledge of nature requires foregrounding the anthropological forces that inevitably inform and qualify the understanding. Again, reciprocity is the keystone concept: both nature and persons are rightfully grasped within the complex nexus of concrete relationships that interlink them. *To be a person is to be a person-in-the-world.* To reiterate, a person-in-the-world is just a *situated constituent* within complex systems that change over time. With the addition of time to the epistemological equation, ecological humanism historicizes and problematizes the sense and reference of "persons" and "nature." As the historical transformations of persons and their environments are ongoing with no determinate end-in-view, so the meanings of these terms are kept open-ended and finally indeterminate.

Ecological humanism is based on the premise that "persons" and "nature" are mutually defined. It stands as a rejection of the belief that persons and nature have their own ontologically discrete essences. Kerry Whiteside clearly states the critical position along the following lines:

> Nature is never simply "out there," to be encountered in an unadulterated form. Neither is humanity "in here," the essence of an autonomous, reflecting subject. Nature's nature is inseparable from organized human practices. Human nature is inseparable from the influences of a bio-physical reality. (65)

Philosophers of ecology analytically distinguish between two primary senses of the polysemous term "nature": such an analysis may be helpful in explaining Whiteside's position. In the first sense (*nature*[1]), it means unadulterated nature, pristine, apart from human interference. In this sense, the term refers to ecosystems that have not undergone any significant anthropogenic alterations. *Nature*[1] is understood in contradistinction to human presence and activity. Here, the concept "nature" is disjoined from the concept of "human." (In the same vein, "nature" is disjoined from "culture.") As suggested by Whiteside's statement, the very coherence of this concept of "nature" is called into question by the theory of ecological humanism. Though we may imagine or conceive of a mountain vista devoid of human presence, we are yet reconstructing the scene based on our human faculties. As broad and as accurate as it might be, we are confined as it were to a human perspective.

As opposed to *nature*[1], ecological humanism advocates a concept of nature more akin to what philosophers of ecology call *nature*[2]. In this latter sense, "nature" means *humanized* nature. The definition of *nature*[2] asserts the following propositions: Humans are fully natural beings. In other words, persons are part and parcel of nature. They are the results of natural processes, and are themselves natural processes. As such, the products of human activities are the products of nature. Hence, *nature and persons are continuous*. (Or, as Wang Fuzhi would put it, *tianrenheyi* 天人合一.) Ecological humanism recognizes that the natural emergence and presence of persons-in-the-world effectively results in the transformation of the natural world into *humanized nature*. In this context, "humanizing nature" does *not* refer to a unilateral-causal relation in which persons dominate the nonhuman aspects of the natural world; instead, it refers to an open set of reciprocal processes in which persons and their environmental relata mutually transform one another. In this vein, we may say along with the contemporary philosopher Li Zehou that humanizing nature implies a reciprocal process of naturalizing humans.

Humanizing Nature in Chinese Philosophy

Kerry Whiteside writes, "Conventionally, 'humanizing nature' has implied that there is some knowable nonhuman world out there ('nature'), which we then alter ('humanize') to make it better conform to our needs and wishes" (64). To be clear "humanizing nature" for Wang Fuzhi should not be understood in this conventional sense. "Humanizing nature" does not mean "dominating nature." Contemporary scholar, Bai Xi, argues the case in point:

> Wang Fuzhi says it well, "What spontaneously emerges are the heavens and the earth. What sustains them are the persons. Persons are the heart-and-mind of the heavens and earth." Insofar as persons simultaneously institute themselves and take the significant position of the "heart-and-mind of the heavens and earth," they do not possess the authority to dominate all living things. Rather, on their own accord they assume the responsibility and duty of being "what sustains" the spontaneous emergence of all living things. Persons act as "the spirit of all living things." Their extraordinary characteristic is in this. (Bai 2008, 477)[2]

Humanizing nature entails transforming biological and ecological conditions into phenomenal and cultural forms of existence. Though Wang celebrated achievements of culture and human experience, he harbored a cautionary skepticism toward overdetermining nature by reason and volition. That is, he was critical of practices that super-imposed artificial theoretical structures onto the world. Humanizing nature ought to respect the integrity, indeterminacy, and resistance of nature-within-nature. It ought to be carried out with the intention of striking accord and creative harmonization between persons and their environments. Karyn Lai's insight into the Confucian worldview discloses this sense of humanization: "The key operational concepts are adaptation, flexibility, versatility, appropriateness and fit, rather than management, domination, restraint, and control. With the for-mer series of concepts, the focus is not on self-determinacy but on sensitivity to interdependencies and resonances" (156). Those who try to force nature into conformity with overdeterminate principles are no different than Mencius's man from Song—who uprooted his garden by trying to help his plants to grow.

According to Li Zehou's interpretive analysis of traditional Chinese philosophy, "humanization of nature" has at least two mean-ings. In the first sense, "humanization of nature" refers to a purposive ordering of natural-animalistic sensuality, emotions, and behaviors for the sake of establishing an aesthetically ordered, harmonious, community. Humanization of nature, in this sense, is the intentional regulation of persons' psychosomatic activities. The end-in-view underwriting this effort is the sublimation of selfish desires and engenderment of a higher order of qualitative experience. Humanization of nature demarcates an emergence of human consciousness and culture as a unique and creative form of life within the natural world. Secondly, "humanizing nature" refers to the evolutionary capacity of persons to efficiently respond to the forces of their natural environment and shape these forces into material culture.

Li argues that his use of "humanizing nature" is a modern and more nuanced formulation of the "rough-hewn" and "roundabout" traditional expression of "continuity of nature and persons," *tianrenheyi* 天人合一 (2010, 73). Honing in on this claim, Roger T. Ames succinctly summarizes and advances Li's premise.

The argument, simply put, is that Chinese philosophers from classical times have recognized a continuity between human beings and their natural environments. The nature of this continuity, however, has often been misunderstood [. . . .] Instead of being a continuity between subject and object, respecting both the ability of the collective human community to transform its environment productively, *and* the resistance of the natural world to this human transformation, it has been dominated by the belief that the moral subject holds absolute transformative powers over an infinitely malleable natural world. (Ames 2006, 354)

In Wang Fuzhi's language, the reciprocity between nature and persons that Li and Ames are pointing to can be expressed by complementary relations in which persons control nature while nature controls persons. This kind of reciprocity, again, is the starting point for an understanding of persons-in-the-world from the perspective of ecological humanism.

In order to fully come to terms with Li's reconstruction of traditional accounts of the continuity of nature and persons, the humanization of nature (or the capacity for humans to intentionally cultivate natural forces with aesthetic experience as an end-in-view) must be understood as only one side of the coin. The humanization of nature correlatively complements and implicates its antithesis: "the naturalization of humans." According to Li, "The latter argues that to become truly human one must shed sociality, allowing one's natural-ness to remain unpolluted and to expand to achieve unity with the universe" (2010, 79). According to Li's philosophy of history (and history of philosophy), the "naturalization of humans" is profoundly developed in the Daoist layers of China's sedimentary history. Here one finds the celebration and aesthetic valuation of an unrefined nature—a nonhuman perspective, a clod, and an uncarved block.[3]

The dialectical-historical movement between humanization and naturalization achieves a synthesis in the literati achievements of the Song-Ming era (Li 2010, 192). Following Li's lead, I move to argue that Wang Fuzhi's philosophy provides a particular instantiation of this synthetic zeitgeist. Wang rejects any form of reductive equivo-cation between the spontaneous modalities of nature and purposive disposition of persons. In developing this position, he posits the ana-lytical division of nature into "nature-within-nature" 在天之天 and "nature-within-persons" 在人之天. Alternatively, he formulates this distinction as a difference between the way-of-nature (tiandao 天道) and way-of-persons (rendao 人道). The way-of-nature is to act with-out any consciousness or deliberate intent. Nature-within-nature is literally without heart-and-mind (wuxin 無心). By contrast, the way of persons is to act with self-awareness and purpose. Nature-within-persons is marked by the presence of a heart-and-mind (youxin 有心).[4]

Though the orders of things and persons are distinguished by the respective privation and presence of thinking-and-feeling 心, they are not metaphysically independent substances by any means. On the one hand, Wang describes the relationships between nature and persons as an interstice: tianrenzhiji 天人之际. On the other hand, the interstice is necessarily grounded in a fundamental continuum: tianrenheyi 天人

合一. In other words, nature and persons are interconnected through a complex set of relatively disjunctive and conjunctive relationships.

Between Persons and Nature

In his *Du Sishu daquan shuo* Wang Fuzhi asserts and develops the descriptive category of *tianrenzhiji* 天人之际 to add analytic depth and rigor to traditional Confucian discourse on "continuity between nature and persons," *tianrenheyi* 天人合一. Wang's use of the term, *tianrenzhiji*, "indicates the mutual opposition of persons, the heavens, the earth, and the myriad things toward being fully incorporated in the complete structure of the natural world" (Li Xiangjun 2008, 455).[5] Due to the polysemy of the relational term *ji*, the phrase *tianrenzhiji* suggests a number of translations: *between nature and persons; interstice of nature and persons; boundaries of nature and persons; meeting of nature and persons*. The contemporary scholar Zhou Bing (2005) provides a discursive analysis of Wang's terminology, which suggests a warrant for interpreting *tianrenzhiji* as category of ecological humanism:

> The claim of "*tianrenzhiji*" is extremely rich in content. From "nature" to "persons," it covers a range of concepts or categories: including, nature, patterning-energy, *ming*, persons, natural disposition, feelings, heart-mind, *dao*, virtue, and more. The meanings of the "nature-persons" relationships also possess many levels and facets. This slogan, from "nature" to "persons" thus presents a particularly complex and problematic system. (5)[6]

Tianrenzhiji, like Edgar Morin's *la relation écosystémique*, signifies a nexus of conjunctive and disjunctive relations. In one frame of reference, the relata are interdependent and interpenetrating. In another frame, they mutually resist one another, retain a systemic integrity, and refuse to be reduced or equivocated to the other. Xiong Lümao and

Yang Zhengzheng (2003) also provide a succinct statement on Wang's use of the term: "Nature stands opposite to persons (mutually-divided), but they are also systemically unified (continuous). They are related by opposition (division) and systemic unification (continuity)" (26).[7] On the one hand, Wang describes the relationships between nature and persons as an interstice: *tianrenzhiji* 天人之际. On the other hand, the interstice is necessarily grounded in a fundamental continuum: *tianren-heyi* 天人合一. The disjunctive interstice and conjunctive continuum mutually imply one another. Accordingly, though *tianrenzhiji* signifies modes of differentiation, it does not reify persons and nature as discrete self-contained entities.

Tianrenzhiji can be reconstructed from the perspective of contemporary philosophy of ecology to refer to boundaries between two interconnected open systems. As such, both persons and nonpersonal orders of world are recognized to have a relative autonomy, internal structure, or integrity. "Even so, given ontological interconnectedness, the boundaries of ecological entities are imprecise, in part because of the entities' openness (porousness or permeability). Linkages tend to blur the distinctness of ecological objects. The selection of a boundary is always arbitrary because boundaries vary over space and time" (Keller and Golley 23). Wang's philosophy of *tianrenzhiji* problematizes the concepts of 'nature' and 'persons' by signifying manifold dimensions of their mutual entailment; thus, *tianrenzhiji* dialogically foregrounds the *problématique* of ecological humanism.

Wang reformulates the *problématique* of reciprocity and resistance by analyzing *tianrenzhiji* into two categories: *nature within nature* (*zaitianzhitian* 在天之天) and *nature within persons* (*zairenzhitian* 在人之天). The occurrence of "nature," that is, *tian* 天, in both terms is telling. The suggestiveness is identified by Zhou Bing: "With regard to the question of '*tian*,' Wang Fuzhi does not endorse the proposition that persons only have a kind of external relation to nature [. . .] Instead, he advocates a discourse in which "*tian*" cannot be separated from *ren*" (53).[8] *Nature-within-nature* refers to those aspects of the natural world that resist and confound human understanding and influence. *Nature-within-persons* refers to the range of embodied and environmental forces within persons' locus of control and comprehension. Nature-within-persons is humanized nature, or nature², as discussed. Nature-within-persons is the historical development of uniquely human experience and culture. François Jullien provides insight into the significance of humanizing processes of culture in the philosophy of Wang Fuzhi:

> It is clear at least that Wang Fuzhi is conscious of the specificity of human history (qua wen 文) in relation to the cyclical function of nature. Originally, man is only an "animal that holds itself upright," and over the course of its gradual process of grand material invention it began to develop itself into civilization . . . There is thus "evolution" from one epoch to another by constant "adaptation." Each defines itself by a certain stage of customs and civilization . . . [But] his consciousness of human order (rendao 人 道) is never completely affranchised from the more global vision of the course of the world (tiandao 天道). (67)[9]

The extensions of the concepts "nature-within-nature" and "nature-within-persons" change over the course of time. Wang Fuzhi signifies the temporal dynamics of the nature-culture interchange by reconstructing "nature-within-nature" and "nature-within-persons" in terms of way-of-nature and way-of-persons: tiandao 天道 and rendao 人道. "Way" in this context denotes a process, and should thereby be interpreted as gerundive: way-in-the-making.[10] Wang alludes to the historicity of culture in this way: "The activities of the ancients are not our activities, and our activities are not the natural world's activities. The suitability of the five flavors is not fixed; the patterns of the five colors are not fixed; the harmony of the five sounds are not fixed" (SL 275–276).[11] The boundaries of nature and persons, tianrenzhiji, are redrawn throughout history—redrawn by humanizing nature.

Adopting Daoist terminology, Wang identifies nature-within-nature as a force that is without heart-and-mind and without acting:

wuxin 無心 and *wuwei* 無為. Whereas he understands the phrase "without mind" literally, he uses "without acting" figuratively. In a manner akin to the *Daodejing*, Wang's "without acting" just means that nature-in-nature is without intentional action. In terms of contemporary ecology, the way-of-nature is stochastic. Conversely, nature-in-persons literally possesses a heart-and-mind, *youxin* 有心. As such, persons act with volition, purpose, or intention—they "have action," *youwei* 有爲.

Again recalling Morin's *relation écosystémique*, persons and their natural environment respectively, possess varying degrees of autonomy. The categorical distinction between "way-of-nature" and "way-of-persons" likewise implies the relative autonomy of nature and persons. Li Zhecheng (2003) alludes to the mutual autonomy in his analysis of Wang's philosophical cosmology:

> First and foremost, he separates nature and nature's constant patterns from persons and persons' reason . . . Wang Chuanshan believes that nature's constant patterns do not shift according to persons' will. He maintains that one must first contemplate persons' reflexive subjective awareness and actions as reactionary responses to the objective world. And only then contemplate the negotiation and systemic unification of persons and nature. (56)[12]

Because persons are volitional and rational, they are able to purposively construct material culture and (at least partially) insulate themselves from effects environmental forces. By the same token, persons have the freedom of will to suspend and sublimate embodied, animalistic, instinctive drives. Thus, Wang writes, "Nature cannot order people to abide by its spontaneity: without thinking, without purposive activity, its way is already complete."[13] On the flipside of the coin, the self-sufficient "complete" way-of-nature indicates that it maintains its own order of autonomy apart from the influence of persons. "Being self-so, it has itself and is so" (Wang ZMZ, 55).[14]

Wang Fuzhi's Critique of
Orthodox and Heterodox Doctrines

Recalling Li Zehou's theory of sedimentation, the history of Chinese philosophy dialectically progresses through antithetical phases of humanizing nature and naturalizing humans. In the taxonomy of schools, the dialectic is one between Confucian humanism and Daoist naturalism. The process achieves a synthesis, on Li's account, in the cultural works of Song-Ming literati. Though Li does not call on Wang Fuzhi to instantiate this last claim, he could. Li Zhecheng 李 哲承 (2002) further corroborates this conclusion. He describes Wang Fuzhi's take on Confucianism and Daoism as critical and syncretic:

> Wang Chuanshan's point of view, in part, synthesizes tra-ditional thought on tianrenheyi with Daoist naturalism; however, in this regard, Wang Chuanshan differs from other Confucians [. . . .] Wang Chuanshan stands in opposi-tion to other Confucian points of view on the continuity of nature and persons; at the same time, he opposes the naturalistic point of view that reduces humanity's condition by blindly returning it to nature [. . .] He believes that a blind "continuity" that does not recognize "separateness" is not the correct idea of systemic unity (tongyi 统一). (56)[15]

Although Wang recognizes a fundamental continuity between nature and persons, he rejects any form of equivocation between the two.[16] Wang sees both schools as guilty of categorical errors in their respec-tive analyses of person-nature relationships. The Confucian makes an initial misstep by literally ascribing anthropomorphic and moral qualities to nature. Thus understood, tian's qualities are identified with those of the sage—a reduction of tian to persons. Daoism, on the other hand, reduces the activities of the sage to spontaneous nature. On this front, Wang charges Daoist naturalism with a fail-ure to see the irreducible cultural, psychological, epistemological, and moral capacities of persons—a reduction of persons to tian. In sum, the critique runs, both schools tend to identify the qualities and functionality of the sage with the qualities and functionality of nature writ-large. Only they disagree as to what those qualities and functions are.

Rejecting Heterodoxy

The *Daodejing* and *Zhuangzi* celebrate nature as an uncivilized and unrefined event (as in Laozi's imagery of "unhewn wood" and Zhuangzi's representation of "the great clod").[17] In the Daoist vision, nature is sublime and spontaneous. As such, it confounds rational apprehension and resists coercive control. In terms familiar to the *Daodejing*, the naturalization of humans is like returning to the experience of a newborn babe: the babe is without prejudice or overdetermined volition, without extraneous desires, without discriminatory and calculating intellection. In terms familiar to the *Zhuangzi*, naturalization of humans entails rejecting one's inherited cultural edifice as "dregs of dead men." Optimal experience is achieved by living in the same way that the wheelwright practices his craft. He acts without intellection, volition, or coercive effort, but through feeling and response, *ganying* 感應. The consummate experience is born out of unmediated intuition of the forces and patterns of change within one's lived-body and environment. Such intuition enables one to efficaciously respond to adverse circumstances and travel the *path* of least resistance through precarious situations. Without projecting any form of volitional, judgmental, or coercive determination onto the transformations of self and world, persons may achieve aesthetic experiences of unobstructed ease, placidity, equanimity, efficacy, and harmonization in their passage through life and the world.[18] Daoism assumes that persons realize their full epistemic potential by deconstructing cultural constructs—with particular focus on linguistically determined analytical distinctions. Like the view of the great Peng bird in flight, the Daoist epistemological ideal is to achieve a nondiscriminatory experience in which phenomena continuously blend, merge, and transform into one another.

Pace the so-called "heterodox schools," Wang writes, "For no reason at all the Buddhist and Daoist randomly lump the body and function of the sage together with the heavens-and-earth. Their broken down understandings and fantastical actions are based on wanton pretexts and falsifiable words" (DSS 709).[19] He contests the Buddhist existential negation of the differentiating qualities, forms, and concrete particulars of the phenomenal world. From Wang Fuzhi's point of view, the Buddhist is ultimately committed to an unjustifiable reduction of persons and the myriad things to a metaphysical state of nondifferentiated emptiness. He applies the same reasoning in his critique of Daoism:

> Lao confuses this and states that *dao* exists within void, void by way voiding concrete particulars. Sakyamuni confuses this and says that *dao* exists within silence, silence by means of silencing concrete particulars. Though one may continuously utter such extravagant words to no end, one will never escape from concrete things (ZYW 1029).[20]

He maintains that phenomenal diversity is irreducibly real. "The world is only concrete particulars and that is all. Dao is dao of concrete particulars. Concrete particulars cannot be called the concrete particulars of dao" (ZYW 1027).[21] The disjunctive relations between nature and persons, which present themselves in prima-facie experience, should be recognized as concrete and real. Wang sees no reason to make the Daoist or Buddhist speculative move toward a world beyond human experience. He fully embraces being-in-the-world.

The person-in-the-world has a perspectival existence:

> The dog and horse see in the darkness of night; the owl is blind in light of day; the dragon uses horns to hear; the ant uses antennae to communicate. There is no determinate auditory or visual modality. Sensations are different in accordance with the many different receptors . . . Tastes are different in accordance with many different benefits . . . Thus,

> what persons know is persons' nature, renzhitian 人之天;
> what animals know is animals' nature, wuzhitian 物之天.
> (Gernet 247)

His belief that knowledge is always leveled from a particular point of view is derived in part from his syncretic reading of the *Zhuangzi* (Gernet 2005, 247). The epistemology of the *Zhuangzi* is aptly described radical relativism.[22] The work's phantasmagoric allegories and deconstructive narratives challenge the assumption that truth, knowledge, or reality amounts to anything more than a matter of perspective. The *Zhuangzi* does not afford any particular significance to *this* human perspective as opposed to *that* perspectival experience of other sentient creatures. On this issue, Wang stands staunchly opposed to the Daoist. He sees Zhuangzi (whom he believed was the historical author of the text) as reducing the epistemological status of the human perspective to a position on par with all other sentient creatures—cicadas, doves, butterflies, fish, and the like. Daoist epistemology, in other words, asserts a reductive equivocation of all modes of experience; consequentially, the uniqueness of any perspective is ultimately negated. And this negation, in turn, renders the very concept of "perspective" meaningless.

As opposed to Daoism, Wang's brand of Confucianism celebrates persons' unique disposition for knowing and transforming nature. Through hard work, and study and practice, *gongfu* 功夫 and *xuexi* 學習, this disposition can be intentionally developed over time. Wang observes:

> In the early stages of an animal's life, the physical development of their awareness arises quicker than that of persons, but in the end they are obtuse. Persons successively fashion clarity in minute details and accumulate functions. With regard to animals, persons' developments are not quicker, but they are greater. Persons come to their adaptations through steadfast effort.[23]

In this context, adaptation is not an ad hoc reactionary response to adversity; instead, it is a creative and active effort to humanize nature. The uniqueness of human experience is demarcated by the presence of heart-and-mind, *youxin* 有心. The faculty enables persons to engage nature (in their embodied experience and in their environment) with volitional purpose, organic intelligence, and valuating emotion; respectively, the heart-mind functions with *zhi* 志, *si* 思, *qing* 性.[24] "Persons have their way," Wang writes, ". . . if it is nature, then it is spontaneous. If it is animal, then it is spontaneous. Appropriate conduct for insects and rituals for mice are not cultivable activities. They are resigned to nature" (DSS1144).[25] Persons are not resigned to nature: their power resides in their ability to continuously cultivate their embodied biological nature and environment to "achieve heights of spiritual culture" (such as religion, ethics, and aesthetics) and "concrete forms of culture" (technology). As Li Zhecheng puts it, "Wang believes that among the countless living organisms, only persons are able to grasp the regular patterns of nature and establish a cultural existence" (Li 2003, 56–57).[26]

Correcting Orthodoxy

In carrying this critique forward, he similarly challenges "conventional Confucian" proposals that fail to recognize the full ontological significance of disjunctive relations:

Though it is said that sages place the common good over their own interests, to reach this place, they must take care of themselves first and stand their ground without regret. Afterward, they can establish the feeling and normative standard. Conventional Confucians do not take this into consideration. They roughly speak of the sage as if he views himself in the same way as he views others, without any distinction or scrutiny. But this takes the different measures of good and bad, merit and criminality, to be loose and open. Moreover, they say that the sage forms a single body with the heavens-and-earth. Those who make such claims slight subtle-distinction by means of candidness and capriciousness. Their claims and what heterodoxy says, "the heavens-and-earth has the same root as me; the myriad things and I share the same lot," are of the same kind. The statements are unfounded and disingenuous deceit, for where is the difference! [. . .] In Hu Wending's commentary on the *Spring and Autumn Annals*, he calls Confucius's Preface its merit. He places it high on a pedestal with exalted status, making the sage take the place of *tian* as if it were his own. Seeing myriad phenomena and differentiated physical forms, he yet identifies them in substance. Indeed, this discussion belongs to lofty fiction.[27] (DSS 1034)

His critique of Confucian discourse is not directed toward the illocutionary force of its descriptions of holistic interconnectivity and cosmological parity among persons and the natural world. His argument problematizes the perlocutionary and locutionary acts of such descriptions when they are left unqualified by conceptual analysis and empirical observation.

He delivers a padded blow to his predecessor Zhang Shi 張栻 (1133–1181) for making a move toward an equivocation of persons and the cosmic force of *tian*. Zhang Shi's commentary on *Analects* 7.27 opens with the claim, "The sage's heart-mind is the heart-mind of the heavens and earth to give life to things."[28] The passage that Zhang is commenting on describes Confucius as being fair and sportsmanlike in his practices of hunting and fishing. Wang finds opportunity to exercise his analytic literal sensibility and correct Zhang's move toward equivocation:

At the outset, he says, "The heart-mind of the sage is one with the heart-mind of the heavens and earth to give life to things." This is fitting in this place; however, it is not exactly correct. In this context, the sage is cultivating and complementing, abiding by the spontaneity of nature's patterns. Did he ever take the heart-mind of the natural world, which gives life, to be his own heart-mind? If he took the heart-mind that gives life to things to be his heart-mind during the time when he employed his methods of fishing and shooting, then he would have had to have given up fishing and shooting all together. (DSS 709)[29]

"Life, consciousness, meaning, purpose, value—these were all implicit in the neo Confucian concept of Nature, either analogically or literally or in a sense that hovered between the two, depending on the individual thinker" (Black 60–61). For Wang Fuzhi, the ascription of heart-and-mind to the heavens and earth can only be a metaphorical representation of its tendency to spontaneously create and sustain life. In this light his argument demonstrates a need for recognizing the functional difference between nature and persons.

In Wang's worldview, the continuity of nature and persons is not an identity relation: it is a relation of mutual complementation, symbiotic support, and creative transformation. He thus lays out his position: "The sage is only the sage. The heavens and earth are only the heavens and earth. The *Zhongyong* speaks of 'matching *tian*,' as in a wife's matching a husband. Certainly, she does not purely take up the way of the husband" (DSS 709).[30] Wang's argument by analogy invokes a standard neo-Confucian strategy for maintaining Confucian orthodoxy while developing it into a cosmology that rivals the comprehensive scope of Daoist and Buddhist speculative metaphysics. The particulars of this methodology include extending the classical Confucian philosophy of relational self and constitutive relations beyond the traditional focus on social ecology (as is found in the *Analects*). This strategy is often grounded by looking to either the *Zhongyong* or the *Yijing* as the locus classicus for the Confucian cosmological vision. With this move, neo-Confucians take up the orthodox position that persons are constituted by their interpersonal relationships, and reconstruct it into the position that persons are also constituted by their relationships to the heavens-and-earth and the myriad things.[31]

He continues, "Although different from *tian*, sages recursively know and recursively match it" (DSS 540).[32] Wang's analogy and terminology of "matching *tian*" is significant in terms of his epistemology of persons-in-the-world. As a wife's interpretive self-understanding is mediated through her relationship to her husband, the sage reflexively understands herself in relation to nature. Conversely, the wife sees the person that is her husband from a unique hermeneutic perspective. Due to the relativity and intentionality of her experience qua wife, the understanding that she has of her husband inevitably presupposes a tacit self-reference. The hermeneutic prejudice of the wife is such that she cannot help but to view her husband as just that—her husband. Analogously, the person-in-the-world is necessarily bound to understand nature from a uniquely human perspective. Given the relativity and intentionality of persons' experience, the understanding that they have of nature (individually and collectively) inevitably presupposes a tacit self-reference. The hermeneutic prejudice of the person-in-the-world is such that she cannot help but to view nature as nature-within-persons—*zairenzhitian* 在人之天. Thus, *renzhitian* 人之天 comes to mean *"the world as humans know it"* (Liu 2010, 360).[33]

The analogy from familial life represents the unity of nature and persons as a kind of mutual reflection and interactive functionality. As matrimony is a relationship of mutual support, negotiation, and complementation, so are persons' relationships with their environing world.[34] Wang advances his premise: "Sages are of themselves sages. *Tian* is of itself *tian*. Thus it is said of sages, 'they can regulate,' 'they can support,' 'as if they are numinous,' 'they match *tian*'" (DSS 540). Persons are in a position to cultivate, develop, and disclose nature's latent qualities. The sage, it may be said, relates to nature through husbandry.

In sum the nature-person continuity, *he* 合, is to be understood as nature-person harmony, *he* 和. *Harmony is not sameness.* It is predicated on plurality and diversity: a harmonization of unique yet interrelated symbiotic powers.[35] Wang's view is that nature and persons are continuous, yet persons and non-human nature play *different* roles in the dynamic transformations of the world at large.

Mencius's Heart-and-Mind and the Human Experience

Wang Fuzhi's philosophical anthropology is predicated on neo-Confucian cosmology and the moral psychology of the classical Confucian

Zisizi-Mencius lineage. To extend the metaphors of Wang Fuzhi's tradition, the way-of-nature and the way-of-persons are not separate paths leading in different directions. The latter is a developmental continuation of the former, *tianrenheyi* 天人合一. The presence of a heart-and-mind distinguishes nature-within-persons from all other orders of the natural world. Though it distinguishes them, it does not alienate them. The presence of the heart-and-mind, rather, qualifies persons as the heart-and-mind of the heavens-and-earth. The development of thinking-and-feeling in persons is viewed as a consummating realization in and of the natural processes that constitute the world. In this light Mencius expresses the continuity between nature and persons, and recognizes nature as the existential ground of persons' thinking-and-feeling: "For a person to give full realization to thinking-and-feeling is for a person to realize his own natural disposition, and a person who realizes his own natural disposition will realize *tian* 天" (Mencius 7A1).

According to Mencius, the difference between persons and beasts is slight (4B19). The difference lies in their *natural dispositions*. "Natural disposition" is here offered as a translation of the Chinese *xing* 性. *Xing* 性 is derived in part from *sheng* 生, meaning *birth, growth,* and *life* in general. As is evidenced in Mencius's debates with Gaozi, *xing* and *sheng* were used interchangeably in pre-Qin China. Given this synonymy, *xing* can mean "direction that a thing develops in its process of growth," "natural tendencies, desires, and characteristic inclinations demonstrated by living organisms," and "tendencies characteristic of a thing" (Shun 37, 180, 183).

Following Mencius, Wang Fuzhi accepts this fundamentally biological signification of *xing*, and he concedes that all living creatures possess *xing* in this sense. In the domain of philosophical anthropology, however, there is much more to the meaning of the term. In addition to the component of biological life, *sheng* 生, the term *xing* 性 also contains the semantic signifier for heart-and-mind. (忄 = 心.) For Mencius and Wang Fuzhi alike, heart-and-mind is unique to the dispositional character of persons.

D. C. Lau notes this point the introduction to his translation of the *Mencius*:

The unique feature that makes up the human being is his heart and so when we speak of human nature we should have in mind, primarily, the human heart. This heart contains incipient moral tendencies which when nurtured with care can enable a man to become a sage. (xlvii)

In agreement, Kwong-loi Shun writes, "Mencius regarded *xing* as constituted by, or at least as having as a central component, the development of the ethical predispositions of the heart [*xin* 心]" (Shun 1997, 10). Based on this analysis three intractable propositions can be stated regarding the heart-and-mind: (1) It is a unique characteristic of human existence; (2) It is dispositional and requires cultivation; (3) It is provides the ground for morality. Whereas Hellenistic-based philosophy takes reason to be the measure of man, Confucianism takes morality (Gernet 331).

The moral processes of *xin* are implicated in emotions or feelings of compassion, shame, deference, and modesty (Mencius 6A6). For Mencius, one must cultivate these emotional qualities to achieve personhood.[36] Thus, *xin* is an emotional and moral activity that is demonstrative of the person-in-the-world. Mencius explains these emotions as "four germs of morality." In this context, moral qualities are given connotations of organic growth, development, and the possibility for cultivation. Indeed, Mencius repeatedly draws analogies between the four germs and the human body: if the four germs are not effectively put to use, they will become crippled, but if they are nourished they will show in a healthy and functional body (2A6, 7A21). The model of the human person given in the *Mencius* is one of an organism, an organism that has natural moral/social inclinations.

Xin is an emotional process, providing persons with impetus to foster a higher moral experience within a community. In passage 2A6, Mencius illustrates this conception of the *xin* by way of allegory: "All persons have thinking and feeling (*xin*) that does not bear the suffering of others, *burenren* 不忍人. Suppose a person were, all of a sudden, to see a young child about to fall into a well. All have the urge to be alarmed by natural sympathies." Emphasis is placed on the spontaneity of the action. In this regard Lau is instructive:

"The reaction was instantaneous, and therefore spontaneous, as there was no time to reflect, and a reaction which is spontaneous is a true manifestation of a man's nature (*xing*)" (xx). Likewise, Shun states, "such [spontaneous] reactions reveal something deep in the heart/mind (*xin*) and show one the kind of person one really is" (140).

"All persons have a heart-and-mind that does not bear the suffering of others," *bu ren ren* 不忍人. To understand the person in this context one must understand the meaning of this "other." The final character, "'ren' 人 (person) is added here, because the discourse is entirely of a man's feelings, *as exercised towards other men*" (ibid.). Shun further supports this view of *buren* 不忍 as fundamentally concerning one's relationships toward other persons (49).

One's *xing* is a disposition to (efficaciously) adapt oneself to social-environmental conditions. This adaptation involves taking on the customs of one's social environment and making them one's own, personalizing them. In this case one acts to create culture and participate in society so as to foster a harmonious balance therein.

Xing, then, is not something unlearned, but it is a process of dispositional development undertaken within the context of preestablished (social) conditions. It is a process of refining, cultivating, and expressing one's moral heart-and-mind in relation to others. The human being in Confucianism is a human becoming.

In light of the Mencius-Zisizi tradition of Confucianism, the person-in-the-world is not born with a determinate and finished essence. Initially, nature endows the human organism with a dispositional trajectory for achieving personhood. "Wang Fuzhi took the further step of defining the totality of *xing* 性 as the emerging, developing state of human existence. In other words, Wang Fuzhi took what we call *xing* 性 to be human potential" (Liu 2010, 364). Wang Fuzhi's form of ecological humanism, describes the ingression of persons-in-the-world in terms as phases of *qi*:

In the *Huowen* "primal *qi*" and "the events under the heavens" are two phases. The position where the transformation of *qi* resides just is the moment of demarcation between persons and base spirit. For this reason, the *Zhongyong* differentiates the language of *tian* and the language of *ming*. *Ming* means "to order" as in a "government order." However, this not the appropriate language for *tian*. Necessarily, the language of *tian* is "to convey." What it conveys is an *event*. This is the bequeathal of nature-within-nature. However, it does not necessarily bequeath the separation between human and animal body. . . .[37]

Persons do not come to exist like a bullet from a barrel. Human nature is not a given. The spontaneous creativity of primordial energy provides the necessary and sufficient conditions for the emergence of life. The natural world provides the human organism with its inchoate beginnings; it gives persons their concrete biological existence, body, and requisite disposition for developing higher cognitive and moral faculties. This initial phase of persons ingression into the world is referred to as "primary disposition of nature," *xiantianzhixing* 先天之性. The consummate achievement of persons-in-the-world is referred to as "later disposition of nature," *houtianzhixing* 後天之性. The person-in-the-world is an undertaking, an unfolding historical event of humanizing nature.

5

Identifying Religiosity in Wang Fuzhi's Neo-Confucianism

Though mundane in certain respects, Wang's worldview nevertheless contains religious reverential foci. His religious reverence is directed toward an ideal of procreativity in nature. He reveres what he envisions to be a procreative drive inherent within the cosmic forces of *yin* and *yang qi*. In this vein, he takes an orthodox position in a long lineage of Confucian scholars concerned with procreativity. In the tradition of the *Yijing*, Zhou Dunyi, Cheng Hao, Zhu Xi and others, Wang Fuzhi represents a Confucian axiology of *ceaseless procreativity*, *shengshengbuyi* 生生不已. This reverence for life and procreativity opens an axiological and spiritual dimension in the neo-Confucian ecological humanism at hand. To explore this dimension in more depth, we here revisit concepts of procreativity and life, *sheng* 生, in the context of *Yijing* and neo-Confucian studies. At the end of the day, Wang Fuzhi believes that the procreative and transformative power of nature is mysterious and unfathomable. As such, it is a sublime inspiration for awe and reverence.

Before advancing into an exposition of Wang's reverence for the sublime and procreative, however, we first advance an axiology of ritual propriety. Ritual propriety in neo-Confucianism serves as a means for integrating and harmonizing persons-in-the-world.

Ritual Propriety as Humanizing Nature

The humanization of nature envisioned in Wang Fuzhi's worldview is a multidimensional phenomenon. Humanizing nature belongs to the domain of moral praxis. In this respect, Confucian humanism is referred to as "Cultivation Humanism" (Cheng 1998). Cultivation of the environment reciprocally entails cultivation of persons' subjective and intersubjective dimensions. Persons humanize nature by methodically sublimating their natural sensuality, emotions, and behaviors. The sublimation is directed toward establishing dynamic emotional equilibrium, experience of social harmony, and mutual concern amongst persons. The praxis assumes a rejection of substance, mind/body, subject/object dualism. Instead it assumes continuity and reciprocity between internal-embodied and external-environmental forces.[1]

From high antiquity forward, the praxis of ritual propriety has been celebrated in China as a defining feature of its civilization.[2] Hence, Li Zehou identifies the ancient traditions of ritual as the initial phase of humanizing nature, superseding prehistoric shamanism. The praxis is a process of humanizing nature in that it purposively integrates and regulates subjective emotions, interpersonal relationships, and the environing world. Ritual propriety is carried out as a means of cultivating and disclosing the individual, society, and the natural world as recursive, mutually complementary forces (Li 2010, 13–14). It is undertaken with the intention of establishing a nested hierarchy of organizational orders: individual, social, natural-cosmic. Li cites the pre-Qin narrative-history *Zuozhuan* 左傳 as an early depiction of this correlation:

> Ritual is the standard of heaven [*tian*], the proper conduct of the earth, and the practice of the people. Heaven and earth have their standard, and the people take this as their model . . . If a man is not amiss in either joy or grief, he is in harmony with the nature of heaven and earth. (Li 2010, 13)

This passage implies a claim, which is adopted by Wang Fuzhi and supported throughout Li's discussion: the individual, society, and the natural world are correlated on multiple levels by *similitude, homology,* and *isomorphism.* In addition, this early text speaks to the potential for persons to act in concert with the forces of their environments by means of engaging the world with a balanced emotional disposition. As Alison Black has demonstrated in her thesis (1989), this continuity or "organic dyad" between the internal-embodied and external-environing dimensions of persons-in-the-world is a prominent theme in the work of Wang Fuzhi.

Ritual propriety and music are prescribed within the tradition as a means for harnessing and creatively expressing one's sensations, emotions, and thoughts (Li 2010, 11). "They calm the violence of the sentiments or excite them according to circumstance" (Gernet 384). The normative demand of the moral praxis is not to eradicate natural sensuousness feelings, or desires, or emotions; rather, the praxis is intended to sublimate, cultivate, and *humanize* the primal modalities of experience so that they are conducive to a higher-quality of shared communal life and cultural achievements.[3] This is the meaning of Wang's statement, "Appetite and lust are the beauties of ritual propriety. Benefits are the dependencies of the masses."[4] Ritual humanizes nature by intentionally transforming biologically based emotive forces into moral sentiments. Rather than antagonistically opposed, nature and culture are understood in this case in terms of continuity. Confucian morality is predicated on an appropriate fusion of ritualized praxis and feeling. Without sincerity, ritual is empty. Without the practice of ritual, sincerity is left uncultivated.[5]

Ritual propriety and music are intended to foster an aesthetic order or harmony within and amongst persons-in-world. The aesthetic experience is predicated on the Confucian mantra: *harmony but not sameness.*[6] Li explains the dictum as such:

Within this system, first of all, "Harmony begets things; identity produces nothing." And, "If sound is singular, it finds no audience; if things are singular, there is no pattern;

if flavors are singular, they have no effect." This is to say, singularity cannot produce harmony; harmony is by necessity the unification of plurality. Second, this unity tends particularly to manifest itself as the "mutual complementarity" of opposing elements. (2010, 20).

The Confucian tradition conceives of harmony as a creative coordination of multiple forces. This fundamental premise is suggested by the pictographic signification of the Chinese character for harmony, *he* 和. The graph is comprised of two components: grain 禾 and mouth 口. That is to say, harmony takes its root phenomenal experience in culinary aesthetics.[7] In this experience each ingredient should contribute its own unique flavor to the holistic sensuous quality of taste. Though each ingredient retains its own flavor, each should mutually complement and enhance one another. Analogously, ritual propriety entails that every human activity and artifice within any given situation should symbiotically support one another. Each situation provides a potential for achieving *an* experience. Though ritual and music are practiced in tandem, they have "a division of labor" (Li 17). Insofar as "ritual propriety" refers to a set of culturally constructed norms or a code of conduct, it "regulates and restrains people externally" (16). Insofar as music directly emerges from and resonates with one's felt-emotions, "it is not an external, coercive institution, but an internal guide" (19). In Confucian discourse humanizing nature entails an integration of the inner dimensions of cognitive-emotional experience and external-environmental states of affairs. The dyadic practice of ritual and music establishes a positive feedback loop between the harmony of one's internal emotional experience and the harmony achieved in one's external social environment. Thus, Li cites the *Rites*: "Music is the ultimate harmonization, the rites the ultimate orderliness; the inner being is harmonized, while the external is ordered" (18).[8] Personal faculties are brought into a dynamic equilibrium *zhong* 中 through their contact with harmony in the environment *he* 和, and harmony develops in a humanized environment through persons shaping it in accord with regulated measures of desires and emotion. Wang Fuzhi expresses the view in the following passage:

Du Yu (222–284) wanted to abbreviate the crown prince funeral ceremony, saying, "In the ritual propriety of the exemplary person, everything internal is all there is." How could he take this savage claim as suitable! Now, consider a person, who in his heart does not lose respect for his father, yet sits obstinately when receiving him. He has a feeling that is not indifferent in his love of his elder brother, yet he angrily twists his arm. Would you also say that everything internal is all there is? The internal and external intersect in mutual establishment and mutual support . . . Thus, the former kings regulated funeral rituals to reach the interior of worthy persons from the exterior, so as to bring them peace within. They regulated the external-environment for those with moderate temperament so as to affectively stimulate them. . . .[9]

Ritualistic music does not only serve to temper the emotions and integrate them into a shared communal experience: it maintains communion with nature (Li 2010, 28). Traditional Chinese music is intended to represent natural patterns. The representation is thought to attune emotional experience so that it resonates with regular transformations and orders of things. "The key was to establish a unifying system of correspondences in which (1) the cadence of music (including song and dance), (2) the activity of the natural world, and (3) the emotions of the human person, found their counterparts in rhythm and meter" (Li 2010, 20). As Wang Fuzhi understands it, ritual is not only a means for establishing a symbiotic harmony between persons and the natural world, it is also a natural development of the world itself—a fulfillment of the natural dispositions unique to persons.

Immanence of Persons-in-the-World

Wang Fuzhi maintains a doctrine of immanence regarding persons-in-the-world: persons are inseparable from the world. He asserts his position as a rejection of Buddhist conceptions of transcendence. In the following passage he alludes to the Mahāyāna Buddhist, Yogācāra

School of ideation only. After outlining premises of their metaphysics and soteriology, he rejects the doctrine as a harmful disdain for
worldly existence:

> Buddhism takes genuine emptiness to be the storehouse
> consciousness of the Thus Come One. It claims that
> within the great void there is not a single thing, and the
> nascent energies of *qi* emerge from illusion, becoming all
> that is harmful. This illusion is the fundamental basis of
> obstruction and hindrance to realizing the true suchness of
> things [. . . .] They are absurd in their wish to annihilate
> the world in order to establish great *nirvana*. After all how
> could they annihilate it? (ZMZ 83)[10]

The Mahāyāna Buddhist *Heart Sutra* captures the Buddhist ideal of
transcendence in "the great *mantra* of the perfection of wisdom."
The *mantra*, which is recited to this day in Buddhist monasteries,
reads: "Gone, gone, gone beyond, utterly gone beyond, Awakening; O
joy" (Mitchell 102). One reaches the "other shore," in the words of
the tradition, by deeply realizing that all conceptual and perceptual
discriminations are ultimately without basis in reality such as it truly
is. In its suchness (Sanskrit, *tathatā*), all phenomena are empty of
own being (*svhabāva-śūnya*). When one comes to such realization,
the phenomenal world is left behind. Technically speaking: the meaningful world as it is interpreted through the structures and lenses of
linguistic constructs and concepts (*prapañca*) is regarded as a mere
provisional truth, which is abnegated by the transcendent experience
and ultimate truth of emptiness.

Arguing on behalf of orthodox Confucianism, Wang takes the
Buddhist call for transcendence and abnegation of distinctions to
be a threat to the coherence of social-and-natural orders. The doctrine is immoral, in his view, for it advocates forsaking the praxis of
cultivating the social and ecological relationships that sustain life
and order. Wang maintains that Buddhist and Daoist commitments
to transcendence are not only immoral, but also metaphysically
unsound. Wang Fuzhi, thus, critiques both the Buddhist doctrine of

emptiness (Chinese: *kong* 空) and the Daoist emphasis on negation (*wu* 無) along the following lines:

> Thus they discard the orders of human relations, denigrate the interconnected patterns of things, hold fast to a recalcitrant void, tread upon death with attractive interest, and say "I find peace in what is peaceful." This abnegates the other, and demonstrates a misunderstanding of the fact that *one cannot break away from the things of this world* [. . . .] *Continuously, whether sleeping or eating, without exception we are all related to other things. Continuously, whether moving or speaking, in each occurrence we are necessarily dependent on other things.* (SYY 237–240)[11]

Accordingly, he offers his own holistic and naturalistic model of persons-in-the-world as an alternative to his understanding of Buddhist and Daoist claims to transcendence.

Critically speaking, Wang Fuzhi's depiction of Buddhism may be parochial. A Buddhist may provide a metaphysical rejoinder to Wang's negative characterization of Buddhist emptiness. Both the Huayan and Tiantai schools of thought could point to their own holistic (causal) models of the universe, such as the Huayan descriptions of reality as "mutually interpenetrating events without obstruction" (*shishiwuai*) and the "non-obstruction of events and patterns" (*shiliwuai*). In this regard, Wang Fuzhi's neo-Confucianism may share more with Buddhism than Wang would care to admit. The Cheng-Zhu school of *lixue*, for example, shares fundamental terminological and theoretical commitments with the Huayan school of Chinese Buddhism. According to both schools, the world is a dynamic, complex, holistic pattern of constantly changing events.

A Mahāyāna Buddhist may have a reply to Wang's moral argument by claiming that it is not the case that the Mahāyāna Buddhist forsakes commitments to this world in pursuit of the other shore; on the contrary, inspired by great compassion (*mahākaruṇā*), the ideal Buddhist commits to the Bodhisattva vow. The Bodhisattva vows to be born again and again into countless lives of embodied suffering for the sake of saving the suffering beings of the world. The Bodhisattva, in other words, is committed to maintaining an immanent presence in this world in one form or another to improve the conditions and experiences of all suffering beings. Though Mahāyāna may reply to Wang's initial critique by invoking the Bodhisattva vow, the Buddhist soteriological commitment to final nirvana for all sentient beings still stands at odds with Wang's positive account of reality and the meaning of life in terms of *yinyang*, energy, concrete particulars and procreativity.

Procreativity in the *Yijing*

Though he maintains a skeptical stance on religious transcendence, his worldview does not lack religiosity. As suggested by Zhang Zai's "Western Inscription," neo-Confucian spirituality is grounded in experiences of being situated within the sublime, fecundate, trans-formative powers of the world system. Zhang Zai (张载 1020–1077) inscribed the following verse on the western wall of his study:

> *Qian* is called "father," *Kun* is called "mother." Now, I am insignificant herein the world, and yet I have a home in the midst of their intermingling. And so that which fills the space between the heavens and the earth is my body; that which controls the heavens and earth (is) my natural disposition. The people and I are of the same womb, and I transform along with things. . . .[12]

Zhang Zai is here presenting a holistic vision of the cosmos as a habi-tat, home, or intimate hearth for persons. With this claim, Zhang Zai expresses a feeling of intimate (familial) connection with the natural world. Zhang Zai's experience of the sublime is not one of fear and trembling, it is one of being at home in the world. In this sense, his statements provide an account of the home or ecology.

Zhang Zai uses the terms Qian 乾 and Kun 坤 to advance his concept of being a person-in-the-world. Qian 乾 and Kun 坤 are the names of the first two hexagrams in the *Yijing*'s series of sixty-four hexagrams. The Qian hexagram (☰) is completely composed of solid "*yang*" lines; the Kun hexagram (☷) is composed of all broken "*yin*" lines. Through categorical resonance (*ganlei* 感類), Qian is a symbol of the heavens and masculinity, and Kun is symbolically refers to earth and femininity. With the conjunction of Qian and Kun, the author alludes to a conception of the natural world as a whole, which is constituted by interacting correlative forces. The interaction of *yin* and *yang* forces in every order of existence drives transformation of things, transformation of energy, and the creation of novel life and experience.

Wang Fuzhi takes an analytical approach to the texts that he comments on. In the case of his *Annotations* on Zhang Zai's "Western Inscription," Wang writes, "It says, 'Qian is *called* father, Kun is *called* mother. It does not say, '*tian is* my father, and earth *is* my mother.'"[13] Wang means that Zhang Zai cannot be taken literally in his ascription of fatherhood and motherhood to the cosmic forces of *yin* and *yang* or *tian* and earth. Instead, Zhang's claim here must be understood as a metaphorical extension of the experience of familial relations and feelings (*qin* 親). In Wang's reading, Zhang Zai should be understood as expressing an appreciation for the life-creating force of nature. All things are born of nature. Wang reads Zhang in particular as expressing a felt intimacy with nature akin to the felt intimacy that one feels for one's parents. Wang Fuzhi compares and contrasts Zhang Zai's work to Zhou Dunyi's (周敦頤 1017–1073). "Master Zhou Lianxi first made the *Taiji Tushuo*, and took up the research into the (cosmological) origins of the continuity of nature and persons as a means for illuminating human life."[14] According to Wang Fuzhi, Zhang Zai's work serves as a development of Zhou's original conception by incorporating the intimate connection that one experiences with the natural world. Thus, Wang argues, Zhang Zai goes beyond Zhou Dunyi by advocating a further cosmological principle of "the continuity of nature and familial intimacy," *tianqinheyi* 天親合一. The filial piety that one bears toward one's parents is thus the basis for the extension of one's service to and intimacy with nature.

Neo-Confucianism celebrates and reveres natural procreativity. In a word, the neo-Confucian affirmation of life and creativity focusses on the Chinese term *sheng* 生. Wing-tsit Chan describes the significance of *sheng* in the works of neo-Confucian authors along the following lines:

> [T]he idea of "sustaining and supporting the life of one another" had been a long tradition in the Confucian school . . . From that idea it was a logical step to the concept of giving life or production and reproduction, not only as [the] way of man's life, but of the universe as well. All these ideas are expressed by the word *sheng*. (Chan 554)

During the Northern Song, an axiological appreciation of life based on the *Yijing* was taken up and developed as a keystone of neo-Confucian theory and practice. Master Zhou Dunyi is said to have exemplified the neo-Confucian orientation to nature in his refusal to cut the grass outside of his windowsill. Cheng Hao 程顥 (1032–1085) followed Zhou Dunyi in this practice.[15] Cheng Hao writes of his senior, "Zhou Dunyi did not cut the grass growing outside his window. When asked about it, he said that he felt toward the grass as he felt toward himself" (Chan 535). Underlying the Zhou-Cheng practice is a belief that all things demonstrate in a propensity to live. In this general way, Master Zhou and the blade of grass share in the same natural disposition for life and procreativity *shengzhixing* (生之性). Zhou refers to this propensity as *shengyi* 生意, which literally translates as "life intention," or "life purpose," and connotes "life meaning." Accordingly, Zhou and Cheng both commit to the belief that the natural world has a general purposiveness for creating and sustaining life.

    Philological analysis demonstrates that the character *sheng* 生 has ancient roots. The character is depicted on the Shang period oracle bones as such: 𡳳 . The character is written on the bronze inscriptions of the Shang and Zhou periods: 𡳳. And it is written in the standardized seal script of the Qin dynasty: 𡳳 (Wang, *Life*, 481). According to the classical *Shuowen jiezi* lexicon (compiled circa 100 CE), "*Sheng* 生," means "to advance. The image is one of grass shoots,

屮, sprouting up from the earth, 土" (Wang, *Life*, 481). The pictograph is decidedly terrestrial and organic. *Sheng* is primarily a biological concept, but in the context of the later strata of the *Yijing*, *sheng* is also used to mean *creativity* in a more general, cosmological, sense.

The term *sheng* is used in two sets of line statements in the early Zhou strata of the text. *Sheng* is used as a noun in the line statements of the Guan hexagram, as in, "Comprehensively observe my *life*, advancing and retreating." The Guan statement implies the need for attaining a sense of propriety, or strategic timing and positioning, vis-à-vis one's social, historical, and natural conditions—as was the case with Wang Fuzhi's reading of the hexagram when he drew his lot and decided to retire into the mountains. *Sheng* is used as a verb in the line statements of the Daguo hexagram: "Decaying poplars *give birth* to grasses . . . Decaying poplars *give birth* to flowers" (ibid.). In addition to the organic/biological sense of birth and life, we find an observation of correlative cycle of life and death—a process philosophy in which every end is a beginning.

Whereas the term, *sheng*, is mentioned only five times in the line statements (and is not mentioned at all in the hexagram statements), explicit mention of *sheng* totals thirty-eight token uses in the *Ten Wings* of later Zhou commentary associated with Confucius. Of the *Ten Wings*, the term occurs most frequently and systematically in the *Appended Phrases Commentary* (twenty-three times in all), thus qualifying this section as the most comprehensive and significant elucidation of life and procreativity within the *Yijing*'s expressed worldview (Wang, *Life*, 481). Beyond the explicit references to the term, the philosophy of procreative life is a ubiquitous theme underlying the text as a whole. Perhaps *sheng* is best understood within an integrated set of mutually expressing axioms. Some members of this set explicitly contain the concept, while others only tacitly contain it. Given the foundational significance of *sheng* in this worldview, the propositions espousing this concept are definitive of the *Yijing*'s process philosophy and correlative cosmology. The following is a partial list of propositions from the *Xici* (*Appended Phrases*) and *Xugua* (*Ordering the Hexagrams*) *Commentaries* dealing with the idea of *sheng*:

1. The sublime virtue of the heavens and earth is *procreativity*; the sublime value of the sage is *positioning*. (*Xici xia* 1.6)[16]

2. There is an intermingling of the genial influences of heaven and earth, and transformation in its various forms abundantly proceeds. There is an intercommunication of seed between male and female, and the myriad things transform with *life*. (*Xici xia* 5.12)[17]

3. One *yin* one *yang* is called *dao*; continuing it is good; developing it is a natural disposition. Humane persons see it and call it humane; knowledgeable persons, see it and call it knowing [. . . .] Everyday novelty is called flourishing excellence. *Procreative creativity* is called change [. . .] Continuous transformation is called an event; *yinyang*, unfathomable, is called sublime. (*Xici shang* 5.1)[18]

4. Vast is the *Yi* and great! [. . .] As for Qian, in its quiescent state it is focused, and in its active state it is undeviating. This is how it achieves its great productivity. As for Kun, in its quiescent state it is condensed, and in its active state it is diffuse. This is how it achieves its capacious *productivity*. (*Xici shang* 6.1)[19]

5. Sages, in establishing the trigrams and hexagrams, *comprehensively observed* phenomena. They appended phrases herein, thereby illuminating good fortune and misfortune. Hard and soft mutually push against each other, thereby *creating* changes and transformations. (*Xici shang* 2.1)[20]

6. The sun and moon mutually push upon on another, and luminescence is born between them [. . . .] Contraction and expansion mutually stimulate one another, and advantage is born therein. (*Xici xia* 5.2)[21]

7. There are the heavens-and-the-earth, so then the myriad things are born therein. (*Xugua* 1)[22]

Such are the slogans of the *Yijing*'s "Life Education," "Philosophy of Procreative Creativity," or "Philosophy of Continuous Life" (Wang Zu-hua 479, 483). Again, the focus, emphasis, and intention of the *Yijing*'s claims are on life and procreativity in general; thus, the text expresses a concerned consciousness not only for human life, but for the flourishing of life in its diverse manifestations. Recognizing the centrality of life in the *Yijing*'s worldview, Wang Zu-hua 王汝華 explains that the text emphasizes "unending fecund procreativity and vitality of ceaseless creative advance" (495).[23]

Each of the claims in each of the above seven passages is polysemous. Looking at the structure of the text, for example, one finds that it often makes a cosmological claim about impersonal forces, immediately followed by statements about how persons ought to conduct themselves. The juxtaposition of cosmological, anthropological, and ethical claims in the above propositions provide insight into the assumption of "continuity between nature and persons" embedded within the text. In addition, the text presents a strategic mode of thinking about persons-in-the-world in terms of the world's propensities of change. Following the idealized model of the sages, the text enjoins the reader to take up methodical comprehensive observation as a means for understanding the changing circumstances of one's environment. Based on this *a posteriori* knowledge, one ought to position oneself in such a way that one may reap profits, rejuvenate oneself, and find ease of passage in a constantly changing, sublime, world.

Like each of the above propositions is polysemous, so each token use of *sheng* implicates a spectrum of concepts—ranging from "birth," "life," and "procreativity," to "creativity." Each token use of the term, *sheng*, simultaneously suggests biological life, biological procreativity, as well as creativity in general. In proposition (3) above we find a reduplication of the character to form a binomial expression: *shengsheng* 生生. The reduplication here serves to intensify, extend, and multiply the sense of life and procreativity. The reduplication certainly implies a conception of "continuous life," where "continuity" here means "spatial and temporal continuity" as well as "holistic interconnectedness." In this case, the binomial term expresses a universal sense of *life everywhere*. Grammatically speaking, the first character in the binomial expression can either be an adjective or a verb; the second character is a noun, thus rendering either of the following interpretations viable: "procreative creativity" and "giving birth to life." As the world is defined by change, and change is defined in terms of *shengsheng*, the change that constitutes the world at every organizational level of existence is considered a procreative process.

Within the process philosophy of the *Yijing*, *sheng* is a primary function (emergent phenomenon) of *yinyang* interactions. The terminology of *yinyang* in the *Book of Changes* is an account of cosmic creativity. The idea is expressed by Wang Fuzhi: "In the direct language displayed in the *Yijing* itself, all is completely embodied in the *dao* of one-*yin*-one-*yang* and persons' natural dispositions. Procreative creativity (*shengsheng*) has its embodiments and movements, which gradually and resolutely germinate."[24]

As previously discussed in chapter two, the creative sense of *yin* and *yang* is directly connected to the concept of *taiji* in the *Appended Phrases* claim: "*Taiji* gives birth to two modes . . ." (*Xici shang* 11.3). Wang Fuzhi reiterates this connection in his discussion of *taiji* as the root-body (*benti* 本體) of *yin* and *yang*.[25] He states:

> *Yinyang* is what the *taiji* manifests [. . .] Movement and rest are the mutually stimulating subtle-mechanisms of *yin* and *yang* [. . . .] Insofar as they are continuous, they are *taiji*; insofar as they are separated, they are *yin* and *yang* [. . . .][26] *Yin* does not have its fetal beginnings without *yang*, and *yang* relies on the material of *yin* to create. Myriad events actualize with concrete form, and their natures are beautiful therein.[27]

Again, *taiji* refers to the creative drive of the constantly changing world. Wang Zu-Hua makes this point in reference to Wang Fuzhi's philosophy:

> We can understand *taiji* as the root-source for the procreative becoming (*shengcheng* 生成) of the myriad things between the heavens and the earth [. . . .] It is the primordial energy (*yuanqi* 元氣) in which there is intermixture without yet

discrimination [. . . .] There is this root-fundamental principle, which constructs the ceaselessly procreative system of the cosmos.[28]

The creativity inherent in *yinyang* interactions is further advanced in discourse on Qian and Kun. In the *Discourse on the Hexagrams Commentary* of the *Ten Wings*, the text states: "Qian initiates. Kun accords."[29] Qian and Kun must be understood correlatively—neither is absolutely primary nor absolutely secondary. The dynamic correlativity of the two events is illustrated by the imagery of the *Yijing*: "a closing door is called Kun; an opening door is called Qian. Continuous closings and openings are called transformations, inexhaustible going and coming is called pervasiveness."[30] Qian refers to phases of increasing energy and activity in any system or process. Qian can also refer to active forces. Kun refers to processes of consolidation, concretion, completion, and entropy. Kun also refers to reactive forces. Through continuous, recursive and reciprocal influences Qian and Kun forces and processes give birth to life and everyday novelty. The Confucian vision from the *Yijing* perspective is a vision of a changing world, into which novel entities are constantly born, and living entities constantly die. The Confucian vision is one of a great transformation of myriad things between the heavens and the earth.

Experiencing the Sublime in Nature

In addition to ideals of life and ceaseless creativity, neo-Confucian literati ascribe positive value to the unfathomable and sublime in nature. In reference to this aspect of Wang Fuzhi's worldview, Alison Black writes, "It was a necessary part of his total conception that one aspect of the universe should elude precise specification . . . This element receives various descriptions at Wang's hands, but it can most comprehensively be described as *shen*" (72). Wang derives his conception of *shen* 神 from the *Appended Phrases* claim, "*Yinyang*, unfathomable, is called *shen*" (*Xici shang* 5.1). In other contexts, the term *shen* may be translated into English as *spirit*; however, given the

Appended Phrases' definition, the term *shen* in this context is closer to the English *sublime*. *Shen* denotes an awe-inspiring, mystifying experience as is expressed in Zhang Zai's *Western Inscription* and the "Sublime Transformations," *shenhua* 神化, chapter of his *Correcting Youthful Ignorance*.

In his commentary on the *Appended Phrases*, Wang defines *shen* in terms of *miao* 妙, meaning *marvelous* and *mysterious*. He writes, "*Shen* is *dao* mysteriously going out through the myriad things" (ZYW 531).[31] Wang's claim suggests an experience of profundity in relation to the complexity and subtlety of the *yin* and *yang* forces that constitute the world and drive its creative transformations. He further discusses the very notion of change, *yi* 易, which titles the *Yijing*, as "numinous and mysterious." *Shen* alludes to the unfathomable finesse and subtlety, complexity, and magnanimity of cosmic change and structure. Along these lines, the extension of the concept further contains nature's boundlessness, *wuji* 無極, and the invisible, *you* 幽, processes of nature's inner-workings. In a word, *shen* functions as *sublime*. The quality of *shen* engenders experiences of profound wonder and awe. It elicits reverence for a natural world that is greater than the individual person and yet provides an intimate place for every thing.

The same point could be made with reference to the Korean neo-Confucian thinker, Yi Yulgok (1536–1584). Yi regarded the hexagram system of the *Yijing* to symbolize "neither a fixed physical object nor a mere mechanical entity; rather, it is a living, dynamic, changing reality" (Ro 177). Moreover, because of the dynamism, procreativity, complexity, and open nature of the world-system and its constituent subsystems, the world is a source of "sanctity and mystery" (ibid.). Ro's description of Yi's cosmology likewise serves as an apt summary of Wang's conception of indeterminacy:

[Yi] believed the universe could not be completely comprehended by human intelligence or through human thought processes. He believed that the universe is a "mystery" not to be reduced to the rational or conceptual framework of the human intellectual system. This dimension of mystery causes us to feel that the universe is sacred; hence, we have a sense of awe toward the universe. The universe "manifests" itself to us as much as it "conceals" itself from us. . . . (ibid.)

Wang finds in the *Yijing* a source and expression of the most profound and transformative experiences—experiences that can rightly be called religious. In the *Inner Commentary*, for example, Wang denotes the relationship between nature and persons using the character *yun* 縕. Elsewhere in his work, he describes the *yun* relationship as a "continuity and efficacy of *qi*." Interpreting this continuity in terms of Wang's text, the energetic relationship integrates nature and persons as correlative forces in a marvelous, fine, subtle, beautiful, and mysterious cosmic pattern:

Patterning is only images of the mystery of the two modes, *qi* everywhere is the actuality of the two modes. Initiating is only the initiating of *qi*. Accordance is only the accordance of *qi*. The profound-mixing of nature and persons is a continuity of *qi*, and that is all. From this efficacy of *qi* then there is patterning.[32]

Wang's denotation of the relationship as *yun* 縕, moreover, suggests in and of itself that he believed the continuity of nature and persons as a source for sublime experience. In addition to the sense of "merging," the term *yun* 縕, like its cognate *yun* 緼 (without the grass-top radical), connotes a "muddled-and-confused, helter-skelter (*fenlun* 紛亂), profound and abstruse (*shenao* 深奧)," state of affairs.[33] In this sense, *yun* 縕 is defined paranomastically as *yun* 緼.[34] Insofar as the former instantiates the latter, the former semiotically refers to Wang Fuzhi's cosmological category of *yinyun* 絪縕, which is glossed above in chapter two as "the creative inchoate co-mingling of *yin* and *yang* in great harmony." The profundity lies in the subtlety and sublimity of the complex set of relationships. The interconnectedness of persons and the world is experienced at its depths as a qualitative feeling. This feeling opens an axiological dimension in Wang's worldview. As a fundamental component of Wang's philosophy, this aspect of indeterminacy must be part of any ecological humanism modeled on the basis of his philosophy.

6

Conclusion

Summarizing Reflections

Neo-Confucianism provides a comprehensive and cogent ecologican humanism, which is applicable in and for the contemporary world. As discussed in the first two chapters, Wang Fuzhi uses neo-Confucian terminology to present a particularly naturalistic cosmology. The terminology of self-so patterning provides a classical Chinese statement of vital materialism: the idea that the world and its myriad inhabitants are structures of self-determining, procreative, energetic transformations. The neo-Confucian belief is that the energy that constitutes the world-system is procreative in the sense that it has the propensity to give rise to life and experience in endlessly diverse forms. In terms of the *Book of Changes*, this "procreative creativity is called *change*," and is further denoted by the term *taiji*. As *taiji*, procreativity is a neo-Confucian category of the *great ultimate* and the sublime. The great ultimate, in short, is the intention of religious reverence in this worldview. Following this line of reasoning, neo-Confucianism can be considered a religiosity oriented toward creativity and life.

Recalling the philosophical specifications for a viable ecology from the discussion of chapter two, a neo-Confucian model of ecological humanism ought to be consistent with naturalism and an epistemology of mitigated scientific realism. Given its commitments to natural causes of natural events and an epistemology of comprehensive observation, the neo-Confucian theory explored in the preceding pages satisfies these specifications. Mitigated scientific realism and the epistemology of comprehensive observation alike advocate empirical and inductive methods; likewise, both pursue high probability with regard to the accuracy of predicted events.

Based upon the preceding discussions of ecological humanism and Wang Fuzhi's neo-Confucianism, we may synthesize an epistemological commitment of neo-Confucian ecological humanism: we should be critical and skeptical of any claim to absolutely determinate or apodictic knowledge. In this domain of epistemology, ecological humanism continuously reasserts philosophical skepticism with regard to the extent and finality of human knowledge and judgment. Again, building upon neo-Confucian spirituality, the determinative judgment afforded by an empirical and rational epistemological method is mitigated and complemented by an awe-inspired feeling that the way of the world (*dao*) is ultimately beyond human comprehension and control. In a synthesized neo-Confucian ecological humanism, moreover, the penumbra of indeterminacy that accompanies any and every determinate judgment provides a source of imaginative, spiritual, sublime reflection (*shensi* 神思).[1] The experience of the boundlessness of the world is profoundly aesthetic and creative for Wang Fuzhi. Thus, in his literary theory, Wang distinguishes between that which is a product of personal effort (*renli* 人力) and that which is received from nature (*tianshou* 天授), "making it quite clear that poetry of the highest order belongs to the latter category" (Wong 1978, 135). The poet's feeling (*qing* 情) merges with sublime scenery of her environment (*jing* 竟), and in this event the poet is subject to experience the unfathomable in nature (*shen* 神).

Wang Fuzhi critically adopts the ideology of indeterminacy (*wu*) from classical Daoist terminology. Using Li Zehou's hermeneutic categories for interpreting classical Chinese philosophy, this Daoist dimension of neo-Confucianism can be seen as a push toward the "naturalization of humans." The naturalization process entails recognition of persons (individually and collectively) as situated constituents within unfathomably complex, subtle, and expansive patterns of the heavens, the earth, and myriad things. As is demonstrated in many of the parables from the *Zhuangzi*, moreover, the process of naturalization also relativizes the human perspective as one among many. Take for example the opening chapter of *Zhuangzi*, in which the reader is introduced to a cicada and a dove, who poke fun at the great Peng bird for daring to have a perspective far greater than their own. What they don't realize is that they are locked into a particular way of looking at the world, but their view is not the only view. Because persons are here recognized as epistemologically limited and relativized as one force of nature amongst many, Wang Fuzhi's school of neo-Confucian philosophy stands by ecological humanism as a challenge to anthropocentric value judgments on the one hand, and an admonishment against the reification of rational judgment on the other. The skepticism and relativism built into neo-Confucianism and ecological humanism alike preclude anthropocentrism and scientism.

Continuing with Li Zehou's categories, neo-Confucian philosophy, such as that of Wang Fuzhi, dialectically synthesizes the "naturalization of humans" with the "humanization of nature." Whereas the former categorically resonates with the *ecological* component of ecological humanism, the latter represents the *humanism* component. As discussed in chapter four, Wang Fuzhi categorizes the subtleties and sublimities of the natural world, which confound human observation and reason, as *nature within nature*. Wang refers to that which lies within persons' locus of understanding and control as *nature within persons*. The former is also referred to as the *way of nature*, and the latter as the *way of persons*. Again, dialogically synthesizing Wang's language with the terminology of ecological humanism, these categories refer to ongoing events within a complex dynamic process of *co-evolution* of nature and persons. "Nature within persons," or the "way of persons," denotes the processes through which persons come to understand and consciously transform themselves and their surroundings.

The humanistic dimension of neo-Confucianism and ecological humanism entails an injunction for persons to explore novel experiences of human flourishing. In exploring novel engagement with the self and environment, the humanist is still seeking to creatively advance culture—to broaden the way, *hongdao* 弘道.[2] Contrary to

the strong anthropocentric tendencies of modern humanism, however, "humanizing nature" in our present context does not advocate
advancing culture by the conquest or domination of nature.

From a complex systems theoretical perspective, the logic of
the 'domination' concept is questionable at best. As maintained in
the preceding exposition of a paradigm, ecological humanism asserts
that persons and nature are reciprocally interrelated, such that any
human attempt to dominate nature can reciprocate in a consequen-
tial adversity to which humans will then have to adapt. The reading of the ongoing interactions between persons and their biological
and ecological conditions is based on the interpretive assumption
that "nature" reciprocally causes persons to transform in reaction to
the transformations that persons enact in and on nature. From an
ecological point of view, persons are situated within a nested hierarchical structure of local and global ecosystems. An ecosystem is
a complex system constituted by structures of energetic processes.
Energetic structures transfer energy through positive and negative
feedback loops. Based on this insight and empirical data to confirm
the model, ecological humanism can only advocate "humanizing
nature" with the informed understanding that persons' actions have
holistic repercussions throughout their environing systems.

Ecosystems are complex. Ecosystems are open and porous systems constituted by open and porous systems. Energy flows through
and between the systems. For example trophic structures through
which matter flows can be complex and difficult to measure. As a
result of the complexity of the world, the ecological repercussions of
human actions have often been unforeseen, reactionary, and diffuse
over time and space. For example, empirical data demonstrates that
people have polluted the Pacific Ocean with particles of plastics.
One ecological question that immediately emerges in this context
is this: How are these plastics ingested by and transferred through
organisms in the trophic web of the system? The humanist further
presses the question with concern: To what extent are we polluting
the fish that people eat with the plastics that we produce and leave
in the ocean?

Application of a Theory

The contemporary epoch of human civilization has recently been referred to as the Anthropocene age. "The new Anthropocene moniker is to mark the never-before significance that an animal species has had such an impact on the ecology of the entire planet that it has fundamentally changed the whole climate" (Irwin 2). Again, recalling the introduction to the philosophy of ecology presented in the opening of our discussion, an ecological worldview must take into account the post-industrial revolution anthropogenic impact that persons have had on the global environment. Moreover, it has been argued in the foregoing discussion that the humanism of neo-Confucianism is ripe for this recognition. In the context of neo-Confucian philosophy, the power of persons to intentionally transform themselves and the world is part and parcel of the idea that persons are a cosmic power on par with the heavens and the earth. Unfortunately, in the face of our current condition of global climate change, we are now in the position of recognizing the consequences of our use and abuse of this power.

Presently, the most recent measurements of global mean temperature has led climatologists to conclude that 2015 was the hottest year on Earth since scientists began collecting the data in 1880:

Released on 20 January [2016], the global temperature data come from three independent records maintained by NASA, the US National Oceanic and Atmospheric Administration (NOAA) and the UK Met Office. All three data sets document unprecedented high temperatures in 2015, pushing the global average to at least 1°C above pre-industrial levels. (*Nature*, Jan. 20, 2016)

These data sets all demonstrate a steady trend of global warming over the past 135 years. According to NOAA, "The global annual temperature has increased at an average rate of 0.06°C (0.11°F) per decade since 1880 and at an average rate of 0.16°C (0.28°F) per decade since 1970."[3] Of course, the average temperature for any given year is determined by a complex cluster of causes. Annual temperature differentiations are influenced by non-anthropogenic climatic and oceanic occurrences, such as the presence of El Niño water temperatures and weather patterns in the Pacific region. Nonetheless, conclusive evidence demonstrates that anthropogenic carbon emissions produced by human combustion of fossil fuels significantly contributes to global warming. Data taken from glacial ice-core samples and other means demonstrates that increases in global mean temperatures are positively correlated to the increase of gaseous carbon dioxide in the Earth's atmosphere. Carbon in the Earth's atmosphere absorbs infrared radiation produced by the sun, thereby trapping this radiation and its heat within the Earth's atmosphere—a phenomenon popularly known as "the greenhouse effect." The industrialized nation-states of the Anthropocene era have significantly increased gaseous carbon emissions into the atmosphere through their unprecedented, large-scale, combustion of carbon-based fuels:

> Global warming, effected by a global rise in greenhouse gas (GHG) emissions, has been accelerated significantly by the growth of emissions of carbon dioxide (CO_2)—the most important anthropogenic GHG—since pre-industrial times, with a global increase of 70% between 1970 and 2004. Among the anthropogenic emissions almost two thirds of the global emissions are estimated to have resulted from the use of fossil fuels for power generation in industry, transportation and individual households. (Meinert 2)

Moreover, in addition to the increase of post-industrial production of carbon emissions, people have further compounded the greenhouse effect by effectively deforesting large swaths of land for the purposes of urban settlement and agriculture. Vegetation on the Earth's surface and in the Earth's oceans naturally regulates the amount of CO_2 in the atmosphere by absorbing it during the process of photosynthesis. In short, the Earth's forests serve as a natural "carbon sink" for Earth's atmosphere. As we continue to consume the forests for anthropocentric purposes, we effectively inhibit the Earth's capacity to remove CO_2 from the atmosphere.

Phytoplankton, vegetative microorganisms that populate the Earth's oceans, likewise serve as a carbon sink for the Earth's atmosphere. Phytoplankton will rise to the ocean's surface during daylight to absorb the radiation of the sun and CO_2 that they require for life. In the complex flow of information through the oceans' ecosystems, much of the CO_2 stored in these organisms is transferred through trophic webs so that it becomes stored in sea-animal tissue and fecal matter. The carbon stored in plankton, feces, and dead-animal tissue is forced (or "pumped") downward by physical pressure to the depths of the ocean. "Once there, about 0.1% of it gets buried in the seafloor, trapped in sediment. When conditions are right in Earth's crust, the fossil phytoplankton are turned into oil over a period of several million years" (Falkowski 2012). During the Anthropocene epoch of natural history, persons have discovered and devised ways and means to extract this oil from the seafloor, burn it to fuel our industries, homes, and automobiles, and thereby release the once-buried carbon back into the atmosphere. The effects of this oil extraction and consumption are manifold. The increased greenhouse effect of an industrialized civilization increases the atmospheric temperature, which in turn increases the temperatures of the oceans (as solar radiation is reflected back into the water). Researchers have observed that warmer top-waters at regions of the oceans' surfaces have altered the flow of nutrients through oceanic ecosystems. Marine biologists Paul Falkowski and Michael Behrenfeld have concluded from their study of oceanic warming that these ecosystemic alterations (reduced nutrients) have inhibited phytoplankton growth in areas, which in turn poses a threat to the yet another one of Earth's means for regulating the CO_2 in the atmosphere. "As our climate warms," they hypothesize, "we can expect lower ocean carbon fixation in much of the world's oceans. If that happens, it will alter ecosystems, diminish fisheries, and leave more carbon dioxide in the atmosphere" (ibid.).

The rise in atmospheric and oceanic temperatures is causing glacial melt at an astonishing rate. The polar ice caps of Greenland and Antarctica are receding as their melting water steadily flows into the oceans. Polar ecosystems that have remained stable for millennia are now destabilized and diminishing at alarmingly visible rates. Animal inhabitants of these habitats, such as species of penguins that have evolved in adaptation to these icy regions, are becoming increasingly endangered.

What Wang Fuzhi and ecological humanism both teach us in their respective ways is that the fate of polar ecosystems and life-forms is not isolated or insulated in these far reaches of our globe. The continuity of energy interconnects us all. These extreme polar reaches serve as microcosmic foci of the anthropogenic adversities that threaten life forms and ecosystems throughout the globe. Indeed, as a direct result of global warming and the melting of glacial ice, the world's oceans are rising. In conjunction, with the destabilization of the earth's energy patterns (e.g., carbon cycles), the world is witnessing extreme meteorological phenomena with increased intensity and frequency. The effects are particularly poignant for China, the world's chief producer of carbon emissions.

> Climatologists expect China to experience in the course of the 21st century a rise in mean surface temperature that is well above the expected global average. This is supposed to lead to more intense impacts, such as a further rise in extreme weather events and desertification, and severe water stress, particularly in the north and northwest of China. Negative impacts might be especially felt in the agricultural sector; the glaciers on the Tibetan Plateau, the source area of the main Asian rivers that water 40% of the world population, are also expected to be severely impacted by global warming. Not least, the rise of the sea level—with a predicted rise up to 60 cm—is likely to impact some of China's most important economic zones along the coastline. (Meinert 9)

One need not spend too much time in a major Chinese industrialized city like Beijing to palpably taste the industrial emissions that cloud the air. The rate and scope of China's industrialization, in short, pose immediate threats to public health and environmental integrity in China and beyond.

A number of questions confront us at the conclusion of our discussion: Where did we as global citizens of the modern world go wrong? Is there a path toward curbing carbon emissions, slowing global warming, and reestablishing ecosystemic stability in the world? What conceptual resources do we have to redirect us toward a harmonious coexistence with environmental forces of our world?

With regard to the first question, we may again reiterate an argument stated at the outset of our present inquiry. The ethos of modernity has been dominated by strong anthropocentric sensibilities. This ethos is a kind of human egoism in which persons have exercised technocratic control of nonhuman natural forces with the intention of satisfying immediate and growing desires for energy consumption. Since the 1970s, philosophers have recognized the need for a novel environmental ethics to assuage the ills of modernity. Some have advocated replacing anthropocentrism with an ecocentric point of view in which nonhuman nature is meant to be understood as intrinsically valuable. In the lights of neo-Confucian ecological humanism, however, the ecocentric alternative is riddled with epistemological and ontological problems. For instance, a question arises in response to ecocentrism as to whether or not it is even possible to conceive of a nature that exists and has value in and of itself. Approaching this critique of ecocentrism from the position of Wang Fuzhi's philosophy, one may argue that we do not have direct epistemological access to any thing in itself. The world as we know it is just that: the world as we know it. Our understanding of the world is necessarily mediated through human constructs of what "nature" is. In Wang Fuzhi's point of view, the value of and in the world arises through the interactions of a subjective heart-and-mind with an environing reality. Value arises in the event of a heart-and-mind's prehension of reality. Thus, in Wang's aesthetic theory, value is understood as a felt experience (qing 情) of one's environment (jing 竟). With the conjoined skeptical and axiological critique of anthropocentrism and ecocentrism alike, a neo-Confucian ecological humanism endorses a via-media alternative to the environmental ethics of a European-American based discourse.

In this alternative, the categories of intrinsic and instrumental value, which are fundamental to anthropocentrism and ecocentrism alike, are abandoned and replaced by a relational conception of value as an emergent property of person-world interactions. Value is found between nature and persons (*tianrenzhiji*).

In addressing the questions of where to go in our theories and practices in relation to nature, we must acknowledge that China is presently the world's chief producer of carbon emissions, followed by the United States. Both nations have achieved this ignominy due to their respective embraces of anthropocentrism and its warrant to industrialize in the name of modernization. In November of 2015, representatives of the PRC, the USA, and the EU convened in Paris, France, to reach an agreement on a course of action to curb their respective release of atmospheric pollutants and thereby attempt to stabilize the increase in global mean temperatures. In this event, we find the suggestion that effective domestic and international policies are in order to reach a goal of sustainable development. Governmental policy must be grounded in a cultural ethos in order for the people of each respective nation to willingly endorse and abide by the law. Accordingly, the need for justifying and promoting policy requires an articulation of a culturally agreeable, axiological understanding of the world. Effective enactment of policy, in other words, requires what Mary Evelyn Tucker refers to as "attitudinal changes toward nature." As Tucker writes in her article, "The Relevance of Chinese Neo-Confucianism for the Reverence of Nature," "The Chinese in particular have a significant contribution to make in this regard." From the origins of Confucian thought, Tucker argues, philosophers of this tradition have developed a reverence for the natural world in the name of the earth (*di* 地) (136). By fleshing out the Confucian reverence for the natural world along with the life and experience that it engenders, Confucianism provides a salient perspective for shifting away from the damaging anthropocentrism and enabled-avarice of modernity, and into an ethics of respect for the social and impersonal forces of our natural world.

The practical injunction of the neo-Confucian ecological humanist in the case of carbon emissions is not necessarily to stop the combustion of these fuels altogether; instead, the injunction is to pragmatically and creatively harness the world's energy in a sustainable and procreative manner. The Confucian injunction is to find balance—to hit the mark in our everyday affairs (*zhongyong* 中庸)—in our drive to broaden the way of persons. Indeed, the ecological humanist is to be differentiated from an ecocentrist in that the former retains a principal concern for increasing the quality of human life. For Wang Fuzhi our technocratic harnessing of fossil fuels is not intrinsically problematic. To the contrary, the practice of harnessing natural resources is a natural process of humanizing nature, of bringing nature within nature into the domain of nature within humans. The fault lies in our short-sightedness: our push to develop too quickly at too grand of a scale.

Whereas anthropocentrism may be characterized with Protagoras's ancient slogan, "Man is the Measure," neo-Confucian ecological humanism recognizes the unfathomable, limitless, procreative cosmos as the ultimate measure. Neo-Confucianism, in this sense, offers a humble vision of persons-in-the-world. In this view, persons are called upon to advance "this culture of ours" in coordination with and deference to the forces that lie beyond our locus of control. Rather than control, the injunction is to abide, adapt, and appreciate the creative forces of change that constitute our environments. The injunction is not to enforce our will upon the world. As in Wang's understanding of the *Yijing* and in his aesthetics of poetry, persons ought to acknowledge the limits of their capacities to organize the world in accordance with their preferences. Rather than exercise coercive power, we ought to cultivate our world in a sustainable and symbiotically procreative manner. We have to continuously remind ourselves that in the unified patterns and continuity of energy that interconnect all processes, our actions have lasting repercussions for us and the myriad living things.

Wang would point out that there is a point where human interactions with the impersonal orders of the world become intrusive, obstructive, and coercive. Such is the case with our altering of the Earth's carbon cycles. Rather than hitting the mark in our everyday affairs, which is a principal intention of Confucian virtuosity, we have overstepped the bounds with our over-consumption of fossil fuels. Due to the misunderstandings and disregards of carbon emissions since the industrial revolution, human civilization has brought about an imbalance in natural patterns of energy flow over the earth's surface and under its oceans. The unhinging of these patterns is proving to be inhospitable for human and nonhuman animals alike.

In 2008, while working at the Confucius Institute in Indianapolis, I had the opportunity to attend a lecture by Ren Jiantao, who was then Dean of the School of Government at Sun Yat Sen University. The title of Ren's talk was "Traditional Chinese Philosophies and Sustainable Development in China." His thesis was that China's leaders and others ought to draw from the fountainhead of Chinese philosophies for spiritual and ethical guidance in persons' interactions with their environments." Similarly, philosophers such as J. Baird Callicott, James McRae, and Roger T. Ames have demonstrated with their works in comparative environmental philosophy that "Asian traditions of thought have something vital to contribute to environmental philosophy." In this vein, Callicott and McRae make the case for sustained, informed, professional work on the part of philosophers trained in Asian cultures and languages to provide in-depth analyses of Asian philosophies as paradigms for thinking about nature outside of the narratives that have developed over the course of European-American intellectual history. Callicott and McRae argue that at the very least, if Asian traditions of thought are found to be unconvincing by those locked into a particularly European-based cultural worldview, then philosophies such as neo-Confucianism are still significant for the fact that "they are certainly viable in their own cultural and historical contexts. And Asian cultures and civilizations need an environment-friendly worldview and an environmental ethic quite as much as these are needed in Western culture and civilization" (Callicott, McRae xix). Although Chinese culture embraced the ethics and methods of modernity over the course of the past century, its traditional ethos of "continuity between persons and nature" may provide a more viable ethics and epistemology for sustainable development. In recognition of the potency of Confucius' ideals for enjoining people to work for harmony within society and harmony between society and its environment, China's leaders have very recently reinvested their political capital in Confucian rhetoric. With their entering into an international agreement to mitigate their carbon emissions in the decades to come, the case can be made that contemporary PRC environmental policy is aligning itself with the historically rooted ethos of its indigenous philosophical traditions.

In the end, persons and all living creatures are going to have to live and die with the conditions that humans significantly help to create: let us be clear on our goals and values, and let us be clear on actual and potential effects of our actions throughout our ecosystems. Ideally, through informed deliberation, persons will strike upon sustainable, procreative, courses for the creative advance of human knowledge and cultural achievement. Ideally, with an understanding of the continuities between nature and persons, the ways of persons, and the ways of nature, persons will be able to engage in harmonious, symbiotically beneficial, interactions with our natural conditions.

Notes

Introduction

1. Wang Fuzhi. *Du Sishudaquan shuo* 讀四書大全說, hereafter referred to as DSS. Translation based on Wang's text: "盈天地之間, 人身以內人身以外, 無非氣者" (DSS 857).

2. Translation based on Wang's text: "天人之蘊, 一氣而已" (DSS 1052).

3. Translation based on Wang's text: "萬理統於一理, 一理含夫萬理, 相統相含" (DSS 1110).

4. Translation based on Wang's text: "氣稟与物相授受之交也" (DSS 962).

5. As we shall see below, "Chuanshan" is Wang Fuzhi's pseudonym.

6. Translation of Chen Lai's original text: "其实, 船山对于儒学传统, 对于儒家经典, 对于孔孟程朱, 都怀有真实的尊重, 其传承发扬孔孟之志 [. . .] 而船山的《读四书大全说》乃是对朱子学派的" 批判的总结" [. . .] 事实上, 通过《读四书大全说》可见, 船山与同时其它著名思想家相近, 也是以承认四书的经典性, 程朱的权威性, 儒学的正当性, 道学概念的意义性为前提的" (45–46).

7. See Chen Lai, "与明代为朱学者和王学者宗派性地依傍朱熹和王阳明不同, 王船山学术既具有鲜明的批判性格 (critical), 又有其孤发独诣的创造诠释 (creative)" (45). Parenthetical inserts are original to the author.

8. Ames and Rosemont translation (78). Original Chinese characters read, "溫故而知新."

9. Claim based on Wang's original text: "新故相資而新其故" (ZYW 1008).

159

10. This claim is based in part on Wong Siu-kit's 黃兆傑 "Introduction" to his translation of Wang Fuzhi's *Notes on Poetry from the Ginger Studio* (Hong Kong: Hong Kong University Press, 1987) viii. Wong's "Introduction" provides a concise and informative sketch of Wang Fuzhi's early biography.

11. Cf. Kang Chuan-Cheng: "王船山 . . . 學識淵博, 對天文, 曆法, 數學, 地理學均有研究, 尤其精於經學, 史學. 文學; 治經於《易》致力最深" (87).

12. For a corroborating account, see Wong (viii).

13. For a corroborating account, see Platt (10).

14. For an extended discussion of the existential crisis faced by Wang Fuzhi and his contemporaries, see Wai-Yee Li (2006).

15. Yan Shoucheng demonstrates that Wang Fuzhi heeded the Confucian injunction to "save the world by putting it in order (*yi kuang tianxia* 一匡天下)" (*Analects* 14.17). Yan continues, "In the late-Ming crisis, Wang Fuzhi's high-spirited forwardness was rather for 'saving the empire from collapse' than for his own career or fame" (1994, 81–82).

16. In order to penetrate Wang's experience, it is important to understand that he shared this crisis with his compatriot scholar-officials. "There were intense debates on the meanings of, and justifications for, martyrdom and survival. This may in part explain the popularity of the genres of 'self-elegy'—the tomb epitaph inscription written for oneself (*ziwei muzhi ming* 自為墓誌銘)" (Li, 2006, 4).

17. Wang's original text reads, "死生, 天事也, 於人何預？行藏者, 吾之生死也." Li notes that her translation and citation is "Quoted in the account of Wang's life by his son, Wang Yu 王敔, "*Daxing fujun xingshu*" 大行府君行述, in Wang Fuzhi 王夫之, *Chuanshan quanshu* 船山 全書 (Changsha: Yuelu shushe, 1989–92), 16: 75" (Li, 2006, 5).

18. For a historical account of the redaction and transmission Wang Fuzhi's complete works, see Platt "The Rediscovery of Wang Fuzhi," in his *Provincial Patriots: The Hunanese and Modern China* (Cambridge, MA: Harvard U. Press, 2007, 8–33).

19. Jacques Gernet calls attention to the same point: "*L'ouvrage principal de Zhang Zai, L'initiation correcte* (Zhengmeng), *est une explication générale de l'univers fondée sur une interprétation du livre des Mutations et tout spécialement sur son Grand commentaire ou Appendice, le Xici. Il peut être considéré lui-même comme une sorte de commentaire philosophique au livre des Mutations*" (33). In translation, "The principal work of Zhang Zai, the *Zhengmeng*, is a general explication of the universe founded on an interpretation of the

Book of Changes, especially on its *Great Commentary* or *Appendix*, the *Xici*. It could be considered, in itself, as a sort of philosophical commentary on the *Book of Changes*."

20. Similarly, Gernet writes, *"Il lui a consacré de façon exclusive un importante partie de son œuvre"* (104). Kang Chuan-Cheng (2008) also notes Wang's esteem for the *Yijing*: "王船山 . . . 學識淵博, 對天文, 曆法, 數學, 地理學均有研究, 尤其精於經學, 史學, 文學; 治經於《易》致力最深" (87).

21. See Kang: "其《易》學著作有《周易內傳》六卷, 《周易外傳》七卷, 《周易大象解》一卷, 《周易稗疏》四卷 . . ." (87).

22. See Gernet: *"Wang Fuzhi y est sans cesse revenu dans ses réflexions et se réfère á lui dans tous les domaines"* (104).

23. This line comes from the *Book of Songs* 詩經, song number 240, titled "Si Qi 思齊." The song quoted here is an ode to King Wen and his mother.

24. The original claim reads, "又以其義例之貫通與其變動者, 為〈繫辭〉,〈說卦〉,〈雜卦〉. . ." (Wang, ZYFL, 649). A more literal translation of this line treats term *"guantong* 貫通" nominally: "Then he used the continuous thread of his moral precedent along with their alternations . . ." Wang's reference to the continuous thread *"guan* 貫" alludes to *Analects* 4.15: "The Master said, 'Zeng, my friend! My way (dao 道) is bound together with one continuous strand (*guan* 貫).' [. . .] [Explaining this comment,] Master Zeng said, 'The way of the Master is doing one's utmost (*zhong* 忠) and putting oneself in the other's place (*shu* 恕), nothing more'" (Roger T. Ames and Henry Rosemont translation, 92).

25. Wang's original text:

伏羲氏始畫卦, 而天人之理盡在其中矣. 上古簡樸, 未遑明著其所以然者以詔天下後世, 幸筮氏猶傳其所畫之象, 而未之亂. 文王起於數千年之後, 以「不顯亦臨, 無射亦保」之心得, 即卦象而體之, 乃繫之〈彖辭〉, 以發明卦象得失吉凶之所繇. 周公又即文王之〈彖〉, 達其變於〈爻〉, 以研時位之幾而精其義. 孔子又即文, 周〈彖〉,〈爻〉之辭, 贊其所以然之理, 而為〈文言〉與〈彖〉,〈象〉之傳; 又以其義例之貫通與其變動者, 為〈繫辭〉, 〈說卦〉,〈雜卦〉, 使占者, 學者得其指歸以通其殊致。蓋孔子所贊之說, 即以明〈彖傳〉,〈象傳〉之綱領, 而〈彖〉,〈象〉二傳即文, 周之〈彖〉,〈爻〉, 文, 周之〈彖〉,〈爻〉即伏羲之畫象, 四聖同揆, 後聖以達先聖之意, 而未嘗有損益也. (Wang, ZYFL, 649)

26. "*Comme la majorité de ses contemporains, Wang croit que les docu-ments les plus anciens de la tradition chinoise, ceux qui ont été promus au rang de Classiques à la fin du Ier siècle avant notre ère, provenaient de sages d'exception*" (Gernet 104). In translation, "As the majority of his contemporaries, Wang believed that the most ancient documents of Chinese tradition, which were in fact promoted to the rank of Classics at the end of the first century BCE, had come from exceptional sages."

27. For a clear, concise, and complete account of the different exegeti-cal takes on the *Yijing*'s genesis, see the article 王船山《易》學索源, by Kang Chuan-Cheng 康全誠 (2008).

28. Contrary to Wang's narrative of the four sages, for example, Ban Gu 班固 (32 CE–92 CE) writes in his *Book of the Former Han* 漢書 that the *Yijing* was composed by "three sages during three ancient epochs, 人更三聖, 世歷三古." One contradiction between Ban's and Wang's beliefs lies in the conjunction of Wang's claim that Fu Xi composed the sixty-four hexa-grams and Ban's claim that King Wen is responsible for this achievement 班固.《漢書》in 百衲本二十四史 (臺北. 臺灣商務印書館, 1996) 436. Full text for the entire *Hanshu* is online at Donald Sturgeon's Chinese Text Project <www.ctext.org>. See the *Hanshu*, "藝文志" passage 16. As in Wang Fuzhi's "history," Ban also recounts that Fu Xi originally discerned and tran-scribed the eight trigrams, and he claims that Confucius authored the Ten Wings. King Wen is here said to have paired each of the eight trigrams with one another, established the received order sixty-four hexagrams, and authored the hexagram and line judgments. Ban transmits this line of tradi-tion: "King Wen used feudal vassals; he complied with what had to be done, and traversed the *dao*. He was able to grasp and model the forecasting of *tian* and persons, and thus layered the six lines of the *Changes* and composed the verses from top to bottom." "文王以諸侯順命而行道, 天人之占, 可得而效, 於是重《易》六爻, 作上下篇" (Ban Gu, qtd. in Kang 2008, 88).

29. Translated from, Wang's original text: "根極精微, 發天人之蘊, 六經, 語, 孟, 人之性知天, 未有如此 [易] 之深切著明者, 誠性學之統宗, 聖功之要領, 於易而顯" (Wang, ZYN, 532). The passage is referenced and para-phrased by Yan Shoucheng: "None of the other *Classics*—even the *Spring and Autumn Annals* or the *Mencius*—inquires into what is subtle and what is refined so perfectly as the *Book of Changes*" (Yan 88). Aside from Yan's exclusion of certain key terms from the text, it is unclear why he chooses to translate the term, "*yu* 語," as "*Spring and Autumn Annals*." Three rea-sons can be cited in rejection of his translation: (1) The term "*yu* 語" does not appear in the Chinese title of the *Spring and Autumn Annals*; (2) The

term is integral to the Chinese title of the *Analects*; (3) The *Annals* is one of the *Six Classics*, which Wang mentions under their collective heading; thus, it would be redundant for him to cite the same text back to back as Yan reads him.

30. The *Five Classics* are the *Book of Changes*, *Yijing* 易經; *Book of Songs*, *Shijing* 詩經; *Spring and Autumn Annals*, Chunqiu 春秋; *Book of Documents*, *Shujing* 書經; *Book of Rites*, *Liji* 禮記. Wang was of the persuasion that the *Book of Music*, *Yuejing* 樂經, which was almost completely destroyed in the Qin dynasty (221–206 BCE) Burning of the Books, should be considered a sixth Classic. Thus, his preferred term to refer to the set is *Six Classics*.

31. Although scholars do not always agree on the time frames in which the appended *Commentaries* were written, they concur in the belief that the "individual *Wings* actually date from different periods" (Lynn 3; cf. Adler, 2002, xxi). Some of the *Yi Commentaries* probably predate Confucius; some are roughly contemporaneous with his life; while others, such as the *Appended Phrases*, appear to have been written (or rewritten) one to two centuries after his death (Lynn 3; Field 50; Gernet 104).

32. Gernet specifies the case of Yan Ruoju: "During Wang Fuzhi's time, Yan Ruoju 閻若璩 (1636–1704) had infamously demonstrated by textual critique that key passages from the Classic *Book of Documents* (*Shangshu* 尚書 or *Shujing* 書經, thought to have been composed in the Xia) were false compositions of a later date. . . ." "[À] l'époque même de Wang Fuzhi, Yan Ruoju (1636–1704) avait démontré par ses travaux de critique textuelle que des passages importants du livre des Documents (Shangshu) étaient des faux composés à date tardive. . . ." (104).

33. From the time of its redaction in the Han (206 BCE–220 CE), the received text was the only known version of the *Yijing* (i.e., the Zhouyi) in existence up until the 1973 archeological discovery of another version of the text, "written on two pieces of silk." The latter is referred to as the "Mawangdui" version after the site at which it was discovered, Mawangdui, in Changsha, Hunan. The Mawangdui text was uncovered from the "tomb of Li Cang, Lord of Dai (d. 168 BCE)" (Shaughnessy 1, 14–16). The *Appended Phrases* is the only *Commentary* found in both the received *Yijing* and the Mawangdui manuscript. In the Mawangdui manuscript, this commentary is not subdivided as it is in the received redaction. In addition, the Mawangdui text contains four commentaries that are not contained in the received edition. (See Shaughnessy 20–26; and Field 45.) The King Wen order of the sixty-four hexagrams is presented in the received version of the *Yijing*. The order of the hexagrams in the Mawangdui text differs from the received version.

34. Though accounts may differ on this point (see Adler 2002), I refer to the following subdivided commentaries: Judgment Commentary, *Tuan zhuan* 彖傳; Image Commentary, *Xiang zhuan* 象傳; and the *Appended Phrases Commentary, Xici zhuan* 繫辭傳. The latter is divided into an "upper" (*shang* 上) and a lower (*xia* 下) part.

35. Bracketed insert inside quotation is original to Shaughnessy.

36. For a supporting account of *yinyang* in the *Yijing* and Wang Fuzhi, also confer the section of Gernet's text "*Opposés complémentaires: La notion de phase*" (85 ff.). Also, Jullien (1989) takes the exposition of correlative cosmology and process philosophy in the *Yijing* and Wang Fuzhi to be his thesis, and provides a comprehensive and illustrative account of these themes.

37. For an excellent analysis and exposition of the development of the "dominion" concept, see William Leiss, *Domination of Nature* (Montreal, QC, CAN: McGill-Queen's University Press, 1994). For an account of the concept in *Genesis* in particular, see especially Leiss (31 ff).

38. Descartes's claim to dominion is made in Part 6, paragraph 2. Source-text for Descartes's *Discourse on Method* is found online through Project Gutenberg: http://www.gutenberg.org/ (accessed Dec. 21, 2011). See also, Whiteside (2002) for brief discussion of Descartes as a foil to *ecological* humanism.

39. "Art" is here used in the sense of its etymological roots in the Greek term "*techne.*"

40. *The New Organon*, in *The Works of Francis Bacon*, vol. IV, 247–248. Quoted in Leiss (58).

41. Feuerbach, Ludwig Andreas. *Sämtliche Werke*. Vol. 3. W. Bolin and F. Jodl, eds. (Reprint edition, Stuttgart: 1959–64), 65. Qtd. in Leiss (48).

Chapter 1

1. Translated from the Chinese text, "凡物不能自成. 必須外為者以成之. 樓臺房屋不能自成. 成於工匠之手." Qtd. in Gernet (84).

2. Translated from Gernet's original text:

L'argument reproduit par tous les missionnaires chrétiens d'après lequel il fallait que l'univers eût été créé par un être extérieur à la nature ne pouvait au' étonner dans un monde où l'on n'admettait pas un au-delà de la nature. L'explication de la complexité et de l'évolution permanente de phénomènes vitaux par le modèle grossier de l'action d'un artisan sur la «matière» y semblait d'ailleurs difficilement recevable. (83)

3. Cf. Jullien (16–17) and Black (6 et passim).

4. Translated from Zhou Bing's text: "在 '理气' 的问题上王夫之提出了 '一统于气' 的气本体论以及 '理气无分体' 的新理气观" (5).

5. Translated from Jullien's text: "*La justification minimale de Dieu au sein du rationalisme occidental est de lui attribuer l'impulsion initiale dans l'enchaînement des causes et des effets qui constituent le cours du monde*" (79).

6. Source text found at http://www.fordham.edu/halsall/source/aquinas3.html (accessed Feb. 20, 2010).

7. Translation of Jullien's claim:

Deux traits au moins me paraissent avoir contribué essentiellement à la conception d'une telle représentation: d'une part, la valorisation anthropologique d'une catégorie du sujet-agent comme instance unique et volontaire; et, d'autre part, la valorisation idéologique d'une différence radical de statut entre le Créateur et sa création. (82)

8. Translation of Jullien's claim: "*Le récit de la Genèse, si important soit-il, ne représente somme toute qu'une version possible de l'avènement du monde au sein de la panoplie des conceptions occidentales*" (83).

9. Translated from Li Zhecheng's original text: "中国先秦时期哲学中主张自然天的学派是老庄学与荀学" (56).

10. Li writes of Xunzi's influence: "荀子的这种科学的自然观, 对以后的中国哲学产生了很大影响. 这种影响在王船山身上亦有反映" (56). That is, "Xunzi's kind of scientific naturalism held a considerable influence over later generations of Chinese philosophy. This influence is also reflected in the corpus of Wang Fuzhi."

11. Wang's text: "荀卿五十始學, 朱雲四十始受易與論語. 乃以其所知者, 與世之黠慧小兒較, 果誰為上而誰位次也？. . . 必將推高堯, 舜, 孔子, 以爲無思無爲而天明自現, 童年靈異而不待壯學, 斯亦釋氏誇誕之淫詞, 學者不察, 其不亂人于禽獸也鮮矣!" (DSS 852).

12. The definition of *tian* 天 qua *ziran jie* 自然界 is stated in the Peking University Press *Classical Chinese Character Dictionary* (785). The lexicon cites Xunzi to instantiate and contextualize this sense of the term.

13. The similarity between Xunzi's notion of *tian* and Daoism is also noted by Wing-tsit Chan (153).

14. See Li Zhecheng's claim along these lines: "老庄学批评孔孟的道德天思想，强调自然天的无意志性" (56). In translation, "The Lao-Zhuang school criticized the Confucian-Mencian line of thought on a moral nature, and they emphasized the non-purposive character of a spontaneous nature."

15. For a focused discussion on the differences between *tian* according Confucius and *tian* according to Wang Fuzhi, see Zheng Xiong's article, "王夫之对孔子天命论的改造" (2006).

16. See Roger T. Ames and Henry Rosemont, Jr. (1998) for a reconstruction of Confucius's nuanced understanding of *tian* as a non-theistic anthropomorphic force (47).

17. Zheng Xiong connects this aspect of Confucius's belief in *tian* as an assertion of the general belief of the Western Zhou period: "孔子继承了西周关于" 天" 的思想，承认天具有主宰人的生死寿夭、富贵贫贱，乃至主宰历史文化的命运" (52). See also Mencius 5A5.

18. This interpretive argument follows Zheng Xiong's discussion of *Analects* 6.28. Zheng states, "这都表现孔子眼中的 "天" 具有人格力量，具有主宰万物的能力. 这也说明孔子所谈的 "天," 指的是主宰之天 (即意志之天)" (52).

19. "宇宙大化没有情感意义，是无心的. 所谓无心，即为自然" (Deng Hui 76).

20.   "王夫之批判了孔子的意志之天， 变意志之天为自然之天" (Zheng Xiong 50).

21. "王船山认为天没有意志，目的，只是其本身内部灵活地运动而已" (Li Zhecheng 56).

22. "天 '无心，' '无为,' 没有意志，没有情感，不能主宰人的命运" (Xiong Lümao and Yang Zhengzheng 27).

23. "天無爲也，無爲而缺，則終缺矣. 故吉凶常變，萬理悉備，而後自然之德全 . . ." (尚書引義，洪範) (qtd. in Li, 2003, 56).

24. "擎拳為敬，箕踞為傲，民之禮也. 若夫天，則寒慄非教以恭，署析非導以慢矣. . . . 五刑傷肌，民之所畏而以討也. 若於天，則蹦蹦者非以盜，不男者非其以淫矣" (Wang Fuzhi 尚書引義，卷一，qtd. in Zheng 52).

25. Chen's claim: "王船山的 《张子正蒙注》 是对张载 《正蒙》 的诠释与发展 . . . 就理论渊源来说，《正蒙》 中的自然哲学的基本概念大部来自 《周易》，主要是 《易传》" (Chen, 2004, 361).

26. "易有太極，是生兩儀，兩儀生四象，四象生八卦." Source text for original Chinese found at Donald Sturgeon's *Chinese Text Project*. Online

at http://chinese.dsturgeon.net/text.pl?node=46908&if=en (accessed Feb. 28, 2010).

27. Jullien writes on this topic:

[A]u sein d'une telle tradition, Wang Fuzhi a poussé le souci encore plus loin que tout autre, pour évacuer des anciennes représentations cosmologique toute possibilité d'interprétation cosmogonique. Son attention critique est ici des plus rigoureuses et porte essentiellement sur la notion de limite suprême (taiji) *qui a joué un rôle primordial dans toute la pensée néo confucéenne (à partir de Zhou Dunyi, au XIᵉ siècle)"* (Jullien 69).

[I]n the midst of this tradition, Wang Fuzhi pushed the concern even further than all others, for evacuating the ancient cosmological representations of all possible cosmogonic interpretation. His critical attention is here most rigorous and essentially concerns the notion of the supreme limit (*taiji*) which plays a primordial role in all neo-Confucian thought (beginning with Zhou Dunyi in the eleventh century).

28. "此太極之所以出生萬物, 成萬理而起萬事者也, 資始資生之本體也." Wang's language of "beginnings and growth, 資始資生" here alludes to the *Yijing*'s *Image Commentary, Xiangzhuan* 象傳, which attributes these characteristics of fecundity and sustainment to the Qian and Kun hexagrams, respectively.

29. Translation of Jullien's text: *". . . le fondement de leur représentation du cours du monde, et de l'avènement de toute existence, en tant que limite ultime en amont de tout procès"* (70).

30. Zhou's original text reads, "無極而太極. 太極動而生陽, 動極而靜, 靜而生陰. 靜極復動. 一動一靜, 互為其根; 分陰分陽, 兩儀立焉." Source of Chinese text found at http://sangle.web.wesleyan.edu/etext/song-qing/zhou.html (accessed March 1, 2010).

31. Jullien's text: *"On ne peut aller plus loin, remonter plus haut : parce qu'il n'y a pas plus loin ni plus haut. Cette limite ultime est celle du « vide » lui-même, en tant que non-actualisation (wuji) au départ de toute actualisation : non pas le vide en tant qu'inexistence, mais au contraire comme absolue plénitude – à son stade de non-actualisation mais contenant toutes les actualisations possibles"* (Jullien 70).

32. Translated from Jullien's text: *"on peut l'interpréter dans un sens plus cosmogonique, en conférant à cette limite un statut de point de départ et d'origine, ou dans un sens purement cosmologique, par éradication de tout statut exclusif d'antériorité . . ."* (70). Emphasis added to the body text.

33. "And yet it is the pure cosmological sense that precisely provides support for Wang Fuzhi, because according to him the thought of process excludes from itself every notion of a point of possible departure for process" (Jullien 70). Translation of Jullien's text: *"Or c'est le pur sens cosmologique que soutient précisément Wang Fuzhi, puisque chez lui la pensée du procès exclut d'elle-même toute notion d'un point de départ possible du procès"* (Jullien 70).

34. See Chen (2004) 368, for reading 情质 as 性质.

35. My translation of Wang's text: "误解《太极图说》者, 谓太极本未有阴阳, 因动而始生阳, 静而始生阴. 不知动静所生之阴阳, 乃固有之蕴, 为寒暑之润燥男女之情质, 其絪緼充满在动静之先, 动静者, 即此阴阳之动静" (ZMZ 24). This passage is also quoted in Chen (2004) 368–369.

36. Here I paraphrase Chen Lai's claim: "这里的太极即是太和絪缊" (368). See also Black 71.

37. Black's translation of Wang's text: "陰陽, 無始者也, 太極非孤立於陰陽之上者也" (ZYN 562). Quoted in Black 66, and Jullien 70.

38. My translation of Jullien's claim:

> La «vertu» inhérente au grand procès qui est continûment à l'œuvre dans le monde est qu'il «embrasse tout», du plus grand au plus infime, et qu'il est aussi à l'origine de tout (c'est-à-dire de toutes les actualisations particulières). Mais il n'y a jamais «un moment ou un existant qui puisse servir des point de départ du procès», de sorte que «toute le reste en soit la suite» . . . De même qu'il ne saurait avoir de fin, le mouvement en cours ne saurait avoir de début . . . (Jullien 9).

39. My translation here is based on Black 66. Wang's original passage runs as follows:

> 生者, 非所生者為子, 生之者為父之謂. 使然, 則有有太極無兩儀, 有兩億無四象, 有四象無八卦之日矣. 生者於上發生也, 如人面生耳, 目, 口, 鼻, 自然賅具, 分而言之, 謂之生耳. . . . 太極即兩儀, 兩儀即四象, 四象即八卦, 猶人面即耳目口鼻; 特於其上所生而固有者分言之, 則為兩, 為四, 為八耳" (ZYBS 789).

40. Cf. Jullien (1989), 70:

En commentant l'expression ancienne du Livre des mutations : «La limite suprême engendre les deux instances (c'est-à-dire le yin et le yang)», Wang Fuzhi précise bien que le terme «engendrer» ne signifie pas ici « donner naissance à », en un sens cosmogonique où la limite suprême jouerait le rôle de « parent » par rapport au yin et au yang, qui seraient en position d' «enfants». Non pas «genèse» ou «filiation», mais essor ou déploiement, en tant qu'essor de la dualité à partir de l'unité que cette dualité constitue totalement. Au sens où l'on pourrait dire que la dualité « sort » de l'unité (en même temps que l'unité n'est que la somme de cette dualité).

In commentating on the ancient expression of the *Book of Changes*, "The supreme limit engenders the two instances (that is to say *yin* and *yang*), Wang clarifies (specifies) that the term "engender" does not here signify "giving birth to," in a cosmological sense where the supreme limit plays the role of parent in relation to yin at yang, which would be in the position of "children." Not "genesis" or "filiation," but emergence or development, the emergence of the duality from the unity, which this duality totally constitutes. . . .

41. The above interpretation follows Jullien:

La notion ne désigne – ne peut désigner – rien d'autre que ce rapport (puisque effectivement il n'y a rien d'autre que le yin-yang), mais elle évoque ce rapport sous son aspect unitaire et global et non pas sous l'angle de la différenciation (yin opposé à yang et inversement) ; c'est-à-dire qu'elle sert à appréhender le réel non seulement sur son mode d'actualisation déterminée (telle qu'elle « émane de l'interaction du yin-yang), mais aussi sur son mode de latence généralisée, où yin et yang, bien qu'implicitement différents, ne manifestent pas activement leur différence et sont intimement confondus. La notion de yin-yang d'une part, celle de limite suprême de l'autre signifient exactement la même chose, mais l'une sous l'angle de la dualité, l'autre sous l'angle de l'unité – l'une sous l'angle de la différenciation actualisatrice et l'autre sous l'angle de la résorption régulatrice . . . (Jullien 71).

The notion [of *taiji*, or supreme ultimate] does not designate—
is not able to designate—anything other than this relationship
(because effectively there is nothing other than *yin* and *yang*),
but it evokes this relationship under its unitary and global aspect,
and not under the angle of the differentiation (the inverse opposition of *yin* and *yang* vice versa); it is to say that it serves
to apprehend the real not only under its mode of determinate
actualization (such as it emanates from the interaction of *yin* and
yang), but also under its mode of generalized latency, where *yin*
and *yang* although implicitly different, do not actively manifest
their difference and are intimately commingled (*confoundus*).
The notion of *yinyang* on the one hand, and the notion of
supreme limit on the other hand, mean exactly the same thing,
but one is under the angle of duality, the other under the angle
of unity—one under the angle of actualizing differentiation and
the other under the angle of the regulating resorption.

42. See Black 66, Jullien 72, Chen 64 ff. Wang makes this claim in
his *Inner Commentary on the Zhouyi*: "太極也, 張子謂之太和" (ZYN 561).
"*Taiji*, Zhangzi calls it '*taihe*.'"

43. The above is based on Jullien's text: "*Or il y un double advantage . . . D'une part, l'effacement de l'idée de limite permet d'évacuer le risque,
toujours présent, de penser cette limite comme origine et point de départ ; et,
d'autre part, la notion d'harmonie met plus nettement en évidence le caractère de
relationallité constitutif de tout procès, comme fonds commun de toute actualisation . . .*" (Jullien 72).

44. Translation based on Wang's text: "未有形器之先, 本无不和, 既
有形器之后, 其和不失" (ZMZ 15).

45. Following Chen Lai, "浑沦" should be read as "混合的均匀"
(2004, 364).

46. Wang's text: "太和, 和之至也. 道者, 天地萬物之通理, 即所謂太
極也. 陰陽異撰, 而其絪縕於太虛之中合同而不相悖害, 渾淪無間, 和之至
矣" (ZMZ 15).

47. Chen Lai's text: "太和絪縕是万物产生的初始本源. 这是太和絪
縕的观念所蕴涵的. 因为在船山的宇宙理论, 太和代表最原始的存在和状
态, 阴阳的分化和万物的产生, 都是后于太和才有的. 不过, 太和并不是只
存在于万物产生之先并仅仅作为宇宙的初始本源, 实际上, 万物产生之后
太和仍然存在" (365).

Chapter 2

1. Quoted in Cooper 4–5. Cooper comments, "the Haeckel passage . . . remains today, nearly a century and a half later, a good abstract characterization of what ecology is all about . . ." (6).

2. Situating a life form in an environment in this way is a method that Wang Fuzhi would have found agreeable. He would have seen this as a means of demonstrating that the inner dimensions of the personal experience and the outer dimensions of the environing world interpenetrate and mutually inform one another.

3. Cf. Morin, 1973, 30–31; cf. Golley 35.

4. "Systems are embedded in the world" (Auyang 60).

5. I translate this passage from Morin's French text:

La relation écosystémique n'est pas une relation externe entre deux entités closes ; il s'agit d'une relation intégrative entre deux systèmes ouverts où chacun est partie de l'autre . . . [L]'écologie, ou plutôt, l'écosystémologie . . . réhabilite la notion de Nature et y enracine l'homme. La nature n'est plus désordre, passivité, milieu amorphe : elle est une totalité complexe. L'homme n'est pas une entité close par rapport à cette totalité complexe : il est un système ouvert, en relation d'autonomie/dépendance organisatrice au sein d'un écosystème. (1973, 30)

6. For further discussion of the distinction between internal relations and "bare particulars," see Callicott (60).

7. Qtd. in Golley 25–26; also qtd. in Ziporyn 27–28.

8. My translation of Gernet's text:

Appliqué aux lignes interrompues et continues du livre des Mutations ou Zhouyi, il semble qu'on ne puisse mieux traduire le mot qi, terme sans équivalent dans nos traditions, que par celui d'énergie. C'est le sens qu'il a dans la langue moderne où le composé dianqi désigne l'électricité . . . La notion chinoise d'énergie a pour étymologie celle de "vapeur" et a conservé au cours de l'histoire les sens divers de vapeur, souffle, air, émanations, climat, ou même vigueur et force vitale qui peut être affaiblie ou renforcée. (Gernet 158–159)

9. Translation from the Chinese: "盈天地閒, 人身以內人身以外, 無非氣者, 故亦無非理者. 理, 行乎氣之中 . . ." (DSS 857).

10. Translation from the Chinese text: "理即是氣之理, 氣當得如此便是理, 理不先而氣不後 . . ." (1052).

11. Gernet's claim: "*Zhu Xi imagine en fin de compte un li idéal, indépendant des énergies et antérieur à la formation des êtres*" (Gernet 201).

12. Gernet's claim:

Hostile aux abstractions et soucieux d'analyse à partir des réalités concrètes, Wang estime à la suite de son maître Zhang Zai que les produits de l'activité de l'énergie universelle démontrent de manière irréfutable que cette énergie possède en elle-même le pouvoir de former des êtres organisés puisque ce pouvoir se révèle clairement à nos yeux . . . (206).

13. "理一分殊" (*Siku Quanshu, zibu* 27, v. 721, p, 364). See Gernet's French rendition "*le li est unique et se divise en li différent*" (201).

14. Gernet's claim: "*Mais cette raison n'est pas la raison la raison logique du discours qui exclut toute contradiction: elle garde des liens avec l'idée de mise en ordre et d'ordre naturel. Elle n'est ni logos grec ni ratio latine*" (Gernet 199).

15. Gernet's text:

La notion d'organisation (li) et, par suite, celle de système s'appliquent chez Wang aussi bien aux sociétés humaines qu'aux êtres vivants. Les institutions de tout genre, les mentalités, les habitudes collectives, les idées dominantes . . . forment un ensemble qui est l'aboutissement de l'adaptation de ces éléments entre eux, au cours d'une longue évolution, et constituent dies systèmes qui se modifient de façon plus ou moins progressive ou soudaine. . . . (Gernet 145)

16. Hall and Ames translation of the following text: "道生一, 一生二, 二生三, 三生萬物 . . ."(Hall, Ames 142).

17. I make a similar, albeit abridged, case for a new materialist reading of Confucian cosmology along with my colleague, Taine Duncan, in our co-authored chapter, "Contemporary Ecofeminism and Confucian Cosmology," *Feminist Engagements with Confucius*. Mathew A. Foust and Sor-hoon Tan, eds. (Boston: Brill, 2016), 228–232.

18. Tucker, 189.

19. Tucker, 188.

20. Translated from Gernet's text. Also quoted in Barsovan and Duncan 232.

Toutes les choses du monde ne sont donc, pour Zhang Zai, que des «corps transitoires» formés d'un assemblage d'énergies, il n'y a, en fin de compte, ni «matière», ni «causes», ni «architecte», comme l'enseignaient les premiers jésuites arrivées en Chine aux environs de 1600 et formés à notre scolastique médiévale. L'univers n'est, de part en part et sous toutes ses formes, qu'énergie en activité incessante et invisible.

Chapter 3

1. For a discussion on the difference between the *xiangshu* and *yili* schools, also see Joseph Adler, translator, "Introduction" to *Introduction to the Study of the Classic of Change (I-hsüeh ch'i-meng)*, by Chu Hsi (Provo, Utah: Global Scholarly Publications, 2002), v–vii. See also Cheng Chung-ying, "On Zhu Xi's Integration of *Yi Li* and *Xiang Shu* in the Study of the *Yijing*".

2. Confer Adler (2002) and Nielsen (2003) for further discussion of the differences between these two schools: "The *hsiang-shu*, or 'image and number' school, focused on the graphic and numerological symbolism of the hexagrams and other diagrams associated with the *I* [. . .] The *i-li*, or 'moral principle' school, on the other hand, focused on the textual layers of the *I*, deriving moral principles from the hexagram texts, the line texts, and appendices" (Adler 2002, v–vi). "Meaning and pattern studies are primarily based on the textual tradition in its exegesis. The textual tradition is here first and foremost the Ten Wings" (Nielsen 303).

3. On Wang's syncretism of the Xiangshu and Yili schools, confer Yan Shoucheng (89).

4. Translation of Wang's text: "曰 '象者材也, 爻者效也.' 材成斷之, 在車為車, 輪輿皆車, 在器為器, 中, 邊皆器也 . . . 故曰 '同歸而殊塗, 一致而百盧'" (ZYFL 661).

5. For a discussion of the different senses of hermeneutic circle, see Ronald Bontekoe's *Dimensions of the Hermeneutic Circle* (Amherst, NY: Humanity Books 2000). See especially Bontekoe's "Introduction." Bontekoe's account of the basic hermeneutic circle also elucidates Wang Fuzhi's interpretation of the *Yijing*:

> The whole is what it is by virtue of its being composed of these [integrated] parts . . . [T]he individual parts of the object of comprehension are understood, in their turn, in terms of their participation in the whole, and this understanding involves the

recognitions of how the whole contextualizes each of its parts. In the process of contextualization, each of the parts is illuminated in its own integrity. The part is what it is by virtue of its being located here—and consequently serving this function— within the whole. The two "poles" of the hermeneutic circle are thus bound together in a relationship of mutual clarification. (Bontekoe 3)

6. See Bontekoe (ibid.) for an in-depth discussion on the difference between a hermeneutic circle and a vicious circle.

7. "學成於聚, 新故相資而新其故; 思得於永, 微顯相次而顯察於微" (ZYW 1008).

8. Wang's original text:

釋經者得句而忘其章, 得章而忘其篇, 古今之通病也。今世姚紅之徒, 拈單辭片語以伸其妄, 皆此術爾 [. . .] 蓋讀書者一句而求一句之義, 則句義必忒, 況于易之為學, 以求知天人之全體大用; 于以爻而求一爻之義, 則爻義必不可知 [. . .] 執一句一義而論先聖之書, 微言隱, 大義乖, 他經且然, 奚況易哉! (ZYFL 662, 670)

9. For a concise and informative exposition of Shao Yong's method for interpreting the *Yijing*, see Don J. Wyatt, "Shao Yong's Numerological-Cosmological System," in *Dao Companion to Neo-Confucian Philosophy*, John Makeham (ed.) (New York: Springer 2010). For further discussion of Wang's reproach to Shao Yong and Jing Fang, see also Jullien 198 and Gernet 77.

10. It may be interesting and elucidating to note that while Wang was developing his seventeenth-century critique of Shao Yong's binary analysis of the *Yijing*, G. W. Liebniz (1646–1716), the quintessential European rationalist, took up Shao's work as a model for developing his own binary calculus.

11. For an introduction to Shao Yong's numerology, see Siu-chi Huang, *Essentials of Neo-Confucianism: Eight Major Philosophers of the Song and Ming Periods* (Westport, CT: Greenwood Press, 1999) chapter 3.

12. For a concise and informative account of the joint Jamesian-Deweyan-Whiteheadian critique, see Rasmus Grønfeldt Winther, " 'Vicious Abstractionism' and 'the Philosophic Fallacy': James and Dewey on the Promises and Limits of Abstraction" (Department of Philosophy, University of Santa Cruz, 2008). Online at http://www.hum.au.dk/semiotics/docs2/news_archive/2008/winther_reification_discontents/vicious_abstractionism.pdf (accessed March 15, 2011).

13. Gernet writes the following of Wang's critique of numerologists of the Xiang-Shu school:

Dans plusieurs passages de son œuvre, Wang critique les efforts des Shao Yong (1012–1077) et de ses prédécesseurs pour soumettre le livre des Mutations à des régularités inspirées par des calculs numérologiques. Si le monde pouvait être analysé de façon immédiate et intégrale, comme l'imagine Shao Yong, il serait dépourvue de tout ce qu'il comporte, dans sa constitution même, de hasard et d'incertitiude. Les divisions systématiques que Jing Fang, Shao Yong . . . *ont introduites dans leurs interprétations du livre des Mutations sont artificielles et, par suite, contraires à son esprit.* (Gernet 77)

In more passages from his oeuvre, Wang critiques the efforts of Shao Yong (1012–1077) and his predecessors for submitting the book of changes to regularities inspired by numerological calculations. If the world could be analyzed in this fashion, as imagined by Shao Yong, it would be deprived of all that constitutes it, that is, of its precarious and uncertain nature. The systematic divisions that they introduced in their interpretations of the *Yijing* were artificial and accordingly contrary to its spirit. (Gernet 77)

14. These three principles are expressed in the following propositions: (1) "日新之謂盛德. Daily novelty, this is called flourishing virtue" (*Xici shang* 5.1). (2) "生生之謂易. Procreation of life, this is called change" (*Xici shang* 5.1). (3) "易有太極, 是生兩儀, 兩儀生四象, 四象生八卦. The *Changes* have a *taiji*; this engenders the two norms (*yin* and *yang*); the two norms engender four images; four images engender eight trigrams" (*Xici shang* 11.3).

15. Translated from Jullien's text:

"Le jour et la nuit sont comme la respiration du ciel, l'été et l'hiver reproduisent le rythme du jour et de la nuit. Seule l'échelle diffère, toute manifestation d'existence est régie par un va-et-vient ininterrompu: contraction-expansion, déploiement-repli, ouvrir et fermer." (Jullien 27)

16. Wang's text:

古之人教我以極深研幾之學, 而我淺嘗而躁用之, 舉天下萬民之情, 皆以名相籠而驅入其中 . . . 天下之思而可得、學而可

知者, 理也; 思而不能得、學而不能知者, 物也。今夫物名則
有涯矣, 数則有量矣. 乃若其實, 則皆有類焉, 類之中又有類焉,
博而極之, 尽巧历之终身而不能悉舉. 大木之叶, 其数亿万, 求
一相肖而无毫发之差者无有也, 而名恶足以限之？必有变焉,
变之余又有变焉, 流而览之, 一日夜之闲, 而不如其故。晴雨
之候, 二端而止, 拟一必然而无意外之差者无有也, 而数恶足
以期之？(Wang, SL 276, qtd. in Gernet 76–77)

The italicized text in my English translation is based directly on Gernet's
French translation.

    17. Wang'sText:

京房八宮六十四卦, 整齊對待一倍分明, 邵子所傳先天方圖,
蔡九峰九九數圖皆然. 要之天地閒無有如此整齊者, 唯人為所
作則有然耳, 圜而可規方而可矩, 皆人為之巧, 自然生物未有
如此者也, 易曰周流六虛不可為典要, 可典可要則形窮于視,
聲窮于聽, 即不能體物而不遺矣, 唯聖人而後能窮神以知化.
(SWW 440)

The above English translation is here informed by Gernet's French translation (Gernet 77–78).

    18. Wang's text:

《皇極經世》之旨, 盡于朱子 "破作兩片" 之语, 謂天下無不相
對待者耳. 乃陰陽之與剛柔, 太之與少, 豈相對待者乎? 陰陽,
氣也; 剛柔, 質也. 有是氣則成是質, 有是質則具是氣; 其可析
乎? 析之則質为死形, 而气为游氣矣. 少即太之稚也, 太即少之
老也; 将一人之生, 老, 少称為二人乎? 自稚至老, 漸移而無分
畫之涯際, 將以何一日焉為少之终而老之始乎? 故兩片四片之
说, 猜量比拟, 非自然之理也. (SWW 441; qtd. in Gernet 79)

    19. Translation based on original text: "陰陽不測之謂神" (*Xici shang*
5.1).

    20. Translation based on original text: "非氣之外有神也"

    21. "神者, 道之妙萬物者也" (ZYW 531).

    22. Wang uses this language, for example, in the following claim: "King
Wen grasped the meaning of numinous and mysterious transformations, and
named it *Change*." "文王取其變易神妙之旨而名之易" (ZYFL 651).

23. Wang's original text: "天下惟器而已矣. 道者, 器之道" (ZYW 420).

24. In order to avoid confusing Wang Bi with Wang Fuzhi, the former is always referred to herein by his full name, and never by his surname alone.

25. For this aspect of Wang's philosophy, see especially, Wagner 42, 67.

26. Translated from the original: "夫無者, 誠萬物之所資, 聖人莫肯致言, 而老子申之無已, 何邪?" 弼曰 : "聖人體無, 無又不可以訓, 故言必及有; 老, 莊未免於有, 恆訓其所不足" (世說新語, 文學, 8). Source text online at Donald Sturgeon's Chinese Text Project, www.ctext.org (accessed April 11, 2011).

27. Wang Bi *Ming xiang* 明象; Richard John Lynn translation (31).

28. "漢儒說象, 多取附會 . . . 王弼反其道而概廢之, 曰 "得象而忘言。得意而忘象" 乃傳固曰 "易者, 象也" (ZYW 1039). The original quote that Wang Fuzhi accredits to Wang Bi is in Wang Bi's *Zhouyi lueli*. For the full translation the text containing Wang Bi's claim, see Richard Lynne's translation *The Classic of Changes: A New Translation of the I Ching as Interpreted by Wang Bi* (New York: Columbia University Press, 1994), 31. Wang Bi, living in the relatively chaotic and difficult time just after the fall of the Han, was in a unique historical position to shift the discourse away from the Han status quo.

29. Gernet notes that the "three sages" here referred to are Fu Xi, King Wen, and Confucius (128).

30. Translated from Wang's original text:

秦焚書, 而易以卜筮之書, 不罹其災, 故六經唯易有全書, 後學之幸也. 然而易之亂也, 自此事 . . . 乃秦既夷之於卜筮之家, 入者不敢講 . . . 漢人所傳者非純乎三聖之教. 而秦以來, 雜占之術紛紜而相亂 . . . 王弼氏知其陋也, 棄其說, 一以道為斷, 蓋庶幾於三聖之意. 而弼學本老莊虛無之旨, 蓋詭於道, 且其言曰 "得意忘言, 得言忘象," 則不知象中之言, 言中之意為天人之蘊所昭示於天下者, 而何可忘那? (ZYFL 652)

31. Wang's text: "以筮言之, 則有三變以得一書以爲初, 漸積之十八變而成卦, 疑初為始而上爲終。然成卦者, 天地固有之化, 萬物固有之理, 人事固有之情 . . . 非因筮而後有卦也 (ZYFL 666).

32. Cf. Jullien 53.

33. This description of holism is based on the work of Brook Ziporyn (2000). Confer page 28 in particular.

34. In Jullien's account, "*La relation n'est ni extériure ni seconde, c'est elle qui fait exister intrinsèquement: la corrélativité est le sens de la réalité. C'est pourquoi la réalité ne s'analyse qu'en termes d'enchaînement et de procès*" (53). To translate: "The relation is neither exterior nor secondary, it is what exists intrinsically: the correlativity is the sense of reality. It is because the reality is only analyzed in terms of sequence and of process."

35. Translated from the following claim: "*car ce qui se manifeste à l'analyse n'est jamais une existence singulière et autonome mais une certain séquence au sein d'un enchaînement (celui du procès)*" (Jullien 52).

36. Wang's text reads:

天下有截然分析而必相對待之物乎？求之于天地，無有此也；求之于萬物，無有此；反而求之于心，抑未諗其必然也. 天尊于上，而天入地中，無深不察；地卑于下，而地升天際，無高不徹. 其界不可得而剖也。截然分析而必相對待者，天地無有也，萬物無有也，人心無有也. (ZYW 1073–1074. (Qtd. in Gernet 91)

Wang's language here mirrors Cheng Hao's earlier work: "天地萬物之理，無獨，必有對，。皆自然而然，非有安排也，。萬物莫不有對。。" In translation, "With regard to the patterning of the natural world and the myriad things, there is nothing that is alone. Everything must have a (correlative) opposite. Everything spontaneously occurs (*ziran*), and thus it is so. It is not the case that there is a prearranged plan" (*Mingdao xue'an, shang*, 550; qtd. in Gernet 86).

37. Cf. Jullien 194.

38. Wang's text:

"錯 者，金之械器，汰去其外而發見中者也. "綜" 者，繫經之線，以機動之，一上一下也. 卦各有六陰六陽，陰見則陽隱于中. 錯去其所見之陰則陽見，錯去其所見之陽則陰見，如乾之與坤 ... 就所見之爻，上下交易，若織之提綜，迭相升降，如屯 之與蒙" (788–789).

39. Original text: "變動不居，周流六虛，上下無常，剛柔相易，不可為典要，唯變所適" (*Xici xia* 1.8).

40. Wang Fuzhi's text: "易體此以爲道，故乾，坤立而屯 ䷂，蒙 ䷃ 繼，陰陽之交也，無可循之序；十變而的泰 ䷊，否 ䷋，八變而得臨 ䷒，觀 ䷓，再變而得剝 ䷖，復 ䷗，其消長也無漸次之期" (ZYN 605; qtd. in Gernet 110).

41. Along these lines, Jullien writes, "*Chaque figuration peut devenir l'autre puisqu'elle contient déjà celui-ci en son sein.*" In translation, "Each figuration is able to become the other because it already contains the other within it" (Jullien 103).

42. Wang's text: "陰陽之撰各六, 其位亦十有二, 半隱半見" (ZYW 225; qtd. in Gernet 110).

43. Confer Jullien, "*Chaque hexagramme possède donc toujours la même somme de douze traits, six traits yin et six traits yang, et ceux-ci se répartissent toujours différemment mais également entre le visible et l'invisible.* In translation, "Each hexagram always possesses not only the six manifest traits which characterize it, but also an underlying latent modality, the six other traits which lie in waiting" (Jullien 102, 103).

44. Although this form of expressionism is a fundamental aspect of Wang's philosophy, it cannot be considered the organizing paradigm as Black maintains. The expression of the invisible by the visible is a singular modality in a greater holistic system.

45. Jullien's French text, "*. . . sur le seul mode de la latence*" (ibid.).

46. Jullien's text:

> *De même que tout réel possède à la pois un extérieur et un intérieur, un envers et un endroit, l'hexagramme est un structure double, contenant à parité le manifeste et le latent . . . Or toute expérience peut être élucidée globalement à partir d'un tel modèle, par exemple entre le projet d'hier et l'exécution d'aujourd'hui, entre l'exécution d'aujourd'hui et sa transformation un autre jour.* (Jullien 102)

47. Cf. David Hall and Roger T. Ames commentary on the *Daodejing* for an expression of this same idea: "whatever 'goes out' and becomes consummately distinct, also 'returns'" (27).

48. Gernet's original text reads:

> *La position des lignes dans les hexagrammes est à elle seule significative. Or, quand tout élément d'un ensemble n'a de sens qu'en raison de la place qu'il i occupe et que le tout n'est pas la simple addition des parties, c'est qu'on est en présence d'un système. Une des idées fréquemment exprimées par Wang est en effet celle de système.* (143)

49. "道一成而三才備, 卦一成而六位備 . . . 三才之道, 大全統乎一端, 而一端領乎大全也" (ZYW 1064, 1066).

50. "*Un jeune yin (shaoyin) aura en effet tendance à se transformer en vieux yin (taiyin) et ce vieux yin à transformer à son tour en un jeune yang (shaoyang) qui deviendra un vieux yang (taiyang) . . . ce qui donne une succession continue de transformations*" (Gernet 113).

51. Confer also Jullien (195) and Cheng (2011, 408).

52. Wang's text: "天下皆一無非中矣" (ZYW 1065).

53. Gernet's text: "*Le bien est affaire de situation (wei) et de moment (shi) . . . On n'est jamais en présence que de continuités et de réalités relatives*" (91).

54. Cf. Jullien, "*En fonction de deux coordonnées: le moment et la position*" (198).

55. Gernet discusses the notion of *ji* as the point of transition between two phases:

> *La notion de phase, passage insensible de l'un à l'autre de deux termes opposes et indissociables, est symbolisée par le dessin bien inconnu qui représente l'enchaînement des énergies yin et yang à l'intérieur d'un cercle. Leur unité est continuité, puisqu'ils coexistent et que les proportions de l'un varient en fonction inverse de l'autre. Leurs signes ne s'inversent qu'au cours d'un instant infinitésimal. Tel est le sens du mot* ji, *l'impondérable qui, dans tous les domaines, aboutit à une inversion des signes.*

> The notion of a phase, an insensible passage from one to the other of two opposed yet inseparable terms is symbolized by the well-known design which represents the chain of *yin* and *yang* energies in the interior of a circle. Their unity is continuity since they coexist and the proportions of one vary in inverse function to the other. Their signs only invert themselves in the course of an infinitesimal instant. This is the sense of the word "*ji* 幾," the imponderable which, in all domains, leads to an inversion of signs. (86)

56. Translation from the Chinese: "君子見幾而作, 不俟終日" (*Xici xia* 5.10). Source text found at Donald Sturgeon's *Chinese Text Project*. Online at http://chinese.dsturgeon.net/text.pl?node=46908&if=en (accessed Feb. 28, 2010).

57. Henry Rosemont and Roger T. Ames translation (1998) 145: "The Master replied, 'Zizhang oversteps the mark (*guo*), and Zixia falls short of it (*buji*).'"

58. The so called fact/value, is/ought, description/prescription distinction has had its foothold in Western philosophical discourse since David Hume's publication of *A Treatise of Human Nature* (1739). Although analytically useful, especially in the advent of natural science, the distinction compartmentalizes experience, and thus detracts from understanding the fullness of experience.

59. Wang's text: "天下者, 时势而已矣. 乘其时, 顺其势 . . ." (Gernet 296).

60. See Chen Lai (2004) 190–193.

61. "人成位乎中, 则可以效法天地而無憾" (ZYN 1037).

62. Wang's guideline for the good life may be summed up in a principle of practical parsimony: *Seek the path of least resistance*—where resistance is defined as agitation in one's emotional equilibrium and obstruction of one's participation in the procreative harmony of one's environment.

63. See this article in *Confucianism and Ecology*, Mary Evelyn Tucker and John Berthrong, eds. (Cambridge, MA: Harvard University Press, 1998), 265–271.

64. "故人者, 天地之心也" (*Liji* 9.20, "Liyun"; complete text found at D. Sturgeon's Chinese Text Project, www.ctext.org (accessed April 14, 2011).

Chapter 4

1. Persons are a necessary condition for valuation to occur, but they are not sufficient. Valuation also requires a world. The axiology mirrors the metaphysics and epistemology in this regard.

2. Translated from Bai's text: "王夫之说的好: "自然者天地, 主持者人. 人者天地之心." 人在为自己确立了 '天地之心' 的价值定位的同时, 不是拥有了主宰万物的权力, 而是主动承担起了自然万物的 "主持者" 的责任和义务, 人作为 "万物之灵," 其特殊性即在于此" (Bai 473).

3. The nonhuman perspective is portrayed by the many characters in Zhuangzi's parables. Likewise, Zhuangzi speaks of "a clod" as something of importance. The "uncarved block" is of course a popular image presented in the *Daodejing*.

4. Cf. Xiong Lümao and Yang Zhengzheng's discussion on the different attributes of *tian* and persons: "天 '无心, ' '无为' . . . 没有意志, 没有情感, 不能主宰人的命运; 人则 "有心, 有为, 有意志" (27).

5. This description is identified by Li Xiangjun as one sense of *tian-renzhiji* as it is sometimes used in Confucian discourse: "天人之际 . . . 有时指的是与人相对的包括天, 地, 万物在内的自然界全体" (455).

6. Translated from Zhou's text: "'天人之际' 是一个内涵非常丰富的命题：从 '天' 到 '人' 涉及封一系列的概念或者范畴, 如 '天,' '理气,' '命,' '人,' '性,' '情,' '心,' '道,' '德' 等等. '天 . . . 人' 之间也具有多层次, 多角度的意义·匾此, 从 '天' 到 '人' 就是一个非常复杂的问题系统" (2005, 5).

7. Translated from Xiong and Yang (2003): "'天' 与 '人' 既是对立('相分') 的, 又是统一 ('合一') 的, 它们是对立统一的关系 ('分') 的, 又是统一 ('合一') 的, 它们是对立统一的关系" (26). Parenthetical inserts are original to the authors.

8. Translated from Zhou's text: "关于 '天' 的问题, 王夫之不赞成人们对 '天' 只是做一种外在的、与人无关式的理解, 而是主张,言天不能脱离人而言 '天'" (Zhou 53).

9. Translation based on Jullien (67):

> Il est clair au moins que Wang Fuzhi est conscient d'une spécificité de l'histoire humaine (en tant que wen) par rapport au fonctionnement cyclique de la nature. L'homme à l'origine n'est qu'un « animal qui se tient debout » et c'est au fur et à mesure des grandes inventions matérielles qu'a commencé à se développer la civilisation . . . Il y a donc « évolution » d'une époque à l'autre, par « adaptation » constante, chacune se définissant par un certain stade des mœurs et de la civilisation (事随势迁) . . . [Mais] sa conscience d'un ordre humain (rendao 人道) n'est jamais complètement affranchie de la vision plus globale du course du monde (tiandao 天道).

Here the Chinese characters are original to Jullien, but he provides them by way of endnote rather than parenthetical insert.

10. This interpretation of *dao* as a gerund follows from the teachings of Roger T. Ames. For discussion of this interpretive strategy, see Roger T. Ames and David Hall (2003). Jullien's cogent argument for interpreting Wang Fuzhi's thought in terms of process philosophy supports taking the Hall and Ames interpretive strategy for *dao* in the present context.

11. Translated from Wang's text, "古人之行, 非我之行也; 我之行非天下之所行也。五味无定適, 五色无定文, 五音无定和" (SL 275–276; qtd. in Gernet 76)

12. Translation of Li's text: "他首先区分自然与自然规律及人与人的道理 . . . 王船山承认自然规律是不以人的意志为转移的, 主张一定要先考虑人的主观能动性, 然后再考虑人与自然的协调与统一" (Li 2003, 56).

13. "天不能使人处乎自然,無思無為而道已備" (尚書引義, 洪范) (qtd. in Li 2003, 56).

14. Translated from Wang's formula: 自然者, 有自而然也. The claim may be alternatively translated as such: "Anything that is self-so, having a self, is then so." For further analysis of this this formula, see Deng Hui's article on Wang Fuzhi's concept of nature, "论王船山的自然 概念" (2003). "自然者, 有自而然也" (ZMZ 55).

15. Translated from Li Zhecheng's original text: "王船山部分地融合了传统的天人合一思想和道家的自然主义观点, 但王船山在这方面与其他儒家不同. 王船山既反对其他儒家的天人合一观点, 也反对在缩小人类作用的状况下盲目地回到自然的自然主义观点 [. . . .] 他认为不承认 '分' 的盲目 '合一,' 不是真正意义上的统一" (56).

16. Cf. Zhou Bing for a parallel analysis. "王夫之虽然赞同 '天人合一' 的思想观念, 但是反对那种把 '圣人' 和 '天地' 直接划等号的做法" (Zhou 196).

17. The nonhuman perspective is portrayed by the many characters in Zhuangzi's parables, such as insects, birds, tortoises, rivers, etc. Likewise, Zhuangzi (chapter 2) speaks of "a clod" as something of importance. The "uncarved block" and "infant" are popular images presented in the *Daodejing*. (See Laozi, chapters 10, 19, 20, 28, 32, 37, 55, 57, 65).

18. See *Zhuangzi* (chapter 13) for the parable of Wheelwright Bian.

19. "無端將聖人體用, 一並與天地合符, 此佛, 老放蕩借誣之詞, 坏知而妄作" (DSS 709).

20. Translation based on Wang's original text: "老氏瞀於此, 而曰道在虛, 虛以器之虛也. 釋氏瞀於此, 而曰道在寂, 寂以器之寂. 淫詞炙, 而不能離乎器 . . ." (ZYW 1029).

21. Translation based on Wang's text: "天下惟器而已矣. 道者器之道, 器者不可谓之道之器也" (ZYW 1027). This celebrated passage has been interpreted as a statement of *realism*: "realism" in the sense that the empirical world is real. Unfortunately, the term *realism* has been overworked throughout the history philosophical discourse. In contemporary metaphysics, the *realism* is actually reserved for the ontological commitment to the existence of universals as opposed to concrete particulars. This contemporary usage of the term thus applies to the antithesis of Wang's position. Using contemporary metaphysical categories, Wang's statement expresses a commitment that is better referred to as *nominalism*, which asserts the irreducible reality of concrete particulars.

22. See A. C. Graham's *Chuang-Tzŭ: The Inner Chapters* (1989, 4).

23. "物之始生也, 形之發知, 皆疾于人, 而其終也鈍. 人則具體而儲其用, 形之發知, 視物而不疾也多矣, 而其既也敏" (思問錄, 內篇). Qtd. In Li Zhecheng (2003, 57).

24. The presence of the "heart-mind" radical in each of these Chinese characters has semantic significance.

25. "有其道 . . . 天則自然矣, 物則自然矣. 螯蟻之義, 相鼠之禮, 不脩為矣, 任天故也" (DSS 1144).

26. Paraphrase and quotation based on Li Zhecheng's original text:

> 他认为很好地适应自然天的生物虽然感觉功能发达, 但是它不能产生高级的精神文明。而人的感觉功能虽没有动物发达, 但因理性发达能够形成文化. . . . 他认为, 在无数的生命中, 只有人是能够把握自然规律建立起文化的存在 (2003, 56–57).

27. Translation based on Wang's text:

> 雖雲聖人大公無我, 然到此處, 亦須照顧自己先立於無憾之地, 然後可以立情法之準。世儒不察, 便謂聖人概將在己、在人作一視同等, 無所分別, 無所嫌忌, 但以在彼善惡功罪之小大爲弛張, 而曰此聖人之以天地為一體者也. 爲此說者, 巇差等以直情而徑行, 其與異端所云 "天地與我同根, 萬物與我共命" 一流荒誕无實之邪説又何以異! [...] 衕文定傳《春秋》, 謂孔子自序其績, 與齊桓等, 為聖人以天自處, 視萬象異形而同體, 亦是議論太高不切實處 (DSS 1034).

28. Translated from the Chinese, "聖人之心, 天地生物之心也" (DSS 709).

29. Translated from Wang's text: "劈头说个'圣人之心, 天地生物之一', 安在此处, 却不恰好。圣人于此, 却是裁成辅相, 顺天理之自然, 何曾兜揽天地生物之心以为心? 若方钓弋时, 以生物之心为心, 则必并钓弋而废之矣" (DSS 709).

30. Translated from Wang's claim: "聖人只是聖人, 天地只是天地.《中庸》說 '配天,' 如妇配夫, 固不纯用夫道" (DSS 709).

31. Zhang Zai's "Western Inscription" can be viewed as a paragon of this strategy.

32. Translation based on Wang's text: "聖人自聖人, 天自天, 故 曰 '可以赞,' 曰 '可以参,' 曰 '如神,' 曰 '配天' [. . .] 雖異而相知, 相配也" (DSS 540).

33. Emphasis original to JeeLoo Liu's text.

34. "Matching *tian*" is here offered as a literal interpretation of the Chinese phrase, *peitian* 配天, which Wang draws out of the *Zhongyong*, chap-

ters 26 and 31. In their *Focusing the Familiar: A Translation and Philosophical Interpretation of the* Zhongyong (University of Hawai'i Press, 2001), David Hall and Roger T. Ames translate the phrase as "companion to the heavens" (chapter 26, 107) and "complement of *tian*" (chapter 31, 113). Hall and Ames thus highlight the *active* connotation of the term *pei* 配 (and active quality of the relationship denoted by the term).

35. See *Analects* 11.23 for the characterization of harmony in terms of differentiation. Contrary to recent expositions of Wang's work (Yan 1995; Liu 2010), I maintain that Wang's philosophy is committed to an irreducible plurality of existents; therefore, his philosophy is *not* monistic.

36. On this topic, Cheng observes: "Mencius, furthermore, insists that these four feelings are the defining characteristic of a man and that they are internal and inherent in the nature of man, for without them man is not a man" (238).

37. "《或問》'一元之氣,' '天下之物' 二段, 扎住氣化上立義, 正是人鬼关头分界語・所以《中庸》劈頭言天, 便言命・命者, 令也・令猶政也・未尾言天, 必言載・栽者, 事也・此在天之天遺, 亦未嘗遺乎人物而別有其體 [. . .]" (DSS 529).

Chapter 5

1. In Chinese, this expression follows the formulations: 內外合一 and 內外交相.

2. Following Jacques Gernet, "*La Chine se glorifie d'avoir des rites et les a même considérés comme la caractéristique principale de sa civilisation . . .*" (384). Literally, "China glorified herself for having the rites and had even considered them as the principal characteristic of her civilization."

3. Jacques Gernet also makes this point in setting up the function of the rites as seen by Wang Fuzhi:

Contrarier des désirs inhérents à la nature humaine, c'est méconnaît la véritable fonction des rites, car les rites visent à régler les désirs, sans forcer la nature, à les intégrer à l'ordre social et à les y faire concourir. Ils exigent et développent un sens aigu des psychologie et une grande maîtrise du comportements puisqu'ils doivent tenir compte à la fois du moment et des lieux, des hiérarchies et des âges. La bonne entente entre les hommes doit beaucoup au respect de cet ensemble de comportements que nous appelons rites. (381)

4. "食色者, 禮之所麗也; 利者, 民之依也" (SYY 242).

5. "誠是實, 禮是虛" (DSS 616). Also cited in Gernet (384). For a related application and analysis of this concept, see Brasovan and Duncan (235).

6. "和而不同." Cf. *Analects* 13.23.

7. For a parallel argument, see Cheng Chung-ying "On Harmony as Transformation: Paradigms from the I Ching," in *Harmony and Strife: Contemporary Perspectives East & West*. Shu-hsien Liu and Robert E. Allinson, eds. (Hong Kong: The Chinese University Press, 1988). See especially, 227–228.

8. *Liji*. 19.26/104/11.

9. Translation based on Wang's text:

杜预欲短太子之丧, 而曰: "君子之于礼, 存诸内而已." 安得此
野人之言而称之哉. 今有人焉, 心不忘乎敬父, 而坐则倨以待;
情不忍乎爱兄, 而怒则紾其臂; 亦将曰存诸内而已乎? 内外交
相维、交相养者也 . . . 故先王之制丧礼, 达贤者之内于外, 以
安其内, 而制中材之外, 以感其内" (*Du Tongjian lun* 讀通鑑論,
422–423). Also cited by Gernet (386).

10. Wang's text: "释氏以真空為如来藏, 謂太虛之中本無一物, 而氣從幻起以成諸惡, 為障碍真如之根本 [. . .] 妄欲銷隕世界以为大涅盤, 彼亦惡能銷隕之哉" (ZMZ 83; qtd. in Gernet 299)? My translation is informed by Gernet's French translation.

11. "乃以廢人倫, 坏物理, 握頑虛, 蹈死趣, 而曰吾以安于所安也." 此无他, 不明于物之不可绝也。且夫物之不可绝也以己有物物之不容绝也以物有己 [. . .] 一眠一食, 而皆与物俱; 一动一言, 而必依物起" (SYY 237–240) (qtd. in Gernet 296). Gernet further cites the following passage, where Wang makes a similar case: "人之所以爲人, 不能離君民親友以爲道, 則亦不能舍人倫物曲以盡道, 其固然也. 今使絕物而始静焉, 舍天下之惡而不取天下之善, 堕其志, 息其意, 外其身, 于是而洞洞焉, 晃晃焉, 若有一澄澈之境, 置吾心而偷以安. 又使解析万物, 求物之始而不可得" (ibid.).

12. Translation based on Zhang Zai's text, "乾稱父, 坤稱母; 予兹藐焉, 乃混然中處. 故天地之塞, 吾其體; 天地之帥, 吾其性. 民吾同胞, 物吾與也." (Original Chinese text found at Steve Angle's, "Chinese Philosophical Etext Archive": http://sangle.web.wesleyan.edu/etext/pre-qin/pre-qin.html (accessed Oct. 31, 2009). Compare to Wing-tsit Chan's translation, "Heaven is my father and Earth is my mother, and even such a small creature as I find an intimate place in their midst. That which fills the universe I regard as my body and that which directs the universe I consider as my nature.

All people are my brothers and sisters, and all things are my companions"
(Chan 497).

13. "其曰"乾稱父, 坤稱母", 初不曰"天吾父, 地吾母"也" (ZMZ 252).

14. "濂溪周子首为太极图说, 以究天人合一之原, 所以明夫人之生
也 . . ." (ibid.).

15. Cheng Hao is also called Bo Chun 伯淳, which recognizes his role
as Elder Brother (bo 伯). He can also be referred to by his posthumous title,
Ming Dao明道. For an account of his life, influence, and thought see Wing-
Tsit Chan, *A Source Book in Chinese Philosophy* (Princeton, NJ: Princeton
University Press, 1963) chapter 31. For an in-depth study into Cheng Hao's
philosophy, see A. C. Graham, *Two Chinese Philosophers: The Metaphysics of
the Brothers Ch'êng* (La Salle, IL: Open Court, 1992).

16. "天地之大德曰生, 聖人之大寶曰位." Source Chinese text found
online at Donald Sturgeon's "Classical Chinese Text Project," http://ctext.
org/book-of-changes/xi-ci-xia (accessed Feb. 3, 2011).

17. "天地絪縕, 萬物化醇. 男女構精, 萬物化生." Translation based
on James Legge.

18. "一陰一陽之謂道, 繼之者善也, 成之者性也. 仁者見之謂之仁,
知者見之謂之知 [. . . .] 日新之謂盛德. 生生之謂易 [. . .] 通變之謂事,
陰陽不測之謂神."

19. "夫易廣矣！大矣！[. . .] 夫乾, 其靜也專, 其動也直, 是以大生
焉. 夫坤, 其靜也翕, 其動也闢, 是以廣生焉." Richard John Lynne (1994)
translation, 55.

20. "聖人設卦觀象, 繫辭焉而明吉凶, 剛柔相推而生變化."

21. "日月相推而明生焉 [. . . .] 屈信相感而利生焉."

22. "有天地, 然後萬物生焉."

23. "強調生生不息、創進不已的精神" (Wang, *Life*, 495).

24. "正言易之所自設, 皆一陰一陽之道而人性之全體也。生生者有
其體而動幾必萌" (周易內傳,卷五, 廣文書局 1970, 481) (qtd. in Wang,
Life, 486).

25. Wang claims: "陰陽之本體 [. . .] 此所謂太極也" (周易內傳, 卷
五, 廣文書局, 1970, 515) (qtd. in Wang, *Life*, 483).

26. "道謂天道也, 陰陽者, 太極所有之實也 [. . . .] 動靜者, 陰陽交
感之幾也 [. . . .] 合之則為太極, 分之則謂之陰陽" (ibid. 475, 476) (qtd.
in Wang, *Life*, 486).

27. "陰非陽無以始, 而陽藉陰之材以生, 萬物形質成而性即麗焉"
(周易內傳, 卷一, 廣文書局, 1970, 39) (qtd. in Wang, *Life*, 487).

28. "可知太極是天地間萬物生成的根本源頭 [. . .] 也是渾淪未判的
元氣 [. . .] 有此根本先設之理, 而後方能架構宇宙的生生系統" (Wang,
Life, 483).

29. "乾, 健也. 坤, 順也" (*Shuogua* 7).

30. "是故闔戶謂之坤; 闢戶謂之乾. 一闔一闢謂之變, 往來不窮謂之通" (*Xici shang* 11.2).

31. "神者, 道之妙萬物者也."

32. "理只是象二儀之妙, 氣方是二儀之實. 健者, 氣之健也. 順者, 氣之順也. 天人之蘊, 一氣而已. 從乎氣之善而為之理" (DSS 1052).

33. See, Zhang Shuangdi 张双棣 and Chen Tao 陈涛. eds. 古代汉语字典 (1998), entries for 蘊 and 緼, 1018, 1019.

34. For the semiotic principle of paronomasia see Roger T. Ames and Henry Rosemont, Jr. Translator's Introduction to the *Analects of Confucius: A Philosophical Interpretation* (1998)

Chapter 6

1. For further discussion of the concept of *shensi* 神思 in the history of Chinese philosophy, see Nicholas S. Brasovan, "The Aesthetics of Qi: Building on an Internalist-Essentialist Philosophy of Art" in *Dao: A Journal of Comparative Philosophy*, vol. 14.1 (2015).

2. Cf. *Analects* 15.29.

3. This information is according to the NOAA website at https://www.ncdc.noaa.gov/sotc/global/201313 (accessed Jan. 20, 2016).

Glossary of Key Chinese Terms

Dao 道. Way-in-the-making. Used in the context of Daoism and neo-Confucianism in reference to cosmological order and process

Di 地. Earth

Gua 卦. A trigram or hexagram symbol from the *Yijing*

Guan 觀. Comprehensive Observation

He 和. Harmony

He 合. Continuity

Li 禮. Ritual Propriety

Li 理. Patterning

Li yi fen shu 理一分殊. Patterning is Unified, but Divisions are Many

Qi 氣. Energy

Qi 器. Concrete Particular

Qizhili 氣之理. Patterns of Energy, or Energetic Patterning

Rendao 人道. Way of Persons

Shen 神. Spritual, Sublime, Unfathomable

Sheng 生. Life, Birth, Procreativity, Creativity

Shi 勢. Propensity

Taihe 太和. Great/Sublime Harmony

Taiji 太極. Great/Sublime Limits, Great Ultimate

Taixu. 太虛. Great/Sublime Vacuity

Tian 天. Nature (in the context of Wang Fuzhi's philosophy)

Tiandao 天道. Way of Nature

Tianrenzhiji 天人之際. Between Nature and Persons, Interstitial Interrelations between Nature and Persons

Tianrenzhiyun 天人之蘊. Profound Merging of Nature and Persons

Tianrenheyi 天人合一. Continuity of Nature and Persons

Weiwuzhui 唯物主義. Materialism

Wu 無. Indeterminacy

Wuji. 無極. Without Limits

Xin 心. Heart-and-Mind

Xing 性. Natural Disposition

Yang 陽. Driving Mode of Energy

Yijing 易經. Book of Changes

Yin 陰. Receptive Mode of Energy

You 有. Determinacy

Yuanqi 元氣. Originary Primordial Energy

Zairenzhitian 在人之天. Nature within Persons

Zaitianzhitian 在天之天. Nature within Nature

Ziran 自然. Self-So, Spontaneity, Nature

Bibliography

Adler, Joseph A. "Response and Responsibility: Chou Tun-i and Confucian Resources for Environmental Ethics." *Confucianism and Ecology: The Interrelation of Heaven, Earth, and Humans.* Ed. Mary Evelyn Tucker and John Berthrong. Cambridge, MA: Harvard U, 1998. 123–50.

———. "Response to Rodney Taylor, 'Of Animals and Man: The Confucian Perspective.'" Presentation at the "Conference on Religion and Animals," Harvard-Yenching Institute, Cambridge, MA (May 1999). Presentation paper online at <http://www2.kenyon.edu/Depts/Religion/Fac/Adler/Writings/Animals.htm> (accessed June 25, 2011).

———. Translator's "Introduction." *Introduction to the Study of the Classic of Change (I-hsüeh ch'i-meng),* by Chu Hsi. Provo, UT: Global Scholarly Publications, 2002.

Analects of Confucius: A Philosophical Translation. Trans. Roger T. Ames and Henry Rosemont, Jr. New York, NY: Ballantine Books, 1998.

Ames, Roger T., and Henry Rosemont, Jr. *The Analects of Confucius: A Philosophical Translation.* Translator's "Introduction." New York, NY: Ballantine Books, 1998.

Ames, Roger T., and David Hall. *Daodejing: A Philosophical Translation.* New York: Ballentine Books, 2003.

———. *Focusing the Familiar: A Translation and Philosophical Interpretation of the Zhongyong.* Honolulu: U of Hawaii P, 2001.

Ames, Roger T., and J. Baird Callicott. "Introduction: The Asian Traditions as a Conceptual Resource for Environmental Philosophy." *Nature in Asian Traditions of Thought.* Albany: State U of New York P, 1989. 1–24.

———. "Epilogue: On the Relation of the Idea and Action." *Nature in Asian Traditions of Thought.* Albany: State U of New York P, 1989. 279–90.

Aristotle. *Metaphysics*. Books VII and VIII. *Readings in Ancient Greek Philosophy*. 4th ed. Ed. S. Marc Cohen, Patricia Curd, and C. D. E. Reed. Indianapolis, IN: Hackett Publishing Co., 2011.

Aquinas, Thomas. *Summa Theologa*. Source text online at <http://www.fordham.edu/halsall/source/aquinas3.html> (accessed Feb. 20, 2010).

Auyang, Sunny Y. *Foundations of Complex-System Theories in Economics, Evolutionary Biology, and Statistical Physics*. Cambridge, UK: Cambridge U, 1998.

Bai, Xi 白奚. "儒家的人类中心论及其生态学意义" in 当代中国的 "人—自然" 观. "Confucian Anthropocentrism and Its Ecological Significance." *The Intellectual Retrospection of Human-natural Relationship in Contemporary China*. Ed. Zhao Yifeng 赵轶峰. Changtchun: Northeast Normal UP, 2008.

Bennet, Jane. *Vibrant Matter: A Political Ecology of Things*. Durham. NC: Duke UP, 2010.

Black, Alison Harley. *Man and Nature in the Philosophical Thought of Wang Fu-chih*. Seattle and London: U of Washington P, 1989. (Unless otherwise note, all references to Black herein refer to this text.)

———. Book Review: "François Jullien's *Procès ou Création: Une introduction à la pensée des letters chinois: Essai de problématique interculturelle* [*Process or creation: An introduction to Chinese literati thought: essay on an intercultural problematic*]." "*The Journal of Asian Studies* 49.4 (Nov. 1990):. 903–05. Association for Asian Studies.

Bol, Peter K. *Neo-Confucianism in History*. Cambridge, MA: Harvard UP, 2008.

Bontekoe, Ronald. *Dimensions of the Hermeneutic Circle*. Amherst, NY: Humanity Books 1996.

Braidotti, Rosi. *The Posthuman*. Malden, MA: Polity Press, 2013.

Brasovan, Nicholas S. "Aesthetics of *Qi*: Building on an Internalist/Essentialist Philosophy of Art." *Dao: A Journal for Comparative Philosophy* 14.1:75–93 (2015).

Brasovan, Nicholas S. and Taine Duncan. "Contemporary Ecofeminism and Confucian Cosmology." *Feminist Encounters with Confucius*. Eds. Mathew A. Foust and Sorhoon Tan. Boston: Brill, 2016. 218–243.

Callicott, J. Baird. "The Metaphysical Implications of Ecology." *Nature in Asian Traditions of Thought*. Albany: State U of New York P, 1989. 51–66.

Callicott, J. Baird, and James McRae, eds. *Environmental Philosophy in Asian Traditions of Thought*. Albany: State U of New York P, 2014.

Chan, Wing-tsit. *A Source Book in Chinese Philosophy*. Princeton, NJ: Princeton UP, 1963.

Chen, Lai. 《诠释与重建：王船山的哲学精神》北京：北京大学出版社, 2004 年. [*Interpretation and Rehabilitation: The Essence of Wang Chuanshan's Philosophy*. Beijing: Peking UP, 2004.]

Cheng, Chung-ying. "Inquiring into the Primary Model: *Yi Jing* and the Onto-Hermeneutical Tradition," *Journal of Chinese Philosophy*. 30.3–4 (2003): 289–312. Oxford: Blackwell Publishing.

———. "On Harmony as Transformation: Paradigms from the *I Ching*." *Harmony and Strife: Contemporary Perspectives, East and West*. Eds. Shu-hsien Liu and Robert E. Allinson. Hong Kong: The Chinese UP, 1988. 225–48,

———. "On the Metaphysical Significance of *Ti* (Body–Embodiment) in Chinese Philosophy: *Benti* (Origin–Substance) and *Ti–Yong* (Substance and Function)." *Journal of Chinese Philosophy*. 29.2 (2003). Oxford: Blackwell Publishing. 145–61.

———. "The Trinity of Cosmology, Ecology, and Ethics in the Confucian Personhood." *Confucianism and Ecology: The Interrelation of Heaven, Earth, and Humans*. Eds. Mary Evelyn Tucker, and John Berthrong. Cambridge, MA: Harvard UP, 1998. 211–36.

———. "Zhouyi and Philosophy of Wei (Positions)," *Extreme-Orient, Extreme-Occident* 18. Paris, 1996. 149–76.

———. "On Comprehensive Observation (*Guan*) as Onto-hermeneutics in the Zhou Yi." *Guoji Yixue yanjiu (International Studies on the Classic of Changes)*, no. 1, Ed. Zhu Bokun. Beijing: Huaxia, 1995. 156–203.

———. "The Primary Way: Philosophy of the *Yijing*," Vol. 1. (Currently in manuscript form at the University of Hawai'i at Mānoa, Department of Philosophy). Referred to herein as Cheng 2011.

Cooper, Gregory J. *The Science of the Struggle for Existence: On the Foundations of Ecology*. Cambridge, UK: Cambridge UP, 2003.

Deng, Hui. 邓辉. "论王船山的 '自然' 概念" in 衡阳师范学院学报. "On Wang Chuanshan's Concept of 'Nature.'" *Journal of Hengyang Normal University*. 24.4 (August, 2008): 76–78.

Falkowski, Paul. "The Power of Plankton." *Nature*. Nature Publishing Group. Feb 29, 2012.

Feuerbach, Ludwig Andreas. *Sämtliche Werke*. Volume 3. Ed. W. Bolin and F. Jodl. Reprint ed. Stuttgart: 1959–64.

Field, Stephen L. *Ancient Chinese Divination*. Honolulu: U of Hawai'i P, 2008.

Fristedt, Peter Erik. "Gadamer's Hermeneutic Holism." PhD Diss.at Stony Brook University, 2008.

Gadamer, Hans-Georg. *Truth and Method.* 2nd ed. Trans. Joel Weinsheimer and Donald G. Marshall. London: Continuum, 1989.

Gernet, Jacques. *La Raison des choses : Essai sur la philosophie de Wang Fuzhi (1619–1692),* Paris: Gallimard, 2005.

Golley, Frank B. *A History of the Ecosystem Concept in Ecology.* New Haven, CT: Yale UP, 1993.

———, and David R. Keller. eds. *The Philosophy of Ecology: From Science to Synthesis.* Athens, GA: The U of Georgia P, 2000.

Graham, Angus Charles (A. C.). *Chuang-Tzŭ: The Inner Chapters.* Indianapolis: Hackett Publishing Company, 1989.

Gu, Ming Dong. "From *Yuanqi* (Primal Energy) to *Wenqi* (Literary Pneuma): A Philosophical Study of a Chinese Aesthetic." *Philosophy East & West.* 59.1 (January 2009): 22–46.

Hall, David, and Roger T. Ames. "Getting It Right: On Saving Confucius from the Confucians." *Philosophy East and West,* 34.1 (Jan., 1984). Honolulu: U of Hawai'i P. 3–23.

Han, Demin 韩德民. "生态世界观——儒家和后现代主义的比较诠释, Ecological World Views: A Comparative Interpretation of Confucianism and the Post-modernismin" in "当代中国的'人—自然'观," *The Intellectual Retrospection of Human-natural Relationship in Contemporary China.* Ed. Zhao Yifeng 赵轶峰. Changchun: Northeast Normal UP, 2008. 369–387.

Handian 漢典. Chinese dictionary. Online at <http://www.zdic.net/>.

Huang, Siu-chi. *Essentials of Neo-Confucianism: Eight Major Philosophers of the Song and Ming Periods.* Westport, CT: Greenwood Press, 1999.

Irwin, Ruth. *Climate Change and Philosophy: Tranformational Possibilities.* London: Continuum, 2010.

Jullien, François. *Procès ou Création: Une introduction à la pensée des letters chinois: Essai de problématique interculturelle.* Paris: Éditions du Seuil, 1989. (Unless otherwise noted, all references to Jullien herein refer to this text.)

———. *The Propensity of Things: Toward a History of Efficacy in China.* Trans. Janet Lloyd. New York: Zone Books, 1999.

Kalton, Michael C. "Extending the Neo-Confucian tradition: Questions and Reconceptualization for the Twenty-First Century." *Confucianism and Ecology: The Interrelation of Heaven, Earth, and Humans.* Ed. Mary

Evelyn Tucker and John Berthrong. Cambridge, MA: Harvard UP, 1998. 77–104.

Kang, Chuan-Cheng 康全誠. 《王船山《易》學索源》《遠東通識學報.》第二卷,第二期, 頁 85–96. 太南臺灣: 遠東科技大學, 通識教育中心, 2008. ["The Investigation on the Origin of the Book of changes of Wang, Chuan-Shan" (sic). *Far East Journal of General Education.* 2.2. 85–96. Tainan, Taiwan: Far East University, Center for General Education, 2008.] Full text online at <http://www.feu.edu.tw/edu/gec/GE_WEB/c_b/9701/085-096.pdf> (accessed Feb 15, 2011).

Keightley, David N. "Shang Divination and Metaphysics." *Philosophy East and West.* 38.4. Honolulu: U of Hawai'i P, 1988. 367–97.

Lai, Karyn. *Learning from Chinese Philosophies: Ethics of Interdependent and Contextualised Self.* Abingdon, Great Britain: Ashgate Publishing Group, 2006.

Lau, D. C. "Translator's Introduction" *Mencius.* Trans. D. C. Lau: Hong Kong, The Chinese UP, 1984, 2003.

Leiss, William. *Domination of Nature.* Montreal, QC, CAN: McGill-Queen's UP, 1994.

Li, Wai-yee. "Introduction" to *Trauma and Transcendence in Early Qing Literature.* Harvard East Asian Monographs 250. Ed. Wilt L. Idema, Wai-yee Li, Ellen Widmer. Cambridge, MA: Harvard UP, 2006.

Li, Xiangjun. "An Exploration of Confucian Theory about Human-nature Relationship" in "当代中国的 '人—自然' 观," *The Intellectual Retrospection of Human-natural Relationship in Contemporary China.* Ed. Zhao Yifeng 赵轶峰. Changchun: Northeast Normal UP, 454–461, 2008.

Li, Zehou. *The Chinese Aesthetic Tradition.* Trans. Maija Bell Samei. Honolulu: U of Hawai'i P, 2010.

Li, Zhecheng. 李哲承. "New Century's Environmental Protection Problem and Wang Chuanshan's Natural View," *Journal of Hengyang Normal University (Social Science)* 1 (1), Feb. 2003 [Chinese text] 新世纪环保问题与王船山的自然观, 衡阳师范学院学报 (社会科学). 55–58. China Academic Journal Electronic Publishing House, 2011.

Liu, JeeLoo. "Wang Fuzhi's Philosophy of Principle (Li) Inherent in Qi." *Dao Companion to Neo-Confucian Philosophy.* Ed. John Makeham. London: Springer, 2010. 355–79.

Liu, Sky. "Contemporary Chinese Studies of WANG Fuzhi in Mainland China." *Dao: A Journal of Comparative Philosophy*III.2 (June 2004): 307–30.

Liu, Xiaogan. 刘笑敢. "经典诠释与体系建构—中国哲学诠释传统的成熟与特点刍议" [Interpreting Classical Texts and Constructing Systems: The Maturation and Special Features of Chinese Philosophical Hermeneutics] in "中国哲学史" History of Chinese Philosophy. 被引|用次数: 11 次. Beijing: Peking UP, 2002, no. 1. 32–37. (Accessed May 29, 2011 via WanFang Database: www.wanfang.com.cn.)

Lynn, Richard John. The Classic of the Changes: As Interpreted by Wang Bi. New York: Columbia UP, 2004.

Mathews, R. H. Mathews' Chinese-English Dictionary. Rev.American ed. Cambridge, MA: Harvard UP, 2000.

Mencius. Mencius: A Bilingual Edition. Trans. D. C. Lau. Hong Kong: The Chinese UP, 2003.

Meinert, Carmen. "Editor's Introduction." Nature, Environment and Culture in East Asia: The Challenge of Climate Change. Boston: Brill, 2013.

Mitchell, Donald J., and Sarah H. Jacoby. Buddhism: Introducing the Buddhist Experience. 3rd ed. New York: Oxford UP, 2014.

Morin, Edgar. Le paradigme perdu. Paris: Seuil, 1979.

———. Method (Vol. 1): The Nature of Nature. New York: Peter Lang Publishers, 1992.

Muller, A. C. "CJKV-English Dictionary: A Dictionary-Database of CJK Characters and Compounds Related to East Asian Cultural, Political, and Intellectual History." Online at <http://buddhism-dict.net/dealt/index.html>. (Last modified Feb. 5, 2007; accessed Feb. 20, 2010).

Neville, Robert Cummings. "Orientation, Self, and Ecological Posture." Confucianism and Ecology: The Interrelation of Heaven, Earth, and Humans. Ed. Mary Evelyn Tucker and John Berthrong. Cambridge, MA: Harvard UP, 1998. 265–74.

Nielsen, Bent. A Companion to Yi jing Numerology and Cosmology: Chinese Studies of Images and Numbers from Han 漢 (202 BCE–220 CE) to Song 宋 (960–1279 CE). New York, NY: RoutledgeCurzon, 2003.

Platt, Stephen R. Provincial Patriots: The Hunanese and Modern China. Cambridge, MA: Harvard UP, 2007.

Ricci, Mateo. The True Meaning of the Lord of Heaven (T'ien-chu Shih-i), translated with introduction and notes by Douglas Lancashire and Peter Hu Kuo-chen, Institute of Jesuit Sources, St.Louis, MO: Saint Louis U, 1985.

Ro, Young-chan. "Ecological Implications of Yi Yulgok's Cosmology." Confucianism and Ecology: The Interrelation of Heaven, Earth, and

Humans. Ed. Mary Evelyn Tucker and John Berthrong. Cambridge, MA: Harvard UP, 1998. 169–86.

Shaughnessy, Edward L. Introduction. *I Ching: The Classic of Changes.* Trans. Edward L. Shaughnessy. New York: Ballantine Books, 1996.

Shun, Kwong-Loi. *Mencius and Early Chinese Thought:* Stanford, CA: Stanford UP, 1999.

———. "Mencius on Jen-Hsing": *Philosophy East and West.* 47.1 (January 1997): 1–20.

Smith, Kidder. "The Difficulty of the *Yijing.*" *Chinese Literature: Essays, Articles, Reviews (CLEAR),* 15 (Dec. 1993): 1–15.

Smuts, Jan Christian. *Holism and Evolution.* London: MacMillon and Co. Ltd., 1926.

Tansley, Arthur. "The Use and Abuse of Vegetational Concepts and Terms." *Philosophy of Ecology.* Ed. Frank B. Golley and David R. Keller. Athens: University of Georgia Press, 2000. 55–76.

Tollefson, Jeff. "2015 Declared the Hottest Year on Record." *Nature News.* Nature Publishing Group, Jan. 20, 2016.

Tu, Weiming. *Centrality and Commonality: An Essay on Chung-yung.* Honolulu: U of Hawaii P. 1976.

———. "The Continuity of Being: Chinese Visions of Nature." *Confucianism and Ecology: The Interrelation of Heaven, Earth, and Humans.* Ed. Mary Evelyn Tucker and John Berthrong. Cambridge, MA: Harvard UP, 1998. 105–122.

———. "Beyond the Enlightenment Mentality." *Confucianism and Ecology: The Interrelation of Heaven, Earth, and Humans.* Ed. Mary Evelyn Tucker and John Berthrong. Cambridge, MA: Harvard UP, 1998. 1–21.

Tucker, Mary Evelyn. "The Philosophy of *Ch'i* as an Ecological Cosmology." *Confucianism and Ecology: The Interrelation of Heaven, Earth, and Humans.* Ed. Mary Evelyn Tucker and John Berthrong. Cambridge, MA: Harvard UP, 1998. 187–210.

———. "The Relevance of Chinese Neo-Confucianism for the Reverence of Nature." *Environmental Philosophy in Asian Traditions of Thought.* Ed. J. Baird Callicott and James McRae. Albany: State U of New York P, 2014.

Tucker, Mary Evelyn, and John Berthrong. "Introduction." *Confucianism and Ecology: The Interrelation of Heaven, Earth, and Humans.* Ed. Mary Evelyn Tucker and John Berthrong. Cambridge, MA: Harvard UP, 1998. xxv–xlv.

Wagner, Rudolf. The *Craft of a Chinese Commentator: Wang Bi on the Laozi.* Albany: State U of New York P, 2000.

———. *Language, Ontology, and Political Philosophy in China: Wang Bi's Scholarly Exploration of the Dark.* Albany, NY: State U of New York P, 2003.

Wang, Fuzhi. 王夫之. 《周易內傳.》《船山全書.》Vol. 1. 長沙市: 嶽麓書社出版, 1988. 39–684 頁. *Inner Commentaries on the* Zhouyi. *Complete Works of Chuanshan.* Vol. 1. Changsha: Yuelu shu Publishers, 1988. 39–648. Referred to herein as ZYN.

———. 《周易內傳發例.》《船山全書.》Vol. 1. 長沙市: 嶽麓書社出版, 1988. 649–84 頁.

Inner Commentary on the Zhouyi: *Examples. Complete Works of Chuanshan.* Vol. 1 Changsha: Yuelu shu Publishers, 1988. 649–84. Referred to herein as ZYFL.

———. 《周易大象解.》《船山全書.》Vol. 1. 長沙市: 嶽麓書社出版, 1988. 693–744 頁. *Minor Commentaries on the* Zhouyi. *Complete Works of Chuanshan.* Vol. 1 Changsha: Yuelu shu Publishers, 1988. 693–744. Referred to herein as ZYDX.

———. 《周易稗疏.》《船山全書.》Vol. 1. 長沙市: 嶽麓書社出版, 1988. 747–815 頁. *Minor Commentaries on the* Zhouyi. *Complete Works of Chuanshan.* Vol. 1. Changsha: Yuelu shu Publishers, 1988. 747–815. Referred to herein as ZYBS.

———. 《周易外傳.》《船山全書.》Vol. 1. 長沙市: 嶽麓書社出版, 1988. 781–1019 頁. *Outer Commentaries on the* Zhouyi. *Complete Works of Chuanshan.* Vol. 1. Changsha: Yuelu shu Publishers, 1988. 781–1019. Referred to herein as ZYW.

———. 《尚書引義.》《船山全書.》Vol. 2. 長沙市: 嶽麓書社出版, 1988. *Complete Works of Chuanshan.* Vol. 2. Changsha: Yuelu shu Publishers, 1988. Referred to herein as SYY.

———. 《四書稗疏.》《船山全書.》Vol. 6. 長沙市: 嶽麓書社出版, 1991. 17–82 頁. *Minor Commentaries on the* Four Books. *Complete Works of Chuanshan.* Vol. 6. Changsha: Yuelu shu Publishers, 1991. pp. 17–82. Referred to herein as SSB.

———. 《四書箋解.》《船山全書.》Vol. 6. 長沙市: 嶽麓書社出版, 1991. 105–390 頁. *Sub-Commentary on the* Four Books. *Complete Works of Chuanshan.* Vol. 6. Changsha: Yuelu shu Publishers, 1991. 105–390. Referred to herein as JJ.

———. 《讀四書大全說.》《船山全書.》Vol. 6. 長沙市: 嶽麓書社出版, 1991. 391–1135 頁. *Reading the Compendium of Discourses on the Four*

Books. *Complete Works of Chuanshan*. Vol. 6. Changsha: Yuelu shu Publishers, 1991. 391–1135. Referred to herein as DSS.

———.《思問錄外篇.》《船山全書.》 Vol. 12. 長沙市: 嶽麓書社出版, 1996. *Outer Commentaries on Siwenlu. Complete Works of Chuanshan*. Vol. 12. Changsha: Yuelu shu Publishers, 1996. Referred to herein as SWW.

———.《宋論》船山全書.》 Vol. 11. 長沙市: 嶽麓書社出版, 1996. *Discourse on the Song*. Complete Works of Chuanshan. Vol. 11. Changsha: Yuelu shu Publishers, 1996. Referred to herein as SL.

———.《張子正蒙注.》《船山全書.》 Vol. 12. 長沙市: 嶽麓書社出版, 1996. *Annotated Commentary to Master Zhang's Zhengmeng. Complete Works of Chuanshan*. Vol. 12. Changsha: Yuelu shu Publishers, 1996. Referred to herein as ZMZ.

———. *Notes on Poetry from the Ginger Studio*, [薑齋詩話]. Trans. Wong Siu-kit. Hong Kong: Hong Kong UP, 1987.

———. 《張子正蒙注.》北京: 中華書局, 1975. [*Commentary on Master Zhang's Correcting Youthful Ignorance.*] Beijing: Zhonghua shuju, 1975.

Wang, Zu-Hua 王汝華, "Thoughts on Respect of Life in the *Book of Changes*, 《易》尊「生」思想四探," in 台南女院學報 [*Tainan Women's College Journal*], vol. 23 (Oct. 2004): 479–503.

Whitehead, Alfred North. *Process and Reality*. Corrected ed. Ed. David Ray Griffin and Donald W. Sherburne. New York: The Free Press, 1978.

Whiteside, Kerry H. *Divided Natures: French Contributions to Political Ecology*. Cambridge, MA: The MIT P, 2002.

Wong, Siu-kit. "Translators Introduction," *Notes on Poetry from the Ginger Studio*, [薑齋詩話]. Trans.Wong Siu-kit. Hong Kong: Hong Kong UP, 1987.

———. "Ch'ing and Ching in the Critical Writings of Wang Fu-chih." *Chinese Approaches to Literature from Confucius to Liang Ch'i-Ch'ao*. Ed. Adele Austin Rickett. Princeton, NJ: Princeton UP, 1978.

Wyatt, Don J. "Shao Yong's Numerological-Cosmological System." *Dao Companion to Neo-Confucian Philosophy*, Ed. John Makeham. New York: Springer, 2010.

Xiong, Lümao 熊呂茂 and Yang Zhengzheng 杨铮铮. "论王夫之的人文主义思想 in 常德师范学院学报. "On Wang Fuzhi's Humanist Thoughts." *Journal of Changde Normal University*. 28.4 (July 2003): 26–28.

Yan, Shoucheng. "Coherence and Contradiction in the Worldview of Wang Fuzhi (1619–1692)." Diss. Department of East Asian Languages and Cultures, Bloomington: Indiana U, 1994.

Zhang, Shuangdi 张双棣, and Chen Tao 陈涛, eds. 《古代汉语字典》北京：北京大学出版社, 1998 年. [*Classical Chinese Dictionary*. Beijing: Peking UP,1998.]

Zheng, Xiong 郑熊. "王夫之对孔子天命论的改造"《湖南大学学报（社会科学版）》. "Reconstructing the Confucius Theory of Nature and Destiny by Wang Fuzhi." *Journal of Hunan University* (*Social Sciences*). 20.5 (Sept. 2006): 50–54. [Chinese text with translation of title and abstract in English].

Zhou, Bing 周兵. "天人之际的理学新诠释: 王夫之 «读四书大全说» 思想研究," diss. at Beijing Normal University, College of Philosophy and Sociology (March, 2005). (Accessed via WanFang Database, www. wanfangdata.com, June 10, 2011.)

Zhu, Xi. *Reflections on Things at Hand*. Trans. Wing-tsit Chan. New York: Columbia UP, 1967.

———. 朱子語類. Beijing: 中华书局, 1986. (Accessible online through "Wesleyan Confucian Etext Project," <http://sangle.web.wesleyan.edu/ etcxt/cep.html>. Copyright by Stephen Angle, 1996.)

Ziporyn, Brook. *Evil And/Or/As the Good: Omnicentrism, Intersubjectivity, and Value Paradox in Tiantai Buddhist Thought*. Cambridge, MA: Harvard UP, 2000.

Index